The Complete DBT Skills Manual:

3 Books in 1:

The Ultimate Dialectical Behavior Therapy Workbook For Treating Anxiety, Stress, Depression & Anger | Mindfulness & Emotion Regulation For Men & Women

By Barrett Huang

https://barretthuang.com/

© Copyright 2024 by Barrett Huang. Updated 2022. - All rights reserved.

This book contains information that is as accurate and reliable as possible. Regardless, purchasing this book constitutes agreement that both the publisher and the author of this book are in no way experts on the topics discussed and that any comments or suggestions made herein are solely for educational purposes. The information provided is not intended as a substitute for professional medical advice, diagnosis, or treatment. Always consult a professional before taking any action advised herein.

This declaration is deemed fair and valid by both the American Bar Association and the Committee of Publishers Association and is legally binding throughout the United States.

Furthermore, the transmission, duplication, or reproduction of any of the following work, including specific information, will be considered illegal, whether it is done electronically or in print. This extends to creating a secondary or tertiary copy of the work or a recorded copy and is only allowed with express written consent from the publisher. All additional rights reserved.

The information in the following pages is broadly considered a truthful and accurate account of facts. Any inattention, use, or misuse of the information in question by the reader will render any resulting actions solely under their purview. There are no scenarios in which the publisher or the original author of this work can be deemed liable for any hardship or damages that may occur after undertaking the information described herein.

Additionally, the information in the following pages is intended only for informational purposes and should thus be thought of as universal. It is presented without assurance regarding its prolonged validity or interim quality as befitting its nature. Trademarks mentioned are done without written consent and should not be considered an endorsement from the trademark holder.

Table of Contents

Introduction 16
Chapter 1: The ABCs of DBT 21
   What is Dialectical Behavior Therapy or DBT? 22
      RADICAL ACCEPTANCE in DBT 23
      CHANGE in DBT 23
      The Four Pillars of DBT 24
   Conditions Mentioned in this Book 26
   DBT Worksheet Overview 27
   WORKBOOK: WEEK 1 - DBT Basics 28
     Exercise: Self-Acceptance and Change 28
Chapter 2: Boundaries – Self-Care 101 30
   Boundaries with Family 32
   Boundaries with Friends 36
     Top 8 Tips for Establishing Boundaries with Friends 40
   Boundaries with the Digital World 41
     Social Media's Contribution to Our Anxiety 45
     Top 6 Ways to Limit Social Media Use 46
   Boundaries with Work 48
     Work Time Boundaries 48
     Workload Boundaries 49
     Boundaries with Co-Workers 54
   Boundaries with Your Spouse/SO 58
     Asking for space is okay. 61
     Keep in mind that things change. 61
   Boundaries with Self 62
   WORKBOOK: WEEK 2 - Setting Boundaries 65
     Exercise: Setting YOUR Boundaries 66
     Exercise: Boundary Journaling 68
Chapter 3: Anxiety, Stress, and Worry 72

Types of Anxiety 76
Types of Anxiety Disorders 77
Learned Optimism 80
WORKBOOK: WEEK 3 – Learned Optimism 86
    Exercise: The ABCDE Model 86
    Exercise: The Happiness Habit 88
Anxiety and the Wise Mind 89
Wise Mind Qualities 91
The Brain-Altering Power of Mindfulness 92
    Top 5 Ways to Be More Mindful 93
    Top 5 Ways to Make Meditation a Daily Habit 95
WORKBOOK: WEEK 4 – Mindfulness 98
    Exercise: 4-7-8 Breathing Technique 98
    Exercise: 5-4-3-2-1 Grounding Technique 99
    Exercise: Mindfulness Body Scan 100
WORKBOOK: WEEK 5 – WISE MIND 101
    Exercise: WISE MIND 101
Chapter 4: ADD & ADHD 102
    What is ADHD? 102
    Where Things Get Difficult 104
    How to Cope with ADHD 105
    Interpersonal Effectiveness 106
WORKBOOK: Week 6 – Interpersonal Effectiveness 107
    Exercise: D.E.A.R.M.A.N. 107
    Exercise: G.I.V.E. 109
    Exercise: F.A.S.T. 111
Chapter 5: Phobias 113
Distress Tolerance 114
WORKBOOK: Week 7 – Distress Tolerance 116
    Exercise: Turning the Mind 116

Exercise: Radical Acceptance Worksheet 117
  Exercise: Self-Sooth with 5 Senses 119
  Exercise: A.C.C.E.P.T.S. 120

Chapter 6: PTSD & Panic Disorders 122

What is PTSD? 123

C-PTSD 125

Emotion Regulation 127

WORKBOOK: Week 8 – Emotion Regulation 131

  Exercise: Opposite Action for Overwhelming Emotions 131
  Exercise: Check the Facts 132
  Exercise: P.L.E.A.S.E. 133

Chapter 7: OCD & Compulsive Behaviors 134

What is OCD? 135

OCD Causes 136

OCD Misconceptions 138

OCD Categories 140

  1. Organization 140
  2. Contamination 140
  3. Checking 141
  4. Hoarding 142
  5. Ruminations 143
  6. Intrusive Thoughts 143

DBT and OCD 144

The Importance of Stress Management 146

WORKBOOK: WEEK 9-12 - DBT for Your Healing 150

  WEEK 9 – Mindfulness 150
  WEEK 10 – Interpersonal Effectiveness 151
  WEEK 11 – Distress Tolerance 154
  WEEK 12 – Emotion Regulation 155

Chapter 8: Supplements and Medications 157

Disclaimer 157
Supplements 157
   Supplements that Help with Anxiety 157
Medications 160
   Medications Used for Anxiety, Stress, and Worry 160
   Medications Used for ADD & ADHD 162
   Medications Used for Phobias 162
   Medications Used for PTSD & Panic Disorders 163
   Medications Used for OCD & Compulsive Behaviors 163

Conclusion 166
Review Request 168
Glossary 169
References 171
Introduction 181
  My Story 182
  Who Should Read This Book 187
  Goals of This Book 187
  Content Warning 188
  Safety 188
  Be Kind to Yourself 189
Depression 101 190
   Depression vs. Sadness 191
  What Causes Depression? 192
  Depression Signs & Symptoms 194
  What are the Different Types of Depression? 198
  Depression Recommended Treatments 201
   Medication 202
   Brain Stimulation Therapy 203
   Light therapy 205
   Exercise/Physical Activity 205

Psychotherapy 206
Living with Depression 209
    Depression and the Brain 210
    Depression and the Body 211
    Depression and Relationships 212
    Depression in Women 214
What is Dialectical Behavior Therapy? 217
    Dialectics 218
    Why DBT for Depression? 222
    DBT Core Concepts 222
        Radical Acceptance 223
        Change 227
    DBT Core Skills 232
        Mindfulness 232
        Distress Tolerance 252
        Emotion Regulation 285
        Interpersonal Effectiveness 313
Continuing the Road to Happiness 329
    Self-Esteem: The Link Between Self-Perception and Depression 329
    Nutrition: Eat to Beat Depression 335
Conclusion 337
Appendix A – PHQ-9 Depression Self-Assessment 339
Appendix B – Journaling for Depression Relief 342
Review Request 345
References 346
Indexes 353
Contents 357
Introduction 360
    Who Should Read This Book 364
    Goals of This Book 364

How to Use This Book 364
What is Dialectical Behavior Therapy? 366
   DBT Fundamentals 370
      Acceptance and Change 370
   DBT Core Skills 375
      Mindfulness 375
      Distress Tolerance 382
      Emotion Regulation 386
      Interpersonal Effectiveness 394
   DBT for Anger Management 406
What is Anger? 409
   Anger 101 409
      Amygdala Hijack 410
   The Anger Cycle 411
   The 10 Different Types of Anger 415
   Male and Female Anger 417
      Brain Biology 417
      Societal Norms 417
      Premenstrual Syndrome 418
      Menopause 419
Why Are You Angry? 421
   The Source of Your Anger 421
      Worksheet: Anger Triggers 1 425
      Worksheet: Anger Triggers 2 426
      Worksheet: Anger Iceberg 429
   How Your Anger Grows 430
   How Do You Express Your Anger? 433
   The Costs of Your Anger 435
   Physical Costs of Anger 435
   Emotional Costs of Anger 436

- Mental Costs of Anger 437
- Social Costs of Anger 438
- Financial Costs of Anger 438
- Relationship Costs of Anger 439

REAL LIFE Tools to Effectively Manage Your Anger 443

- Anger and Vulnerability 443
  - Top 8 Tips to Be More Vulnerable 444
  - Worksheet: Vulnerability List 450
- Mindfulness Skills for Anger Management 454
  - Worksheet: Mindful Body Scanning (Anger Observation) 455
  - Worksheet: Mindfully Angry (Anger Description) 457
- Distress Tolerance Skills for Anger Management 458
  - Worksheet: Radical Acceptance 459
  - Worksheet: STOP 465
  - Worksheet: ACCEPTS 468
- Emotion Regulation Skills for Anger Management 472
  - Worksheet: BPE 473
  - Worksheet: PLEASE 475
  - Worksheet: COPE AHEAD 481
- Interpersonal Effectiveness Skills for Anger Management 483
  - How to Set Boundaries 484
  - Worksheet: FAST 488
  - Anger and Unfairness 490
  - How to Prevent Yourself from Exploding 491
  - Healthy Ways to Communicate Your Anger 493

Living a Life Less Angry 495

- HANGRY is Real 495
- Get Enough Sleep! 496
- Be Accountable for Your Own Emotions 498
- Setbacks 499

Let It Go 500

Live a Positive Life 502

Conclusion 505

Appendix A – Miller-Patton Anger Self-Assessment 506

Review Request 511

Further Reading 512

About the Author 513

Referenc 514

Indexes 520

DBT Workbook for Adults

Develop Emotional Wellbeing with Practical Exercises for Managing Fear, Stress, Worry, Anxiety, Panic Attacks, Intrusive Thoughts & More

(Includes 12-Week Plan for Anxiety Relief)

By Barrett Huang

https://barretthuang.com/

Contents

Introduction 16

Chapter 1: The ABCs of DBT 21

  What is Dialectical Behavior Therapy or DBT? 22

    RADICAL ACCEPTANCE in DBT 23

    CHANGE in DBT 23

    The Four Pillars of DBT 24

  Conditions Mentioned in this Book 26

  DBT Worksheet Overview 27

  WORKBOOK: WEEK 1 - DBT Basics 28

    Exercise: Self-Acceptance and Change 28

Chapter 2: Boundaries – Self-Care 101 30

  Boundaries with Family 32

  Boundaries with Friends 36

    Top 8 Tips for Establishing Boundaries with Friends 40

  Boundaries with the Digital World 41

    Social Media's Contribution to Our Anxiety 45

    Top 6 Ways to Limit Social Media Use 46

  Boundaries with Work 48

    Work Time Boundaries 48

    Workload Boundaries 49

    Boundaries with Co-Workers 54

  Boundaries with Your Spouse/SO 58

    Asking for space is okay. 61

    Keep in mind that things change. 61

  Boundaries with Self 62

  WORKBOOK: WEEK 2 - Setting Boundaries 65

    Exercise: Setting YOUR Boundaries 66

    Exercise: Boundary Journaling 68

- Chapter 3: Anxiety, Stress, and Worry 72
  - Types of Anxiety 76
  - Types of Anxiety Disorders 77
  - Learned Optimism 80
  - WORKBOOK: WEEK 3 – Learned Optimism 86
    - Exercise: The ABCDE Model 86
    - Exercise: The Happiness Habit 88
  - Anxiety and the Wise Mind 89
  - Wise Mind Qualities 91
  - The Brain-Altering Power of Mindfulness 92
    - Top 5 Ways to Be More Mindful 93
    - Top 5 Ways to Make Meditation a Daily Habit 95
  - WORKBOOK: WEEK 4 – Mindfulness 98
    - Exercise: 4-7-8 Breathing Technique 98
    - Exercise: 5-4-3-2-1 Grounding Technique 99
    - Exercise: Mindfulness Body Scan 100
  - WORKBOOK: WEEK 5 – WISE MIND 101
    - Exercise: WISE MIND 101
- Chapter 4: ADD & ADHD 102
  - What is ADHD? 102
  - Where Things Get Difficult 104
  - How to Cope with ADHD 105
  - Interpersonal Effectiveness 106
  - WORKBOOK: Week 6 – Interpersonal Effectiveness 107
    - Exercise: D.E.A.R.M.A.N. 107
    - Exercise: G.I.V.E. 109
    - Exercise: F.A.S.T. 111
- Chapter 5: Phobias 113
  - Distress Tolerance 114
  - WORKBOOK: Week 7 – Distress Tolerance 116

- Exercise: Turning the Mind 116
- Exercise: Radical Acceptance Worksheet 117
- Exercise: Self-Sooth with 5 Senses 119
- Exercise: A.C.C.E.P.T.S. 120

Chapter 6: PTSD & Panic Disorders 122
What is PTSD? 123
C-PTSD 125
Emotion Regulation 127
WORKBOOK: Week 8 – Emotion Regulation 131
- Exercise: Opposite Action for Overwhelming Emotions 131
- Exercise: Check the Facts 132
- Exercise: P.L.E.A.S.E. 133

Chapter 7: OCD & Compulsive Behaviors 134
What is OCD? 135
OCD Causes 136
OCD Misconceptions 138
OCD Categories 140
1. Organization 140
2. Contamination 140
3. Checking 141
4. Hoarding 142
5. Ruminations 143
6. Intrusive Thoughts 143

DBT and OCD 144
The Importance of Stress Management 146
WORKBOOK: WEEK 9-12 - DBT for Your Healing 150
- WEEK 9 – Mindfulness 150
- WEEK 10 – Interpersonal Effectiveness 151
- WEEK 11 – Distress Tolerance 154
- WEEK 12 – Emotion Regulation 155

Chapter 8: Supplements and Medications 157
   Disclaimer 157
   Supplements 157
      Supplements that Help with Anxiety 157
   Medications 160
      Medications Used for Anxiety, Stress, and Worry 160
      Medications Used for ADD & ADHD 162
      Medications Used for Phobias 162
      Medications Used for PTSD & Panic Disorders 163
      Medications Used for OCD & Compulsive Behaviors 163
Conclusion 166
Review Request 168
Glossary 169
References 171
Index 177

Introduction

"Be kind to yourself, then let your kindness fill the world."- Minna

So

My dad was a hoarder, and my mother had undiagnosed anxiety. As a child, I was understandably extremely anxious, living in an environment that felt chaotic and confusing. The unrest I felt as a kid shaped me into an adult who now has Generalized Anxiety Disorder (GAD) and Obsessive-Compulsive Disorder (OCD).

One of my earliest compulsions was to make sure I never stepped on any lines or cracks on the pavement because I felt something terrible would happen to me.

Obsessions, negative thoughts, and constant worrying can be debilitating, and I have felt all of them. That feeling of dread, like something terrible will happen, is wired deeply into my psyche.

I sometimes still think that if I don't double-check the stove, the entire house will burn down. I check that the tap is turned off by tapping it 2-3 times. I still triple-check the door to make sure it's locked when I leave, or my brain tells me someone will break in and steal everything. I live in a safe, gated neighborhood. You would think my rational brain would take over and set me straight—but it doesn't. It's a constant struggle.

In the past, I'd be so nervous approaching and talking to a girl I was interested in that I would hyperventilate. This is because my brain tells me she will laugh in my face and humiliate me. I know these thoughts are irrational and unlikely to happen, but my mind and emotions get the better of me at times.

Thanks to working with professionals and using anti-anxiety medication, I have improved my symptoms over time. But for me, anxiety never truly goes away.

I live with these conditions daily, but I manage them well with the right tools and support.

I've done [cognitive behavior therapy (CBT)](#) and [dialectical behavior therapy (DBT)](#), and I believe both are beneficial. This book is for those who have tried CBT and other methods and haven't found much help. We will significantly focus on DBT in this book since it was the method that changed my life. I hope this book helps you better understand your anxiety and acquire the tools you need to better manage and improve your condition as I have.

Today, I'm calmer, more level-headed, and capable of handling challenges better than before. I've run a successful online business and have self-published numerous bestselling books. Even though it can be stressful, and I still get anxious, it's more manageable now.

Our upbringing and environment play a huge role in how we react to situations. It's clear to me now that my family was a significant source of my stress and anxiety, and the way I was brought up resulted in my brain being shaped into this ball of anxiety. Once I got older, I realized that the things I experienced were not normal, and I needed to get away from the situation to improve my life and mindset. Once I left home and began traveling the world, everything changed for the better.

I traveled around Asia, to Thailand, Manila, and Hong Kong. During my travels, my eyes were opened to different ways of life. I witnessed poverty, corruption, injustice, and strife that I wouldn't have seen otherwise. Through these experiences, I began to realize how privileged my life was.

I met people who had no arms or legs and were begging for change. I imagined their life as miserable, yet every last one of them had a smile on their face. This made me realize that whatever I am anxious about in my life is likely not as bad as what they are going through. And so began my journey into healing myself and rebuilding my life.

One of the biggest goals of this book is to show you, dear reader, that you are not alone.

Millions of people suffer from varying degrees of anxiety disorders, and no two are the same. At times, the way you are feeling may make you feel very much alone, but you are not.

If you or someone you know is in crisis, resources are available to you. Call a trusted friend or family member, Google your local crisis line, and if those methods do not seem to be enough to support you at the moment, head to your nearest Emergency Department. Anxiety and panic are no joke, and you do not have to suffer alone.

If you're in a state where you're ready to take control of your anxiety, let's get into it. To get the most out of this book, I advise reading one chapter at a time and completing the exercises I have shared with you at the end of each chapter. You can then re-read sections until you feel you've mastered them.

Note that the 12-week workbook included does not have to be completed in 12 weeks. It is essential to work through each chapter at your own pace.

Like everything else, some days will be easier and more beneficial to you than others. And there are going to be times that you need a break. During those times—take a break!

Addressing anxiety and helping yourself can take a lot out of you. There will be times when you're faced with your past, faced with debilitating emotions, and faced with tasks that seem physically and mentally impossible to do at that moment. Believe me, I've been there, and I genuinely get it.

But here's my number one rule: **BE KIND TO YOURSELF**.

Say it out loud—**I WILL BE KIND TO MYSELF**.

Write it down on a sticky note, make it your desktop background or phone wallpaper, write it on your bathroom mirror; place it everywhere to remind yourself to be kind and forgiving to yourself.

Whatever got you to this point, whether it was childhood trauma like me or another trauma later in life, I'm so very sorry that happened to you. But please know this—you are not your trauma, and you are not a reflection of whoever raised you.

YOU ARE INCREDIBLE just to pick up this book and want to better yourself. Take some credit for your first step!

In the following pages, we will cover the basics of anxiety. Don't worry; we will not dwell on that too long. We will then discuss DBT and how to get the most out of it, the major task of setting boundaries, and then dive into some more specific diagnoses as they relate to anxiety.

We will go through some DBT exercises that I found particularly helpful in my journey. Even if you don't have specific diagnoses, I suggest going through the chapters and the exercises anyway. Someone who does not have OCD may still benefit from the DBT exercises included in that chapter. DBT can help anyone with anxiety and anxiety-related conditions, such as phobias, social anxiety, PTSD, and ADD.

THANK YOU for being here, and please know that **YOU ARE NOT ALONE**.

I often felt that I was struggling in this world alone in dealing with my anxiety, so I found tremendous inspiration in others' stories. Just the thought that people out there understood what I was going through helped me.

I sincerely hope this book helps you on your path to healing too.

Chapter 1: The ABCs of DBT

"Let go of what you can't control. Channel all that energy into living fully in the now."
- Karen Salmansohn

We all want to be happy and think positive thoughts all the time. In reality, life is hard. But please remember this: it's never as bad as you fear. In fact, one study has shown that 91.4% of our worries don't come true at all.[1]

Still, I understand you. Often, even though we know specific facts (like our fears won't likely come true), we still feel the way we do. I'm usually asked WHY I feel anxious, and frequently my answer would be, *"I don't know. It's just there."*

Like me, you probably feel a tidal wave of emotions when you're anxious. Before, when this happens, I get paralyzed, feel lost, and quite frankly, get stuck in the moment, or worse, spiral down into even more anxious thoughts.

ACCEPT the Tidal Wave

One of the things that I learned is to simply accept—and not fight—that tidal wave of anxious feelings. Why? Because waves come and go. So I started to cope by letting the tidal wave hit me… and then wash over me.

CHANGE to Move Forward

Another coping mechanism that has helped me is understanding and applying the word *perspective*. Whenever my mind gets polluted with fear and negative thoughts, I try very hard to imagine a different perspective or possibility.

For instance, say I'm at some party. I meet someone, we get into some small talk, and then the other person moves on. I would get very anxious about how that person thought of me. Did they like me? Did they think I was weird? Stupid? Too friendly? Not friendly enough?

To slowly divert my anxious thoughts, I'd start to think of other possibilities. *What else could be true?*

Perhaps the other person was also nervous about meeting someone at a party.
Perhaps the other person had a bad day, so they weren't in the mood to be chatty.
Perhaps the other person was just shy.
Perhaps they have anxiety too.

By looking at the SAME situation from a different angle, I slowly changed my thoughts and emotions about the event. No, it's not that there's something wrong with me; something else may be happening in that person's life.

ACCEPTANCE and CHANGE are the two strategies at the heart of dialectical behavior therapy.

What is Dialectical Behavior Therapy or DBT?

Dialectical behavior therapy (DBT) was developed by Marsha M. Linehan[2], Ph.D., in the 1980s as a result of her and her colleagues' work with patients with borderline personality disorder (BPD).

Working with BPD patients who were suicidal, Linehan realized that, unlike cognitive behavior therapy (CBT), which focuses primarily on detecting negative thought patterns and changing them to positive ones (change-focused), it is far more effective to employ two opposing (dialectical) strategies: acceptance AND change.

RADICAL ACCEPTANCE in DBT

DBT teaches people to accept their feelings, emotions, and realities AS IS without judgment.

You have a right to feel what you feel. Your emotions are valid. There's nothing wrong with you.

And there's no need to delve deeper into the source of your pain (or anxiety), figure things out, or pass judgment on yourself, other people, or the situations that may have caused your anguish. Doing this will just make you *stay* in that negative state and may *lead* you to an emotional (rather than logical) reaction that may worsen the situation.

➡ It is what it is.

CHANGE in DBT

Acceptance comes with realizing that your current ways are not beneficial to you. As such, you recognize the importance of shifting your time, thoughts, and energy into learning new behaviors, skills, and techniques to help you cope better with life.

➡ It is what it is. I'm now going to learn new ways to positively move on.

DBT focuses on developing four (4) primary skills. None of these are easy to learn, but the benefits of *retraining your mind* can lead you to a more carefree and fulfilling life.

The Four Pillars of DBT

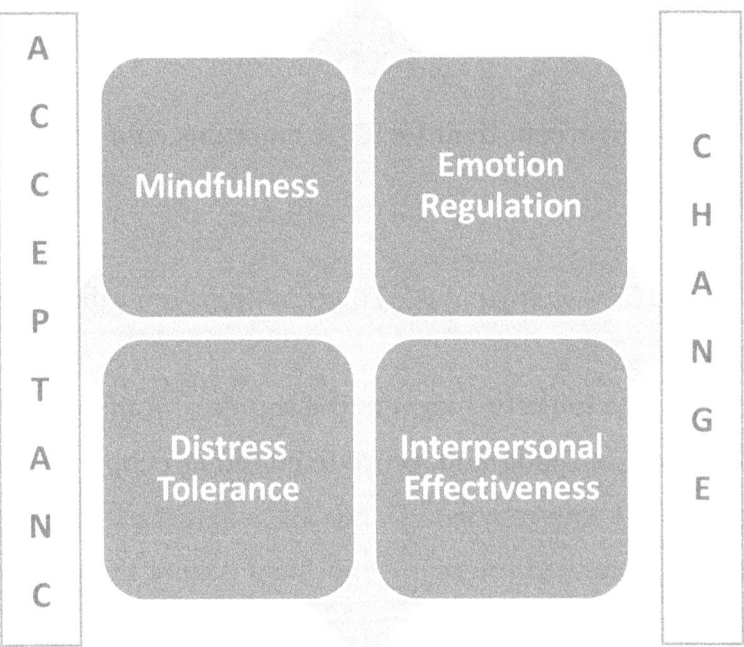

- MINDFULNESS is being aware of the present moment without judgment. It is observing, describing, and participating in the NOW. It can include narrowing your attention or focusing on something specific. Other times, mindfulness involves noticing the world around you or expanding your awareness.

- DISTRESS TOLERANCE is increasing your tolerance of negative emotions (as opposed to denying or trying to escape them) to improve the outcome of a stressful situation.

- INTERPERSONAL EFFECTIVENESS is improving your interpersonal skills to get more of your needs met while maintaining good relationships with those around you. It is about finding a balance between dealing with others without losing your self-respect.

- EMOTION REGULATION is managing negative and overwhelming emotions while increasing positive experiences. To regulate emotions effectively, it is crucial to understand that negative emotions are not necessarily bad or something to be avoided. Experiencing these feelings is a natural part of life, but there are ways to deal with them so they do not control us.

A trigger event activates automatic negative thoughts in people with anxiety who have high emotional sensitivity. As a result, these thoughts trigger an adverse emotional response, leading to destructive behavior choices. In the aftermath of detrimental behavior, shame and self-loathing become more prominent. Emotional regulation helps sufferers learn to cope with their emotions more effectively.

The purpose of DBT is to change the way you perceive the world and how you react to it because the way you are seeing the world right now is not working for you.

If you're in a constant state of anxiety, your fight-or-flight system is always ready to go. You're hypervigilant, and that sense of dread can be incredibly overwhelming, adversely affecting your physical health. Without getting too far down the biological rabbit hole, chronic stress negatively impacts your health and well-being.[3] So, it is in your best interest to learn and adopt the skills we'll cover in this book.

Here's what you will learn in the following pages:

1) **Acceptance Skills.** Learn strategies to cope with people, situations, and emotions in your life. Additionally, you will develop skills to help you improve your interactions and behaviors towards others.

2) **Behavioral Skills.** Discover how to become proficient at analyzing issues or destructive behavior patterns and replacing them with healthier and more effective ones.

3) **Set Boundaries.** Find out how to effectively set boundaries with family, friends, co-workers, spouse, and even yourself.

4) **Cognitive Skills.** Learn how to change beliefs and thoughts that do not serve you.

5) **Collaboration Skills.** Develop your communication and teamwork skills, which can help you with your relationships at home, work, or school.

6) **Support Skills.** This part will be directed toward developing and utilizing your positive strengths and qualities.

Conditions Mentioned in this Book

The content in this book has been broken down into various conditions and how DBT can help address them. Emotional regulation and self-destructive behaviors are prevalent in many mental health conditions, so although DBT has been initially developed for BPD patients, this type of therapy has broad applications[4].

DBT Worksheet Overview

This book includes a 12-week plan for anxiety relief. The goal is to help you begin a self-guided course where you learn to use DBT skills to cope with your anxiety. Most of these exercises are derived or adaptations from Marsha Linehan, Ph.D., the creator of dialectical behavior therapy (DBT).[2]

DBT is based on cognitive behavior therapy with a strong emphasis on mindfulness and emotion regulation. As such, you will learn tools for living in the moment, healthily dealing with stress and emotions, and improving your relationships with others.

The exercises are divided into the four primary DBT skills: Mindfulness, Interpersonal Effectiveness, Distress Tolerance, and Emotion Regulation.

As you move through this book, it's important to remember that you don't have to do these in order, and you can always go back and revisit any of the topics we've covered. This is your journey, and you are in charge.

One last thing before we really get going: some of the following content and exercises will challenge you in ways that perhaps you haven't been challenged before. You may get upset when thinking about or working through difficult subjects. Some of this may be related to trauma, but some could be difficult points you need to accept about yourself.

I just want you to know that it's okay to be upset. It's okay to take breaks. Remember my motto at the beginning of this book: **BE KIND TO YOURSELF**.

WORKBOOK: WEEK 1 - DBT Basics

As mentioned, dialectic behavior therapy (DBT) is about the coming together of two seemingly opposite (dialectic) strategies: Acceptance AND Change. This exercise will help you start practicing these core DBT concepts.

Exercise: Self-Acceptance and Change

I've put some sample statements here for you as a guide.

SELF-ACCEPTANCE:

This is difficult... but temporary.

I AM DOING MY BEST. THAT'S ENOUGH.

Things are not going as planned. That's

It's okay to feel this way.

My feelings are valid.

DESIRE TO CHANGE:

I am not as happy as I know I could be.

I AM OPEN TO IMPROVING MY LIFE.

I know there are other parts of me I can explore to live

I WILL NOT FEEL GUILTY FOR WANTING TO TAKE

There's nothing wrong with wanting 'more'.

YOUR STATEMENT:

"I accept myself as who I am right now. I know I'm like this for a reason even though I don't know exactly why. What I do know is that I don't feel happy or fulfilled living this way. I know this is not my best life. So I accept myself without judgement and I'm open to learning new things and exploring myself further to increase my happiness."

Now, it's your turn...

Fill out the following diagram with your own Acceptance and Change statements.

Important: Don't put any pressure on yourself, ok? Just write whatever you feel. If nothing's coming to you today, that's ok too. You can always return to this exercise whenever it suits you.

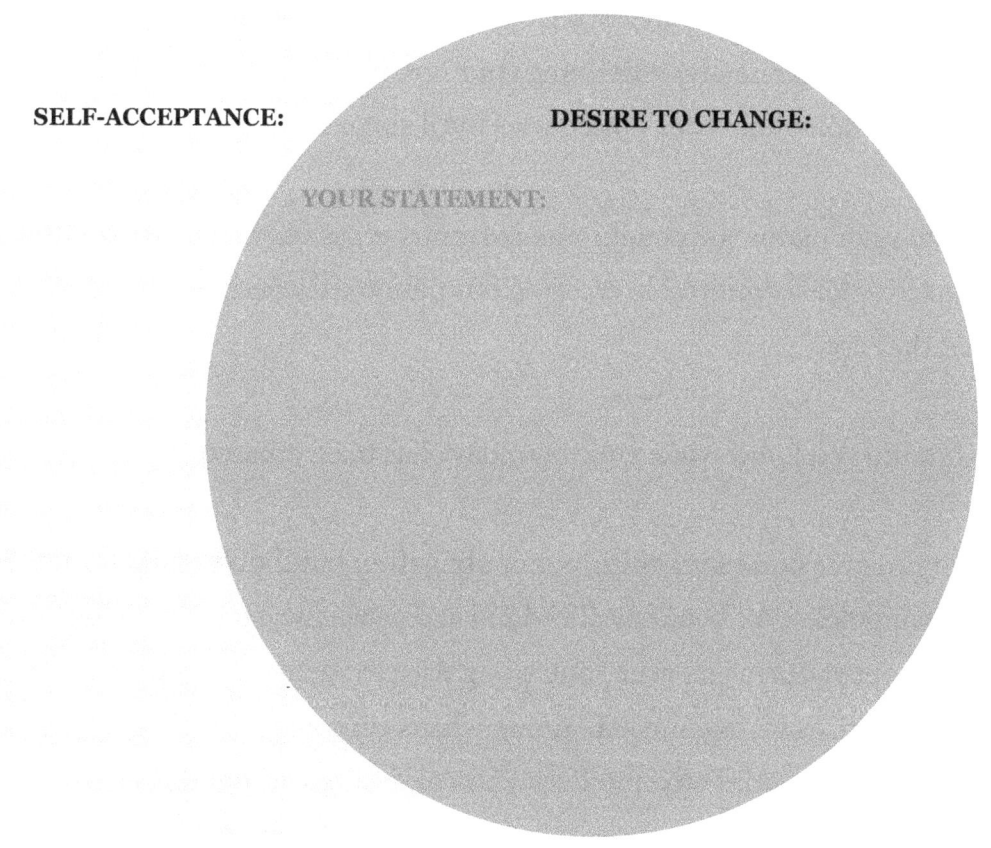

Chapter 2: Boundaries – Self-Care 101

"Daring to set boundaries is about having the courage to love ourselves even when we risk disappointing others." - Brene Brown

Many mental health conditions are *triggered*. As such, it's vital to set healthy boundaries as they set the stage for healthy and positive relationships.

Setting boundaries is a way for us to limit what we tolerate and what we won't. I ask you not to stress about defining your boundaries at this stage. Truth be told, most of us don't know our boundaries until someone crosses them.

And let's not blame the people who currently cross our boundaries. Often, people in our lives feel comfortable crossing our boundaries because they don't know what they are.

So how do you know when your boundary has been crossed?

Have you ever done something out of obligation but didn't really want to? Has your happiness ever been sacrificed to keep peace in a situation where everyone else is happy? Have you ever gone along with someone or a group just because it was easier than saying and explaining what's on your mind? Has anyone ever commented on your body, intellect, choices, or life without any correction from you?

Reflect on at least one of my questions and think about how these situations made you feel. Not good, right?

But here's the thing, not speaking up for yourself will also make you feel "not good". Let's back up a little bit.

Setting boundaries begins with you. You need to decide what is important to you. No one else can figure that out.

For example, imagine saving your money as a young adult and moving into an apartment. Your parents come to help you move, and they criticize everything about the place: it's too far from work; it's too small; there's no bathtub (only a shower); on and on it goes.

Your parents make you feel small about your choices, so you fight, and they leave. A little deflating, right?

Trying to please everyone damages you in the end.

Most of us who identify as people-pleasers or peacekeepers don't want to upset the apple cart and are afraid of conflict. We spend a lot of time and energy managing the perceptions of others and taking more responsibility than is ours. We abandon ourselves to make sure that other people are okay instead of checking in with ourselves to see if we are okay.

To be happy and develop positive relationships, you must reclaim your power! Instead of giving everything away to everyone, including yourself, take care of yourself first by prioritizing what you need. And it begins with self-awareness.

Ask yourself: what do I want? What are my preferences?

Knowing what you want will help you put yourself and your needs first. Many people don't even ask themselves these questions, so you're already ahead of the game. This is how you become self-aware.

Also, if you don't decide what is important to you, others will make the decision for you. And guess what? Their choices are often not in your best interest but theirs.

The second step is to **communicate and express your preferences (boundaries)**.

It's not enough to know your boundaries; you should state them. If you don't, people will keep crossing that line. This is just how things are in life; people will push for what they want.

So despite how uncomfortable it may feel, express your honest opinions, thoughts, and feelings, even if you're scared the other person might get hurt. True, you might offend someone, but what is the worst that can happen?

We are often too afraid of hurting other people or getting into uncomfortable, awkward situations, so we tend to hold back. But who is that hurting and damaging in the end? I think you already know the answer to that one.

Boundaries with Family

Family dynamics are complex. If you were fortunate to grow up in a loving and supportive family and/or were raised in a peaceful environment where you felt heard and validated, congratulations! The majority of people did not.

From an early age, many people had their boundaries crossed. Think of the last time you visited your uncle or another relative, and you were ~~asked~~ told to kiss or hug him. In my family, a common thing is for relatives to ask whom I am dating and when I plan to get married. These questions can be intrusive, no?

When you were a kid, your parents may have crossed boundaries to protect other people's feelings. So you're taught early to "just be polite" or "just smile" and hug or kiss your relatives. One of the most common scenarios is when a parent crosses a child's boundary by not respecting their body autonomy. My point is that we learn early to break our own boundaries for the sake of others.

Growing up, we are taught to do things because Mom would like us to do them or because this will mean we are a good person. Yes, there has to be a balance between being a happy, giving, and loving person who wants to help other people and learning how to fill ourselves up inside and feed ourselves the love and acceptance we deserve.

Even as grown adults, most of us deal with boundaries and power struggles in dealing with older relatives. If you're a grown adult who lives alone or with a partner, and your parent(s) have a key to your home for safety reasons, and they hardly use it, fine.

However, how would you feel if they had a key to your home and showed up uninvited and unannounced? How would you react if they went through your stuff, rearranged the contents of your kitchen cabinets, and threw out all your snacks? How far do you think your parents crossed your boundary in this scenario? You know what? This is what my mom did to me!

What if your parent or loved one criticizes your appearance, lifestyle choices, or career? How would that make you feel? What if you go to your parents' house every Sunday night for dinner because it's a family tradition, and they tear apart your new haircut, outfit, and everything you bring up with them? Would you keep going back? This has been my experience, affecting my decision-making abilities throughout life.

Everyone in my family is super direct. There is no sugar-coating or political correctness here. On the one hand, it's good to have people who directly state how they feel. But if all you hear is negative criticism, it gets annoying, and it chips at your self-esteem.

Parents and relatives say that they do these things out of love. They care about you, so they want to 'correct' you. If you look pale, they say you should sleep more and work less. If you don't look healthy to them, they say you should lose weight (or gain weight). These things can hurt at the moment, and it's sometimes hard to remember that they say these things from a place of love. So it gets very confusing because, on the one hand, you believe this person loves you, but at the same time, they seem to see only your flaws. (Message: You're not good enough.) This is why I advocate setting boundaries.

If we don't set boundaries, the people who claim to love us, and often we love them back, are the ones who will slowly break us down in the end.

Establishing healthy boundaries is good and will give you more peace of mind. Otherwise, your future may consist of your parents determining your every adult decision and undermining your authority with your own kids. Setting those boundaries is going to serve you for a long time.

So, consider what you stand for, what you like, and where your morals are. Get to know yourself to discover your boundaries. Once you've realized that a boundary needs to be drawn, communicate it immediately.

For example, if your parents are overtly religious, and you are not, it's perfectly okay to say, '*Hey Mom and Dad, I love you, but I've decided not to attend church anymore. Organized religion just doesn't align with who I am.*' No explaining further, just a fact.

Your parents will likely have a massive issue with this. Take comfort in knowing that a) people do not like change; b) your parents see the time at church as a way to spend time with you and may feel rejected, and c) if they love you, they will eventually get over it.

Setting boundaries, especially if you've never done them before, isn't easy, and it's likely going to cause issues in your family. But if you want to set clear, healthy boundaries with your loved ones, this is a step you will have to take.

By the way, this doesn't mean that our parents set out to destroy our lives! Remember that our parents are doing the best they can with what they know. They're pretty much carrying over the parenting style of *their* parents.

The difference is that we know and acknowledge that we don't have to subject ourselves to the same rules and do the same things to our children.

Breaking cycles is part of setting boundaries. Your mom may insert herself where she does not belong, such as telling you how to parent, and it's up to you to protect yourself (and your children) when she does.

It's about seeing things from a more holistic point of view, which isn't easy. As I got older and did much self-reflection and gained a better understanding of my Chinese culture, I realized that my parents did the best they could with my sister and me.

They weren't perfect, but I know they love and care for us. I also realized that it wasn't fair to have Western expectations of them. For example, I yearned for them to say '*I love you*' and express their feelings as they do here in North America. But that's not the Chinese family culture. At the same time, though, they had to realize that we are not in China anymore and should respect my feelings and beliefs.

Hopefully, having an honest conversation with your parents helps you better understand each other.

Please remember that as you communicate who you are to them, try to understand them too. Ask *them* about *their* stories. Ask *them* about *their* feelings. Ask *them* about *their* life journey.

For me, taking a course in Chinese history and learning about how my parents grew up were some of the best things I did. It helped me understand where they were coming from and exercise more patience with their ways.

Boundaries with Friends

It's human nature to want to be accepted by our peer groups. When making friends, we tend to be on our best behavior, and some of that includes sacrificing our own needs for the sake of others. No question about it, our parents and society have conditioned us to put other people first. And I think that's where it gets a little twisted.

We focus so much on giving in to other people's wants that we neglect ourselves.

As kids, something as simple as being on the playground and being told to share something makes you share because it's the right thing to do. When making friends, we're told that we should be nice so that others will like us. And often, being friendly means going with what other people like and do.

No one teaches us that thinking of ourselves and sticking to what we like and do is okay.

Of course, it's important to teach children how to share. But on the other hand, maybe the first child just started playing with the ball and the second child needs to learn to wait their turn. Or perhaps both children need to learn how to play ball together. There's a balance that is missing.

When we get older, in adolescence or adulthood, we still want that feeling of belonging. For example, let's say you're with a group of friends and 8 out of the 10 enjoy camping, while the other two despise it. Now, these two tell a joke that they would rather not spend their money living in filth and sleeping on the ground. The rest of the group then pressures these two by saying something like, "*Oh, but it will be fun! Just you guys wait and see*" or "*But it won't be the same without you guys!*", or worse, "*If you guys aren't going, we're not going.*"

What do you think will happen? Most likely, the two anti-camping friends would give in and join because of peer pressure. But what *should* happen is that the pro-camping friends should respect those who don't want to join and that the anti-camping friends should stick to their choices. This is what true friendship is all about.

Now, if you have a friend that puts you down consistently, yells at you, and calls you names, that's a big problem. This is where you should stand up for yourself, right? That's obvious.

But what if you DO stand up for yourself and your friend calls you over-sensitive, selfish, or even stupid? This pushback may shock you, but please expect it if you've never stood up for yourself before.

Once *pushback* happens, would you start questioning yourself and wonder if you are too sensitive or selfish? Would you back down to keep the peace? If you do, what would that make you feel? Don't you think that standing up for yourself and backing down would make your friend respect you more? On the contrary, this move will *empower* your so-called friend not to take you seriously next time.

So what do you do? Establish your boundaries, and if that means losing a few friends along the way, that's okay.

Even if you've been friends for 15 or 20 years, it's okay to want change. It's okay to want to be treated better. If this friend truly cares about you and isn't some psychopath, they will take the time to re-learn how to treat you.

If they are not receptive after your first few tries at setting boundaries, as difficult as it might be to say goodbye to this friend or distance yourself from them, it may be necessary. Surrounding yourself with people who respect you and your boundaries is vital to your health.

You don't have to be mean or rude all of a sudden to make your point; you just have to be firm and confident with what you are saying to protect yourself. It's said that we are the average of our five closest friends, so you want to surround yourself with people who will support and motivate you to become better.[5]

One book I recommend is "*When I Say No, I Feel Guilty: How to Cope, Using the Skills of Systematic Assertive Therapy*" by Manuel J. Smith. I read it back in university, and it helped me set boundaries with friends and family. It also showed me that it's okay to say no and not feel guilty when I don't want to do something others do. Although the book is a bit dated, there are plenty of tips and examples to help you become more assertive in your life.

I won't lie to you; conversations regarding boundaries will make you uncomfortable, but it's essential to stick to them. If a friend is exhibiting negative behavior towards you, tell them to stop and continue stating it until you lose that 'friend' or the negative behavior changes. I know it's hard and will take time, but doing this improves your relationship with others and the one you have with yourself.

Boundaries help improve our confidence and help get rid of some of the anxiety in our lives. It may be helpful to practice what you want to say beforehand, especially if you're nervous or prone to anxiety. If you are prepared for these moments, you will be strong when it counts.

Here are some example starter phrases for you.

- *I'm busy now, so please feel free to do [x] without me.*
- *I'm really not into [x], but you guys have fun!*
- *I tried [x], but I realized it's not really me, so I'm afraid I won't be joining you guys.*
- *Sorry, I can't help you with [x] because my plate is too full as it is.*
- *Thanks for the invite but I'd rather not go.*
- *Hey [friend], I've told you a couple of times before that I don't like it when you [x]. I'm uncomfortable with it, so can you please not do it?*

Yes, it can be exhausting and frustrating to constantly establish your boundaries, but it must be done. And when you do so, the best way is to do it assertively. Apart from the fact that assertiveness increases self-esteem and improves mental well-being,[6] being assertive implies to your friends that they should simply respect your and your wishes. (It's not open for discussion.)

Note that to be assertive is not to be aggressive. You're not in combative mode. Most simply and respectfully, you're just saying what your boundaries are.

Top 8 Tips for Establishing Boundaries with Friends

1. Mentally pump yourself up with positive self-talk. It may sound corny, but if you know you're going to have to stand your ground, try thinking, *'I can do this'* or *'This should be done'*, or *'This is for my mental health'*.

2. Practice the conversation ahead of time to reduce nervousness and the likelihood of you relenting. It's best to do this, whether out loud, before a mirror, or with a trustworthy confidante.

3. Setting your boundaries doesn't have to be verbal only. Be aware of what you are saying through your body language. When we want to please others, being assertive can be challenging, so when you have this conversation, be sure you're sitting or standing straight, your shoulders are rolled back, and you keep eye contact.

4. Feel free to share your *emotions* as you set your boundaries with your friends. Emotions will have more validity if they are expressed. In addition to increasing self-respect, acknowledging one's feelings also serves as a reminder that feelings matter. We create a bridge when we share our emotions and let others know what we're feeling.

5. Take responsibility for what you communicate. Don't accuse the listener since accusatory statements can put them on the defensive and make relaying your message more difficult. For example, you might say, *'I feel humiliated when you tell our other friends what happened to me last summer.'* The 'I' statements express how you are feeling.

6. If you receive a request that could endanger your wellbeing, Just Say No. An apology is not necessary, and it is best to clearly, respectfully, and honestly say 'no'. If you have just recovered from bronchitis, do not go skiing with your best friend. If you are unable to pay your own rent, do not lend your friend money.

7. Whenever necessary, concisely rephrase your words. People may find your boundaries challenging to understand and accept, primarily if you are exhibiting assertive behavior for the first time. However, boundaries should not be negotiable. If someone questions you or shows hostility, repeat yourself firmly.

8. Talk to a therapist if you have difficulty communicating your boundaries. A therapist can identify the underlying factors that make it difficult for you to express what you need, and they can give you new methods of navigating these roadblocks.

Boundaries with the Digital World

Social media addiction and other online-related disorders are real, and many of these conditions include but are not limited to depression, loneliness, anxiety, sleep disturbances, and low self-esteem.

Our real lives are becoming more mixed with our online life, so we should set clear boundaries with digital tasks like email and social media. For example, if you finish work at 5 PM but still answer emails until 8 PM or 9 PM, that can indicate a problem. It's important to shut down your digital world at set times so that you can focus on other aspects of your life too.

Personally, I only check emails a couple of times a day, which allows me to reply to all messages at one time. This lets others know that they operate on my time and not the other way around. To this day, I haven't had anyone get angry with me for replying to a message or email the following day.

You're not the only one who experiences anxiety or stress over email! The inability to complete tasks (the feeling that you aren't accomplishing enough) is one of the most common triggers for social anxiety and productivity-related anxiety.

It's stressful to communicate by email because it's asynchronous, sending messages before receiving replies. We don't know when we will hear back.

A significant amount of context, tone, and emotion is also missing from emails. Email is often perceived as confusing and anxiety-inducing due to these factors.

Here are a few of the most common scenarios regarding email anxiety and what you can do to handle them.

1. **You are not receiving a timely reply from someone.** Our brains tend to make up stories to explain why we're not getting a response. Often, we think of social rejection. Did we say or do something to offend the other? Are we not important enough to deserve a reply?

    In reality, this is not about you. Other people's email behavior is about them and what's going on in their lives at that moment.

    So when someone does not reply to your email, don't take it personally. It may not mean much if a friend or colleague doesn't respond to you. Some people are so overloaded with emails that they cannot reply to all of them right away, even if they want to.

So what do you? Keep a record of times when you have been frustrated by a slow response, and then it turned out you were worried about nothing. As these incidents occur, keep a running list. A great way to convince your brain that you shouldn't be anxious over slow responses is to collect data directly from your own life.

2. **Lack of effusiveness in emails.** Email communication lacks tone of voice and body language, so many people resort to exclamation points and smiley faces to make up for it. In an email, anxious people sometimes worry that the absence of clear emotional signals can indicate something is wrong, and it is not necessarily true.

   Those with an anxiety disorder are more likely to see negativity or hostility when none exists, so keep some balancing self-talk ready when you notice this reaction.

   For example, consider other possibilities. What *else* could be true?

   - Perhaps the responder isn't very expressive over emails.
   - Maybe the responder was tired, distracted, or in a hurry while writing their response.
   - Perhaps the responder was unsure if you were okay with a casual conversation over email, so they used a more formal and direct tone.
   - Maybe something bad happened that day to the other person, so they were not in the mood when they responded to you.

   Look, you'll most likely never find out what happened. And because of that, email is often anxiety-provoking but know that 'not liking you' is often NOT the reason for an email that lacks enthusiasm.

So what do you do? Re-read the email; perhaps your anxious state when reading it caused you to miss any positivity present in the email.

Whenever I talk about anxiety-driven thinking, I usually refer to certain biases we have as 'cognitive blind spots'. When this occurs, we tend to miss positive signals entirely, and instead, we fixate on anything that appears negative or ambiguous.

As mentioned at the start, I have Generalized Anxiety Disorder (GAD), so this pattern of negative thinking happens to me a lot, making me overreact or perceive negativity when it isn't there. However, since I know my biases, I use the *What Else Is True* strategy I described here, which is very beneficial!

3. **You worry about email overload.** When your inbox takes up so much of your time and energy, it makes you feel anxious and frustrates you when you can't get to meaningful work.

   So what do you? Monitor the time you spend e-mailing with a timer or an app. Do this for about a week to see how much time you email on average. From there, try to spend 5% to 10% less time on email each week to avoid getting overwhelmed. How? Writing shorter emails is one way to achieve this. Another tip is to separate important and less important emails and reply only to the important ones first. If you have more time, only then do you get the time to respond to the less important ones.

   Also, try not to be too hard on yourself. Individuals with differing schedules don't always expect a response to emails sent in the evening or during the weekend. It might be an unnecessary psychological pressure you're placing on yourself if you feel the need to respond to emails over the weekend or late in the evening.

You can also ask others for advice. See what other people are doing to solve their email overload problem. Family, friends, and coworkers are likely facing the same problem as you, so ask if anyone has advice on how to handle this.

Then there's that giant time suck: **social media**.

Social Media's Contribution to Our Anxiety

Comparing ourselves to others is in our nature.[7] We do it all the time: we compare our current situation to our previous situation, our current self to our old self, ourselves to others our age, and our knowledge and abilities to others in our niche.

However, in the online world, we compare our realities to an *illusion*, specifically an illusion of the perfect life.

People say they don't care about the images they see because they know they are edited. Still, they admit to using several filters on their pictures every day and taking multiple photos from different angles before choosing which ones to share. We want to put out our 'best selves' and 'best life' because when others see our social media feeds, we don't want to be judged as 'less'.

Sharing snippets of our life in pictures and text is not without purpose. What are we hoping to achieve? We want people to like us, and the absence of approval or validation in the form of likes, positive comments, and re-tweets can lead to low self-esteem, body image issues, and self-consciousness. Numerous studies have also linked social media to anxiety and depression.[8]

FoMO, or Fear of Missing Out, is a phenomenon that has been worsened by social media, with a reported 69% (7 in 10) of millennials experiencing it.[9] With

FoMO, you're always checking what your friends and followers are doing because you don't want to miss out. You want to know what they know. You want to do what they do.

People who have FoMo report feeling anxious, lonely, and inadequate. The most common example is when you notice friends at a particular location (because they have their GPS location turned on), and you are not invited.

Those who don't have a strong social media presence may still experience an anxiety condition called *nomophobia* or Fear of Being Offline (FoBO).

We are constantly distracted by the *beep*, *buzz*, and *ding* of our devices, yet we're addicted to hearing them. This is because every time we respond or get a notification that someone liked, commented, or re-tweeted something about us, our brains release dopamine, a neurotransmitter that's also called the 'pleasure chemical'.[10]

So if the presence of notifications boosts our moods, the opposite is also true; their absence deflates us.

Of course, not all notifications elicit positive emotions. For example, people become even more anxious and depressed if they receive notifications about their former partner and their new love interest.

So what do you do? I suggest you cut down on your social media use, especially if you notice that it's affecting your quality of life and contributing to your anxiety.

Top 6 Ways to Limit Social Media Use

1. Resist the urge to share everything. Enjoy an evening with friends for the sole purpose of being with friends, not to have an opportunity to snap something and post it on social media. Live in the moment and concentrate on those around you.

2. If you spend most of your time checking other people's accounts, limit the number of platforms you use on social media.

3. Turn off notifications. Disable or limit push notifications for social media or enable the Do Not Disturb mode on your mobile device. Trust me, that FoMO feeling you may have now will dissipate. After a couple of days, you will wonder why you ever had your notifications on in the first place. It's much more peaceful without them!

4. Take frequent digital timeouts during the day. Use apps to control your screen time or set the amount of time you plan to spend on social media. My limit is 20 minutes a day. I set a timer, and once that timer goes off, I shut down my social media apps.

5. Take a digital day off. Set one day in the week when you're off the grid. If you're a frequent poster, liker, or commenter, let family and close friends know so that they don't worry.

6. Go on a digital detox. Don't participate in social media for at least seven days. This will rehabilitate your brain from craving it. Out of sight, out of mind.

A word of caution: Sometimes, people are active online because of a sense of belonging and self-importance. If you go offline for an extended period and no one notices, that's okay. Please remember that you're going offline to take care of yourself and get back in touch with the REAL world, so go ahead and do that. Visit your mom, call a friend to meet up for drinks or dinner, or be quiet and read a book or clean your house. REAL LIFE has so much to offer, so be an active part of it.

Note: If you can't go on a digital detox because you use social media for your work or business then set some boundaries so that your work and personal lives don't overlap. Here are a few tips:

a) Consider delegating social-media related work to staff, a team member or even hire someone to do your social-media tasks for you.
b) Limit your use of social media for work only. This means you shouldn't check them outside work hours, nor access them for personal use. If possible, have a separate work phone where you install work-related social medis apps, and be sure to leave that device at the office.

Boundaries with Work

Whether you are a surgeon or a garbage collector, you have career responsibilities, work hours to adhere to, daily tasks to perform, and co-workers to deal with. Some co-workers are incredibly helpful and are great to work with, while others may need a lesson in teamwork and/or professionalism.

If you're struggling to set boundaries in the workplace, let me help you with this section. We will break this down a little into three categories: **work time boundaries**, **workload boundaries**, and **boundaries with co-workers**.

Work Time Boundaries

Like most of the population, you have set working hours. These hours are set by your employer and are usually part of a contract or a collective agreement. The expectation as to when you start and end working is clear (unless you have a workplace culture that fosters flexible working hours).

I have a friend who was an administrative assistant and payroll clerk for a small excavating company owner. Her boss, let's call him Paul, would call her at all hours, way past her 9-5 schedule. He would call as late as 1 a.m. on a Friday or on various hours during weekends, even if he knew she was away visiting family or me.
He would expect her to answer whatever question was on his mind at the time. He would call her to pick up his kids. He would call her when he was drunk and having marital issues. He even had her book a trip for him and his mistress. Boundaries? What boundaries?

Eventually, my friend had enough. She quit her job, and guess what? He continued to call her for a solid month afterward. He had handed so much of his work and personal business off to her that he needed information on many issues like where to find a certain contract, the status of certain bills, etc. He even asked for the contact information of his own divorce lawyer!

When she explained the situation to me, she told me she didn't quit sooner because *'the crew wouldn't get paid on time"*. She was worried that the men who worked for this guy wouldn't get their paychecks because no one knew how to do it. She even trained a new person at the job for a solid week after her scheduled exit date.

Bottom line, you need to set work time boundaries because if you don't, your life will be about taking care of someone else's life.

Workload Boundaries
When it comes to workload, don't accept it when a co-worker tries to dump their work on you. Some of these people are sly and might say something like, *'but you're so much better at it than me'*. That may well be the case, but don't be a

victim of your kindness here. Remember that if you give in, you may always be this colleague's 'go-to person'.

And difficult as it may be, you need to set boundaries with your boss too. If you don't, the goalpost of your responsibilities will move further all the time.

Workload boundaries function in a variety of ways and serve many purposes. The first benefit is that they clarify everyone's responsibilities. They help us maintain our emotional and physical well-being, remain focused on our individual principles, and identify our limits. Further, having clear workload boundaries will enable us to work more efficiently and effectively.

Workplace Boundary Examples

Workplace boundaries can only be set if there are clear-cut rules, to begin with. This establishes accountability and leaves little room for blame or excuses. Employees should be able to answer the following questions:

- What's your work schedule?
- To whom do you report?
- What's the scope of your work?

With the above examples, you can set the following sample boundaries.

- What's your work schedule? Once you know…
  Boundary: No calls to your home.
  Boundary: No calls beyond work hours.
  Boundary: No reading or replying to emails or messages after office hours.

- To whom do you report? Once you know…
  Boundary: No to projects handed by others.

Boundary: No to tasks co-workers want to pass on to you.

- What's the scope of your work? Once you know…
  Boundary: No to projects you cannot take on due to a full schedule.

Of course, projects evolve, and flexibility is also required in the workplace. But when you feel you are doing more than you should, it is time to speak out.

Workplace Interpersonal Boundaries

Working together effectively requires the establishment of good, motivating, and respectful interpersonal boundaries in employee-coworkers and employee-management relationships. Without them, there is a possibility of one side taking advantage of the other, or workplace bullying may occur in the worst-case scenario.

Here are some examples of workplace interpersonal boundaries you may want to adapt.

- To avoid your personal and workplace lives from overlapping, consider NOT adding colleagues to your social media accounts. (And don't follow them either!)
- You may want to avoid talking about your personal life or anything you don't feel comfortable sharing at work (e.g., important family events, your anxiety, your religion, your political beliefs, etc.)
- During disagreements with colleagues or managers, always advocate for respect. This means no one should be ridiculing or scolding others. Also, remember to focus on the *issue*, not the people you're disagreeing with.
- If possible, close your office doors to indicate you don't want to be disturbed or when you simply need some quiet time to focus.

- When receiving feedback, state clearly that constructive feedback is welcome, but negative criticism is not.

Work-Related Personal Boundaries

You may not realize it, but you may be contributing to your work anxiety by NOT setting work-related personal boundaries. Following are a few things to consider.

- Leave your laptop and any work-related files or documents at work so that you don't reach for them at home.
- You've informed co-workers that you don't want to be reached at home or beyond work hours. Still, someone calls. What do you do? Don't answer. **Note**: If you feel that not being available puts you in a situation where you don't get as much involved in a project or any work-related decisions, consider having these calls go to voicemail. However, when you do this, restrict the times you check them (e.g., only from 5-6 PM) and reply only to issues that truly cannot wait till the next workday.
- Take time off when you need it; it's your right as an employee, and you deserve it. A 2016 poll in the United States found that the average employee with the ability to take paid time off (PTO) only took about 16 days, leaving 662 million vacation days unutilized.[11] Don't feel chained to your desk. If you need a break to take care of yourself—take it.
- Work smart, not long. This means you may need to take a step back and re-evaluate how you work. Are you prioritizing the right tasks? Are you easily distracted by less productive issues? Are you taking on tasks you should delegate to others? Consider *how* you work and see if your current methods are serving you.

As always, the first step to setting boundaries is to know what is personally important to you. For example, if you want to focus on your physical health, that means ensuring you have time to do that. So you may want to set a personal work-related boundary regarding the time you leave work to have time to exercise before dinner.

So how do you establish clear boundaries work?

You may feel anxious about letting co-workers know what you like and don't like, but honestly, it's not as hard as you think. Communicate your boundaries one conversation at a time or as the need arises. For example, if you notice that lunch breaks are becoming political debate times, say simply that you prefer not to discuss your political beliefs at work and that you'd much rather have a peaceful lunch. If colleagues continue to do this, then remove yourself from the situation.

What do you do when people violate your boundaries?
Speak up right away. Imagine your boundaries as a 'No Trespassing' sign on a gate. When people ignore the sign and cross over, point to the sign and close the gate again.

Still, when someone does not respect your boundaries the first time, try to remain compassionate. Most people don't realize how their actions affect you, so let them know they crossed the line so they won't make the same mistake again. Use specific rather than personal explanations.

Don't speak from your perspective when discussing work boundaries. Instead of saying, *'I'm stressed'* or *'I have a lot to do'*, which sounds whiny, explain the reason for your boundary by stating how it will affect other projects, your clients, or your bottom line. For example, say something like, *'If I focus on X, I'll not be able to focus on Y.'*

Have a game plan. A person suffering from anxiety will be uneasy when a boundary is crossed. Often, the stress is not just about the boundary violation itself but about how to handle it. We don't want the conflict. However, I've found that one of the best ways to handle this is to have a plan. Think about how you will handle the situation. List down the step you want to take and visualize what will happen.

For example, suppose your boss sends you a dozen emails while you're on vacation when they know that you're away.

Think about the best way to handle such a situation.

Step 1: I'll create an Out of Office reply so that anyone who sends me a message while I'm gone knows that I will only reply by [date].
Step 2: When [date] arrives, and my boss asks me why I didn't reply, what should I say?
  a) I've properly informed everyone before I left that I would be on vacation; I expected that people would respect that.
  b) I don't work on weekends, let alone during vacation days. But please do let me know if there was anything unsatisfactory before I left.

By being prepared, you will be better able to handle conflict.

Boundaries with Co-Workers
How do you handle your co-workers' laundry list of issues? Let us count the ways.

- If you're new to the team and your ideas are being squashed by long-standing employees, set the boundary that you're not a pushover by asking *why* your idea won't work. Who knows, perhaps you will learn something from their expertise and feedback. But if their response is *'it just won't work'*, or *'we do it this way'*, then you know your ideas aren't the problem–it's them.

You may choose to let it go the first time, but push back if it keeps on happening.

Be ready to state your ideas a second time. If you have to get to the third time, state that you may have to bring your concerns to your boss. Most times, their claims are unfounded, and they will back down at this point. Be confident. Do not waver. Practice beforehand if you feel you need to.

- Workplace harassment or bullying is never to be tolerated. The first time this happens, make sure it's the last time by strongly stating your boundaries. If it happens again, collect evidence and present this to your supervisor or inform human resources.

If you're having boundary issues with your supervisor or boss, here are a few tips on how to handle the situation.

- **Be clear about the boundary being crossed.** It's important to be communicate clearly. For example: I value my time at home so please note that I don't answer emails after 7 PM.
- **Be ready with a non-emotional response.** If your boss has a habit of adding tasks to your list, instead of saying, "*I'm overloaded!*", say "*Just to clarify… if I do, 'B', then I won't have time for 'A', which you gave last week. Do you prefer this?*"

  In short, don't make the issue about you. Show your boss the 'bigger picture'. You can even add, "*I'll prioritize what you tell me but I'm almost done with 'A', just so you know*" or "*I'll prioritize what you tell me but I believe 'A' is needed by Monday.*"

- If your boss is not getting the message and keeps on crossing your boundaries, then do as above, collect evidence and present this to your human resources department.

- Consider how much you want to share. Like it or not, you'll be sending a lot of time with your co-workers. And yes, sometimes, knowing each other as individuals (as opposed to just a colleague) means better teamwork.

  So consider what you're willing to share. If you find the questions too invasive (e.g., Who are you dating? How's your married life? Do you go to church?, etc.), one question I have in my back pocket is: *why do you want to know?*

  This usually tells the person asking that I'm finding their questions inappropriate, stopping them in their tracks. If they do not stop, feel free to repeat your question. They'll get the hint!

Everyone has a right to a stress-free work environment and fair treatment. If you don't feel comfortable where you're working, the first step is always to state your boundaries in a friendly yet firm manner.

Again, be ready to explain what is acceptable to you and *why*. People often set boundaries by saying, '*It's not OK to*' or '*I don't want you to*' without stating their reasons. When this happens, your listener may become defensive and more likely to challenge your boundaries. So when always state your WHY. For example, say something like, '*It's not OK to interrupt my lunch hour with projects because I use that time to collect my thoughts and plan the rest of my tasks in the afternoon.*'

Consider giving your audience clear options, too, such as, '*I appreciate your emails and calls, but I would appreciate it if you email OR I call you at the end of the day if your note is not urgent. Which would you prefer?*'

You should also mention project goals when setting your boundary. For instance, '*If I'm not always in meetings and answering emails, I can focus on our clients better, and we'll hit our quota easier for this month.*' This way, your co-worker gets the big picture and, in doing so, may understand and support your boundary faster.

When all else fails, think if quitting is an option for you. Life is too short to be working with people who don't respect your boundaries. If you don't find going to work enjoyable anymore and view the workplace as nothing but a place of stress, then you should really consider quitting for your mental health.

What should you do when co-workers respect your boundary?

Consider that your co-workers may not be used to some of your boundaries because they've never encountered them before. Further, remember that setting boundaries is also asking others to stop what they are doing for your benefit. So when colleagues change and respect your boundaries, don't forget to say 'Thank You'. Depending on the gravity of the boundary, you may even give a small gift or token of thanks or simply say, "*Hey, just wanted to say I appreciate you respecting my boundary. How about lunch on me?*'

Work boundaries shouldn't divide you from your colleagues. Communicated the right away, you'll find that it helps not just you but also others in establishing a healthy and productive work environment.

Boundaries with Your Spouse/SO

You meet someone. You fall in love. You decide to live with this person for the rest of your life. But sometimes, darn, this person is annoying!

Like any relationship, setting boundaries with your partner should happen at the beginning of the relationship. Still, if you're with someone for a long time already, that doesn't mean you can't set boundaries anymore. There's no deadline for setting boundaries.

For instance, suppose you don't like it when your partner comes home while you're sleeping and makes a lot of noise as they get into bed. Or perhaps they turn the lights too early in the morning, waking you up unnecessarily. Whatever is bothering you, you need to be able to talk about it.

Suppose you and your friends are out together and your partner starts to flirt with someone. Some couples won't be affected by this because they feel secure in their relationship, but this can be a big issue if you have insecurities or have been the victim of infidelity. Although your partner may interact with other people this way when they first met you, you're not comfortable with that anymore. And you need to effectively communicate this with your partner. Otherwise, you'll end up feeling resentment towards them.

Setting your boundaries doesn't have to mean a fight. Your relationship can be strengthened in the long run by letting your partner know about issues that bother you.

Stating your boundaries with your significant other (SO) can require more kindness than with anyone else in your life. This is because you're so entwined with each other's lives, feelings, thoughts, and hopes for the future, that you don't want to hurt their feelings.

You also have to consider that your partner has been raised differently, and what works for you may not work for them. For instance, maybe your partner doesn't enjoy onions, and so instead of putting them into your pasta sauce like you have your entire life, you suddenly need to change things because you're living with somebody you love. Respecting each other's boundaries, communicating each other's needs and wants, and listening well to each other are the basis of any healthy, long-lasting relationship.

This is why it's important to have a clear idea of what you want and don't want in a relationship ahead of time. I've met many unhappy people, yet they stay with their partners because they don't want to be alone.

My first relationship was a disaster because I catered only to my girlfriend's needs and neglected my own. In the end, she lost attraction and respect for me. The funny thing is that a year after we broke up, she was attracted to me again since I had matured a lot. However, I was a different person and knew that she wasn't the right person for me.

I strongly advise you spend time thinking about what you want in a partner and write it down on paper. Think about the most important qualities that you want and don't want so that when you are dating someone, you can filter out people who are a terrible match for you. Knowing what you want is key!

Establishing relationship boundaries can be done in a variety of ways. To get you started, here are some suggestions.

1) **Start early.** Boundaries are much easier to establish at the beginning of any relationship than later because you're both emotionally invested and have established habits and routines by then.

2) **Communication is key.** It's important to remember that setting your boundaries should NOT be a one-way conversation. That's just asking for a fight.

   Start by timing your conversation right. For instance, don't start this when your partner has just woken up or spring this conversation at the end of their day when you know they're tired and stressed. Choose your moment and then say something like, *'Babe, can we sit down and talk?'*

3) **Use 'I' statements.** The way you say something is more important than what you say. So start with statements like *'I feel'* or *'I think'* or *'I am'*. If you begin with an accusatory statement such as *'You always'* or *'You never'*, you will be met with *'I don't want to'*.

   Remember, nobody wants to be rejected or criticized, and getting back on track can be difficult once defensive barriers arise. You should strive to set boundaries with kindness based on how you wish to be treated.

   Also, always state the reason for your boundaries. For example, *'Babe, I am a light sleeper, so when you get into bed noisily, I wake up and have a hard time falling asleep again, making me groggy in the morning. I am just asking you to be mindful of that when you get into bed. Is that okay? Does that sound reasonable to you?'*

   Even though it's a 'boundary' for you, you must get their opinion on this so that your statements don't come across as a command.

   Also, be specific with what you want or need. For example, your boundary is that you want one night a week to be alone, study, or read. If you're specific about why you need this alone time, your partner will receive it a lot better than if you say, *'Can you just leave me alone Thursday nights?'*

Asking for space is okay.

Regardless of how short or long you are in your relationship, know that it's okay to want to have some space. For example, you may need to decompress for half an hour if you have a demanding job when you get home. But instead of saying, *'Can you just leave me alone?'*, isn't it more beneficial to say, *'Babe, I just need 30 minutes when I come home to shift my mind from work. I'll be more useful to you and the kids that way. So when I come home, I'll be moving my ass to the offices first, okay?'*

The important thing is to explain that your request isn't a rejection of your partner. It's just something you need for yourself.

Keep in mind that things change.

Every relationship is different, and everything is flexible. During your relationship, there can be events that cause boundaries to shift, including:

- Becoming a parent.
- Moving into a new home.
- Getting a new job.
- Losing a loved one.
- Making new friends.

So even though a boundary has been stated, keep in mind that there should be room for change, development, and growth

Boundaries with Self

Lastly, let's talk about boundaries we should have with ourselves.

I'm currently transitioning to a work-at-home position, and I am guilty of rolling over and grabbing my phone first thing in the morning. Because of this, I start my day with my brain already churning before my body is even caffeinated.

So, I'm developing a morning routine that includes meditation and yoga so that I don't start my day with stress and demands. Carving out this 'ME time' takes some discipline, but I know it's for my own good, so I make the necessary changes.

For example, I have replaced my phone alarm with a traditional clock. This enables me to leave my phone in my office to charge overnight so that I don't get a chance to start checking my emails the minute I wake up.

Before I even set foot in my office, I start with some coffee, do about 30 minutes of stretching and meditating, and 5 minutes of journaling which includes a grateful practice.

In doing so, I start my workday feeling prepared mentally and physically. My goal is to increase this morning routine to a 60-minute routine where I walk first, stretch, and journal.

Some days, it takes more willpower to avoid my phone because I know emails are waiting from overseas clients who expect an answer before going to bed.

BUT...

My inner peace, mental focus, and physical well-being are more important than any client. I refuse to work before 8:30 AM. This mindset serves me well, but I'm still developing it, and the temptation to dive right into work is there almost every day. Creating these boundaries with myself serve me well in establishing discipline and protecting myself from burnout.

So I urge you to ask yourself these questions.

- *In what ways can I care for myself that I'm not currently doing?*
- *Are there needs in my life that I'm ignoring for the benefit of other people?*
- *What do I want to do if I had a FULL DAY all to myself?*
- *What do I want to do if I had a FULL WEEK all to myself?*
- *What new habits have I been thinking about that I just don't have time for now?*

Write down your answers on a sheet of paper. Analyze them. Are they really not doable? Chances are, THEY ARE. And if they're not ALL doable now, I guarantee there will be at least a few things you can do starting today. It's just that you haven't prioritized yourself before and set boundaries with yourself.

If you've been telling yourself, *'I really need to lose a little bit of weight'* or *'I should really get some good-quality sleep'*, now is the time to set some of these self-care and self-love goals that need to happen.

You can set a deadline for yourself to get you to commit to your goals. For instance, I used to work until 10 or 11 at night. Now, I stop working at 7:30 pm. Then I work out, eat dinner, listen to an audiobook, and relax for the rest of the night.

I suggest you start by trying to establish a morning routine. Science says that it's extremely beneficial to making us more productive and less stressed during the day.[12]

Start with small changes, and don't shock your system. For example, if you wake up at 8 AM, set the alarm for 7AM and then give yourself about 20 minutes each day where you can't be disturbed. This time is only for you, and you can do anything you want.

Life is too short to work yourself to the point where your body shows signs of stress. Your anxiety levels will decrease if you take the time to care for yourself and love yourself the way you deserve to be cared for and loved.

Setting boundaries is one of the most important ways you can practice self-care. If you don't set boundaries with yourself and the people around you, you'll find yourself running on empty soon because you will give and give and give… until there's nothing left.

Communicating boundaries does not mean you're selfish. It just means you're not self**LESS**.

Many people are concerned that setting boundaries means losing relationships. On the contrary, my friend, it means establishing better and stronger relationships with people who really care about you. And if you lose someone, that's okay. Any person who doesn't respect your boundaries will only contribute to your anxiety or any mental health issue you may have.

So, protect yourself. Identify and communicate your boundaries. Define your space and look after your mental well-being, and you will be rewarded with better relationships.

WORKBOOK: WEEK 2 - Setting Boundaries

Boundaries are personal 'No Trespassing' signs you raise to promote your well-being and help ensure that we are not affected by others' actions and behaviors.

Although boundaries aim to protect you, you should ensure that you set **HEALTHY BOUNDARIES** and not unhealthy ones.

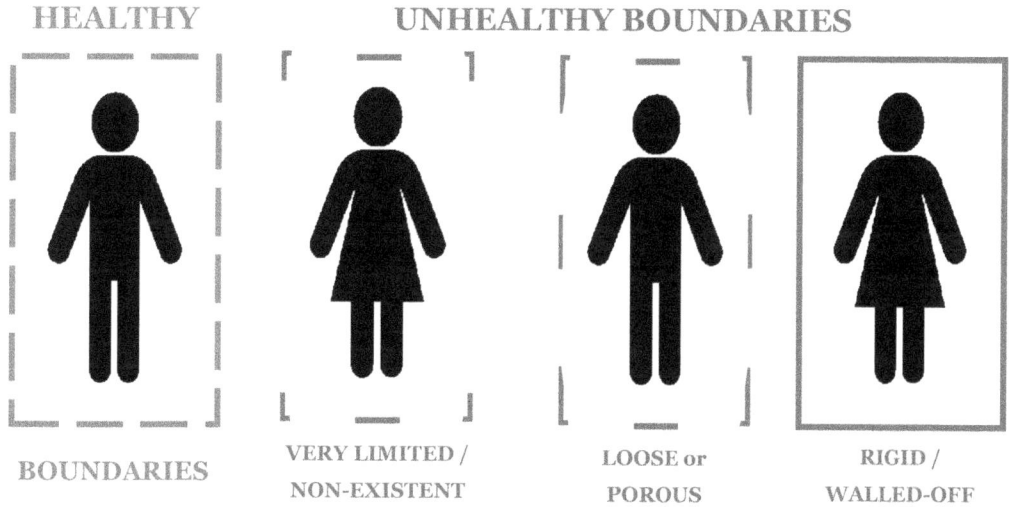

With the above in mind, please do the following exercise.

It indicates different types of boundaries and what they mean. Note there may be other boundaries you want to set that are not covered in the diagram (e.g., financial, internal spiritual, etc.) If so, then please feel free to add them to below or to a separate **My Personal Boundaries** sheet.

Remember, there are no right or wrong statements here.

All you need to do is consider what YOU want.

Exercise: Setting YOUR Boundaries

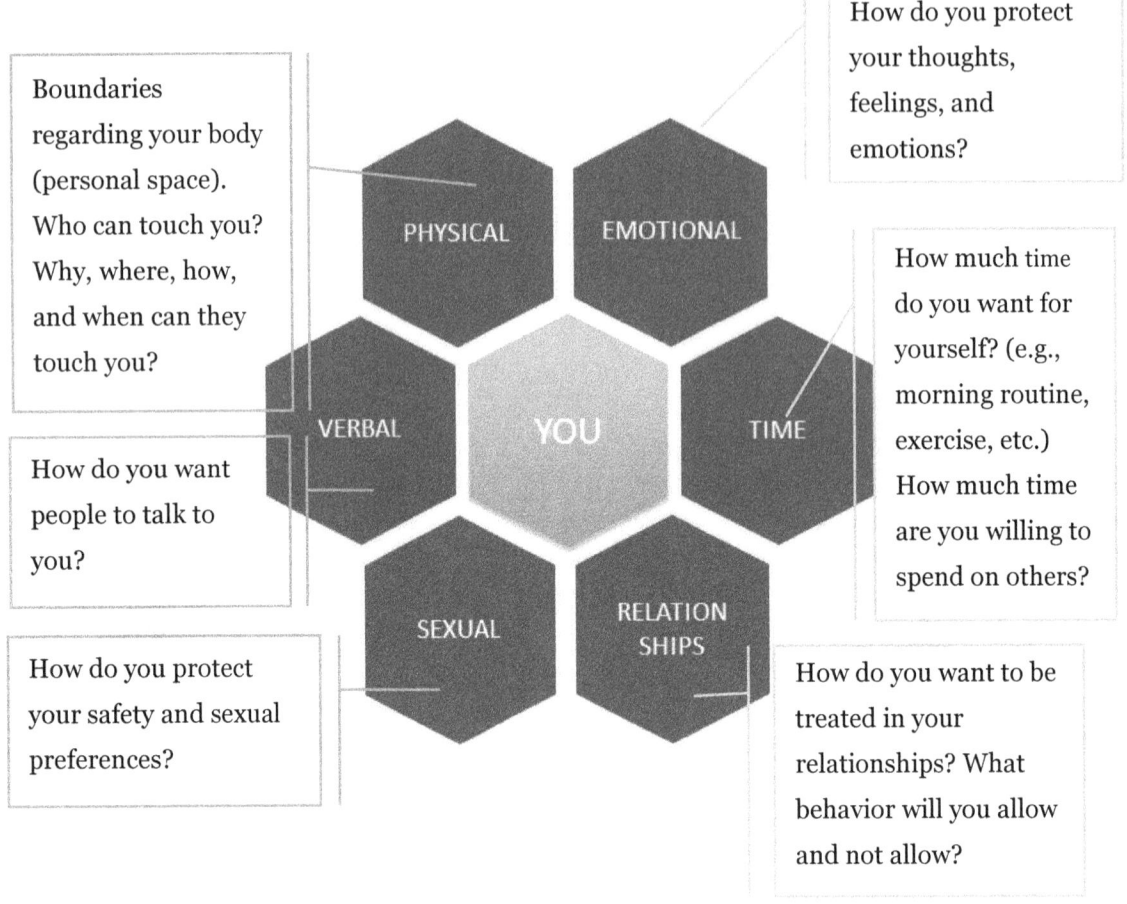

Write your personal boundaries below. If necessary, get another piece of paper, label it your **My Personal Boundaries** and lay it all out there.

Physical Boundaries:
1.)
2.)
3.)

Verbal Boundaries:

1.)

2.)

3.)

Sexual Boundaries:

1.)

2.)

3.)

Emotional Boundaries:

1.)

2.)

3.)

Time Boundaries:

1.)

2.)

3.)

Relationship Boundaries:

1.)

2.)

3.)

Exercise: Boundary Journaling

If you're struggling to set and maintain boundaries, then you may want to sit down and make some notes about why and with whom you're having trouble setting boundaries with.

Take note of your feelings. Is someone or something triggering these emotions? Write everything down.

Next, answer this question: *what else is true?* This will give you a new perspective on the situation, and you may begin to see the person or circumstance differently as a result. If you feel a boundary has been crossed, develop a game plan on how to address the person or issue causing your distress.

STEP 1. Pick an area in your life making you anxious now.

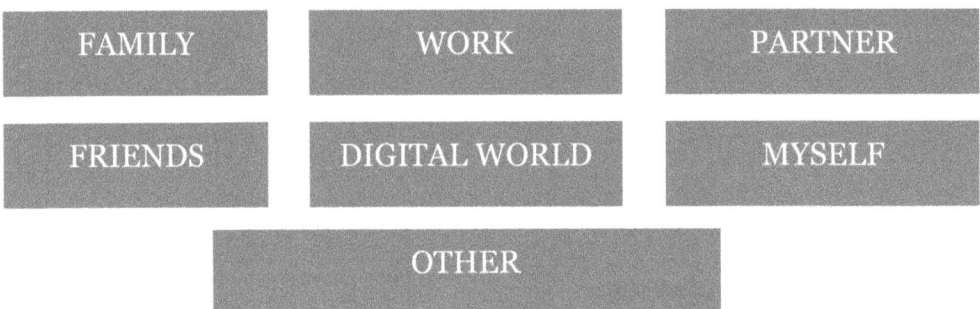

STEP 2. What are you feeling? (You can choose more than one.)

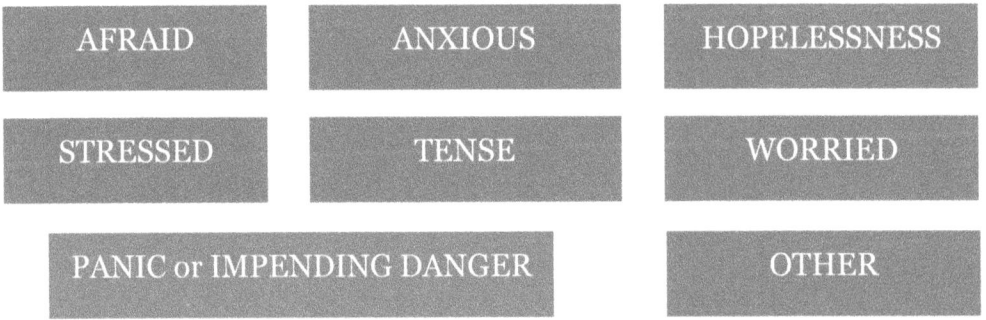

STEP 3. Is a specific person or event making you feel this?

Your answer: _____

STEP 4: Which boundary is being violated? (You can choose more than one.)

- PHYSICAL
- EMOTIONAL
- VERBAL
- TIME
- SEXUAL
- RELATIONSHIP
- OTHER

STEP 5: Describe, in the simplest of words, the current situation.
Example:

> **Area:** Family || **Emotion:** Stressed, Tense|| **Person:** Mom
> **Statement**: Mom called and is demanding I attend Sunday dinner and make up with my brother. My brother has told me – over lunch! – that he doesn't value me at all and wouldn't mind no further contact with me.

Your turn:

_____
_____
_____
_____

STEP 6. What else is true?

Example: Mom just really wants me to attend Sunday dinner because we haven't seen each other in over a month.

Your turn:

_____
_____
_____
_____

STEP 7: List down how you can re-instate your boundary.

Example: Mom, I love you, but I will not attend Sunday dinner. I need time to process how I feel about [brother] because he really hurt me. I will see you next Sunday.

Your turn:

Option #1.

_____
_____
_____

Option #2.

_____
_____
_____

Option #3.

Chapter 3: Anxiety, Stress, and Worry

"Anxiety is like a rocking chair. It gives you something to do, but it doesn't get you very far."

- Jodi Picoult

The following is a story from a friend, KR:

When I was pregnant with my first child, I read every book I could get my hands on about pregnancy and babies. The books brought me knowledge, but they also made me a what-if monster. I constantly worried that I was gaining too much weight and causing a problem for my baby. I fretted over if I would be capable of caring for a baby properly. My mother hadn't been the best example, so I was determined to be the Best Parent in the World.

When the baby came, he was a happy, healthy little guy, and soon after he was born, he became very ill with a disease that had nothing to do with anything we had done as parents. Still, I wracked my brain over things I could have done differently to prevent an unpreventable disease.

For years after he recovered, I continued to worry excessively. I once asked my doctor if it was normal to keep my hands locked on my kids at all times while in public. I was hypervigilant about cars, strangers, foods, trampolines; you name it – everything was a danger, and I was a Mama Bear, ready to strike if anything came for my cubs.

In my 30's, my doctor sat me down, and we talked about my fears. I was then diagnosed with an anxiety disorder. I received medication, learned coping strategies to care for myself, and I can confidently say that I am now able to walk into a store with my now 23-year-old son and not worry that he might get hit by a car.

In fact, he's traveled the world with my blessing, starting at age 16! Thanks to my doctor recognizing that I needed help with my anxiety, I and my son both lead healthier lives.

Many different circumstances in our life can lead to anxiety, stress, or worry. It's normal to experience anxiety on the first day at a new job, on your wedding day, or when you're about to sign the closing papers on your first house.
It's when anxiety interferes with your day-to-day functioning that you should evaluate your situation and speak to a health professional.

You are not alone if you're feeling overwhelmed and anxious, and you shouldn't feel shame in seeking professional help. Some of the signs that you need to watch for are:

- You no longer enjoy the things that you once did.
- You avoid situations that you once enjoyed, like socializing.
- You use alcohol or drugs to get through unpleasant situations.
- You experience one or more of the following:
    - A preoccupation with irrational fears and excessive worry.
    - Inability to fall or stay asleep.
    - Panic attacks.
    - Feeling too hot or cold.
    - Feeling restless, agitated, or irritable.
    - Weakness, dizziness, shaking, etc.

- Digestion problems.
- Chest pains.
- Difficulty focusing.
- Increase in heart rate.

A doctor can help you evaluate whether your anxiety is acute or transitory or whether you have an anxiety disorder. The following is a sample self-assessment form a professional may pose.

SELF-ASSESSMENT STATEMENT	Never	Sometimes	Most of the Time	All the Time
I find myself unable to sit still.				
I worry about several things at once.				
I am restless, agitated, skittish, or irritable.				
I am unable to feel calm or relaxed.				
I am unable to let go of feelings of fear or anxiety.				
I have been feeling moody and upset.				
I feel dread or feel that something terrible may happen to me or others.				
I have difficulty concentrating.				
I have difficulty getting to sleep and/or staying asleep.				
I have muscle tension.				

If you find yourself answering a good number of these points with *Most of the Time* or *All the Time*, professional help is advised.

Types of Anxiety

Mild anxiety is a sense that something is not quite right and that something needs extra scrutiny. Stimulating the senses will help you focus, which aids in learning, problem-solving, acting, thinking, and feeling better.

Note that mild anxiety is not always a bad thing. People are often motivated to change their behaviors or work toward a goal when mildly anxious. For example, students who are anxious about their exams can use that nervousness to concentrate better and develop better studying habits.

Moderate anxiety is when a person feels agitated over something (or someone) to the point that their sole focus is on the stressful situation. For example, say that you have a doctor's appointment. You might experience a faster heartbeat, stomach cramps, dry mouth, or even nausea over the appointment. When trying to explain the purpose of the appointment to others, you may talk faster than you normally do, make nervous hand gestures, or even bite your nails. These all point to the fact that your singular focus is the upcoming doctor's appointment.

When the date arrives, and your doctor gives you a clean bill of health, all your anxious symptoms subside.

Severe Anxiety is when a person panics to the point where all their survival skills become more primitive, defensive responses are initiated, and cognitive abilities sharply decline.

For instance, a person with severe anxiety who has suddenly been laid off from work may experience severe chest pains, vomiting, body shakes, scattered thoughts, and an extreme sense of dread over the future.

With severe anxiety, your ability to concentrate and find solutions is drastically impaired, which may lead to even more anxiety. You may not even be able to take care of your own needs, such as getting out of bed or eating on time. Attempts by loved ones to assist you are likely to be futile because you cannot move on from the stressful situation.

Types of Anxiety Disorders

People with anxiety disorders develop maladaptive behaviors and emotional disabilities because anxiety does not signal danger or prompt any motivation for change. Instead, the anxiety has become chronic, taking over their lives.

There are many manifestations of anxiety disorders. Following are some types.

Generalized Anxiety Disorder is characterized by persistent and excessive worry and anxiety for at least six months. During these events, you may experience uncontrolled worrying, significant distress, or social or occupational functioning impairment. In addition, you may suffer from restlessness, fatigue, difficulty concentrating or going blank, irritability, muscle tension, and sleep disturbances.

Panic Disorder is a state in which a person has reoccurring panic episodes. A panic attack is a brief period of acute dread that results in strong bodily symptoms such as hyperventilation, sweating, hot and cold flashes, trembling, rapid heart rate, inability to gather thoughts and speak coherently, feeling detached from reality, etc. Many people experience a panic attack once or twice in their lives. If you're experiencing more frequent panic attacks and find yourself constantly worrying about your next likely panic attack, you may be dealing with a panic disorder.

Social Anxiety Disorder (SAD) is a condition wherein a person experiences extreme fear in social settings. People with this disorder are afraid of being judged by others, so they avoid meeting people and attending social gatherings at all costs. Avoidance becomes their default behavior. Unfortunately, avoidance can make SAD worse because instead of learning coping mechanisms, the resulting isolation makes them even more anxious the next time they're in a social setting.

Obsessive-Compulsive Disorder (OCD) is a state in which a person experiences repeated undesirable views or emotions (obsessions) or the need to perform something again and again (compulsions). Most people with OCD recognize that their obsessions and/or compulsions are excessive and unreasonable, but they can't help but give in to them. Left untreated, it is almost impossible to ignore, suppress, or neutralize obsessions with compulsions. (For more details regarding OCD, please see Chapter 7: OCD & Compulsive Behaviors.)

Acute Stress Disorder is a condition wherein a person experiences a powerful and negative reaction to a traumatic event. Symptoms include feelings of intense fear, helplessness, hopelessness, horror, significant distress, or impaired functioning. There must be at least three of the following symptoms to make a diagnosis: (1) emotional detachment, (2) reduced awareness, (3) derealisation, (4) depersonalization, and (5) dissociative amnesia (inability to recall important aspects of the event).

Acute Stress Disorder can last from two days to four weeks. If you're experiencing this longer than this period, you may have post-traumatic stress disorder.

Post-Traumatic Stress Disorder (PTSD) is a condition that's caused by exposure to a traumatic event that involves intense fear, helplessness, or horror. With PTSD, the person can't help but re-experience or re-live the traumatic event no matter how hard they try to get past it. It typically begins within three months to years after the event and may last a few months or years.

PTSD symptoms include intrusive recollections or dreams, flashbacks, and physical and psychological distress over reminders of the event. Avoidance and disassociation become a PTSD sufferer's recourse. For instance, this person may not want to see or talk to anyone associated with the traumatic event. Character changes are also common such as increased irritability, sudden and unprovoked angry outbursts, hypervigilance, exaggerated startle response, etc. (Please see Chapter 6: PTSD and Panic Disorders for a more detailed explanation of this condition.)

A **Phobia** is when a person experiences severe anxiety over a specific object or situation, which often results in avoidance (of that stimuli). Typically, phobias do not arise due to past negative experiences; you may have a phobia over something you've never encountered before.

Many people who have a phobia over something know that their fear is unusual and irrational, and they may even joke about how silly it is. Despite this, however, they feel powerless to stop their fear of it.

According to behavioral theorists, anxiety is mostly obtained from experiences. So if you *learned* anxiety, you could unlearn it by the same token. And one of the concepts related to this is *learned optimism*.

Learned Optimism

Two hamsters were placed in two separate cages. Hamster 'A' was given light electric shocks, but there's an option to escape the cage and move to another where there are no shocks. He tried; he succeeded and has moved to the shock-free cage.

Hamster 'B' was also subjected to light electric shocks, but unlike Hamster 'A', there were no ways to escape his cage. It becomes clear to 'B' that he has no control over the situation. His only option is to sit and accept the shocks.

After some time, hamsters 'A' and 'B' were removed from their cages and placed in two separate brand new cages. Both cages provided the option of escape. What do you think happened?

After the first light electric shock, 'A', knowing that he was able to escape the first time, quickly moved his ass and escaped. 'B', however, stayed put after receiving the first shock. He didn't even try. He was *conditioned* to accept the poor treatment. This is called *learned helplessness*.

Learned optimism is the opposite of learned helplessness. It's a concept developed by Martin Seligman[13], who's considered the father of positive psychology. It's the idea that you can learn to be optimistic and happy by challenging negative self-talk and replacing them with positive ones.

If you think that this is easier said than done, I can confirm that it is.

Happiness, optimism, and positivity are views that I personally need to keep on cultivating. You see, as a kid, I hated my life.

Anxiety and depression were my constant companions. I longed for that happy, normal family like what I saw on TV. Instead, my childhood was filled with anxiety. I was constantly worried about doing something wrong and making my dad angry. My parents' constant fighting (and eventual divorce) always made me nervous, stressed, and worried.

As I got older, I would complain a lot. I was always negative about everything—the eternal pessimist. In my mind, there was never any hope of things improving. Truth be told, I probably learned that from my mother, who always played the victim card and never took responsibility for her actions. So I, too, always thought that life was just something happening to me. I'm the victim here since I have no control over anything.

After a lot of self-reflection and many attempts at working on myself, I finally started to heal. As mentioned earlier, taking the step to understand my parent's life stories and culture also helped me. (They were not out to cause me stress. They just didn't know better and continued a parenting pattern they learned from their parents.)

Also, traveling, living overseas, and getting to know various people opened my eyes and mind. Suddenly, I realized that most of the things I complained about were within my control, which meant I could change them.

I realized that many of the things that happened to me didn't just 'happen'; they were the results of my own decisions.

I started to look around my social circle. Why did my friends achieve amazing things, and I didn't? I realized that it wasn't because life was hard on me. My friends *chose* to consistently work hard each day and improve their lives. Once I became aware of this, I recognized that I could also achieve the same results, if not more, by doing what they did and putting in the hard work.

As a result of this mindset shift, that I can do anything I set my mind to, I was able to change many aspects of my life for the better. This included my health, dating life, and business.

So **if I can move from *learned helplessness* to *learned optimism*, so can you**!

Studies have shown that learned optimism positively affects a person's psychological and physical well-being.[14,15] It's also seen as effective for handling stress, negative emotions, and pessimism.[16]

Optimists generally achieve more, lead healthier lives, and experience more happiness in life. On the other hand, pessimists are more prone to give up, suffer from sadness, and not enjoy life.

To explain why things are permanent, ubiquitous, or personal, pessimists and optimists have different explanation styles. Let's say you walk up to a lady at a bar and offer her a drink. She declines your offer.

Pessimists believe this is a permanent trend: *I will never get a girlfriend.* Optimists believe that there's no trend here, and it's a one-off situation: *Ah, that didn't work. No sweat. There are plenty of girls out there who'll like me.*

Pessimists: *I'm not interesting.*
Optimists: *She's not interested in me. That's ok. It doesn't mean I'm uninteresting.*

Pessimists will also take this very personally: *I'm ugly. That's why she humiliated me.*

Optimists will not take things personally so easily: *She was probably not in the mood, or I'm just not her type. No harm, no foul.*

When you have a pessimistic explanatory style, you will have your soul crushed. All my friends who were good with women always optimistically explained things.

Optimism is much more helpful than pessimism, but you also need balance. Someone who's too optimistic may become delusional and be unable to see reality.

For example, say you have a business idea and are naively optimistic about it. Even though the business isn't going anywhere, you keep wasting resources on this idea. Nothing has changed after six months of giving it everything you've got. And still, you say, '*Oh, this part of the project is slow, but the business is wonderful!*'

Eventually, you will lose support for your business, so you think, '*Well, maybe they were just in a bad mood today.*'

At some point, optimism needs to give way to reality. Being positive doesn't mean you should be blind, and you need to take responsibility whenever necessary. Otherwise, you will not only lose your business but potentially family, friends, and your life savings.

So, by all means, dive into learned optimism. (It's helped me A LOT!) Trying to see things from different perspectives can be very helpful when dealing with anxiety. Just don't swing too far and lose sight of reality.

So, how do you become a more optimistic person? Here are some things you can do to re-train your brain to be more positive.

1. **Engage in optimistic self-talk.** Promote positivity by modeling positive self-talk. Simple reflections about what you enjoyed about your day, what you're grateful for, and what you intend to do to maximize your next day can be a powerful start to cultivating positive thoughts.

   And don't be shy and give yourself credit whenever you deserve it! For example, did you help a friend? Called someone and made their day? Helped someone cross the street or get something at the grocery store they can't reach? Did you smile at someone?

   Also, think of the strengths or skills you possess. You know there's GOOD in you, and you just need to tune into them more.

2. **Practice self-empathy.** BE KIND TO YOURSELF. Acknowledge your feelings and realize that you deserve kindness, understanding, and compassion just like everyone else. By becoming empathic with ourselves, we can understand better what we are going through.

3. **Put more emphasis on intention and effort rather than results.** Build optimism by having the right attitude, to begin with. Positive thinkers always prioritize the *process* over the results. It is important to encourage yourself to partake in activities without thinking about the outcome. Be grateful for your efforts to become someone who believes in themselves and never gives up.

   And if something didn't turn out the way you planned, don't be too hard on yourself. Instead of judging your participation in it as a 'failure', commend yourself for trying and then use that situation as a learning experience. Next time you'll know better, so you'll do better.

4. *Think of happier times.* Bad times are never-ending—if you keep thinking about them. Instead, remember past experiences that made you happy. Visualize that situation; remember what you felt then. Next, think of a past event that initially left you feeling sad but eventually overcame them. Now, let this motivate you. Think, *'if I overcame that, I can overcome this too now'*. (See related exercise, **The Happiness Habit**, on page 88).

5. *Change your perspective.* *What else could be true?* If you're a pessimist, you need to constantly challenge your automatic negative way of thinking. Over time, you won't even need to shift your perspective. You'll find that you've broken the habit of thinking negatively and that thinking positively is now your nature.

6. *TUNE OUT negativity.* Look around you? Is anyone or anything contributing to your negativity? For example, are you at a job you're miserable in? Does the news depress you? Do you have a friend that does nothing but complain? (I mentioned before that it's said we're the average of our five (5) closest friends[5], so make the effort to find those who support and motivate. Don't surround yourself with people who bring you down.)

List these external sources and plan how you can change *your* situation (not them).

As I've previously shared, I realized at one point that my family was the source of my negativity. So as hard as it was to do, living away from them (I moved to another continent!), at least for a while, was one of the best things I've ever done for myself.

WORKBOOK: WEEK 3 – Learned Optimism

Exercise: The ABCDE Model

The **ABCDE Model** was developed by Martin Seligman[13] to gauge your current mindset and to help you become more optimistic.

Adversity: What difficult situation have you experienced recently?

Example: I'm on a new diet, and it's frustrating me.

Belief: What are the thoughts running through your mind about this adversity?

Example: I just don't have willpower. I'm never going to reach my goals. It's too hard.

Consequence: What consequences and behaviors resulted from your beliefs in step 2?

Example: The thought that I don't have willpower prevented me from meal planning and prepping. (What's the point?)

Disputation: Argue or dispute your beliefs in step 2.

Example: Willpower… I don't have it, or I'm not using/cultivating it? Maybe I just do this one meal at a time. Then it won't be too hard.

Energization: How do you feel now that you've challenged your initial (automatic?) beliefs?

Example: I feel a bit pumped up again. I'll check out IG and Pinterest and look at some simple healthy recipes for inspiration. I'll make a 3-day meal plan and see how I go about that.

Now, it's your turn! Please fill out the following.

A — Adversity

B — Belief

C — Consequence

D — Disputation

E — Energization

IMPORTANT: Please remember that becoming more optimistic in life is an ongoing process. Each time you face a challenge, I encourage you to go through this exercise. Repetition is vital if you want to shift away from one learned mindset to a new one.

You'll find it easier to identify your pessimistic (negative) beliefs and challenge them with continued practice. And in doing so, become more optimistic (positive) about yourself and life.

You've got this!

Exercise: The Happiness Habit

In my journey, I came across a book by *Shawn Achor* called *The Happiness Advantage*[17]. In it is an exercise that has helped me develop the habit of thinking and building happy memories. And in doing so, I was able to adjust my way of thinking from looking at the negative to looking for the positive things in life. I hope this exercise helps you too.

Write down three (3) things that you are grateful for today.
1.)
2.)
3.)

–OR–

Write down one (1) positive event that has happened in the last 24 hours.

NEXT...

> **Select a positive event from either of your lists above and then do this for 30 consecutive days.**

I will _____ for 30 days.

Anxiety and the Wise Mind

Unlike other types of therapy where you're asked to delve into your past, DBT focuses more on the here and now. So, if you're seeing or planning to see a DBT therapist, you'll most likely be asked to respond about current pain points in your life.

The discussion may go into your past and why those pain points developed, but the focus is on how to solve the issues you're currently facing. DBT teaches you to think logically, not emotionally, to respond to problems.

And here's where you learn about the DBT concept called **WISE MIND**.

According to DBT, our minds have two sides: the **EMOTIONAL** and the **REASONABLE** sides. Both sides have their pros and cons, and there is no judgment about which one is better.

The **EMOTIONAL MIND** is when we let our **feelings take control** of our thoughts and actions. Sometimes, people have a sense of self-stigma and wonder why they aren't more 'reasonable'. But being reasonable all the time isn't possible—because we're humans. And humans have emotions.

Further, emotions do not have to be negative. Overly emotional people do get labeled as people who have outbursts but being in your emotional mind could be something as simple as expressing love.

The **REASONABLE MIND** is when **logic takes control**. We weigh the pros and cons and then decide—based on facts—the best way to move forward. For example, you want to fit in a daily exercise routine. There's a gym five minutes away from your office, but you don't like getting caught in rush hour traffic at the end of your day. So, you *reason out* that going to the gym before work is the best solution for you.

DBT states that by combining these two parts of our minds, we create a third mind called the **WISE MIND**. This is taking the best components of our emotional and reasonable minds to arrive at decisions we feel good about, instead of reacting at the moment (knee-jerk reaction) and then having more regret later.

People who suffer from anxiety are prone to let their Emotional Minds rule. However, it's not that you never practice your Wise Mind either. For example, when speaking to your significant other (SO) about what to have for dinner, you're probably using your Wise Mind there.

Your Reasonable Mind is taking stock of the ingredients you have on hand, and you're probably considering what you had yesterday. But because you love your partner, your Emotional Mind is considering what they would want to eat. So, the Wise Mind is the marriage between your emotional and rational minds.

EMOTIONAL MIND

Ruled by emotion, mood, feelings, urges.

anger
sadness
stress
anxiety
bitterness
fear

REASONABLE MIND

Ruled facts, reason, logic.

experience
information
research
data
logic
facts

WISE MIND

I accept these emotions.
My feelings are valid.
I just need to stay calm here.
BREATHE.
I don't need to react now.
ZOOM OUT.
Ok, what do I know FOR SURE?
What's the best solution?

Wise Mind Qualities

The Wise Mind is **calm and peaceful**. It honors the Emotional Mind while adding information from the Reasonable Mind.

With the Wise Mind, you are in control of your emotions. Your feelings are valid, and you are NOT judging them. You're not letting them rule you, and you're not letting logic (Reasonable Mind) be your sole guide. You're being guided by your inner wisdom here.

You can feel your emotions, no matter how extreme they may be.
You are also able to access information and knowledge.
Your emotions and your reasoning guide you.

The Wise Mind is **purposeful**. You use your inner resources (emotion and reason) to decide your next steps, knowing that this will produce the best outcome for you.

The Wise Mind is **flexible and open to change**. Although it draws from past experiences, it's not stuck to a routine. It's flexible, open, and willing to the best solution present at the time.

The Wise Mind is **good at conflict resolution**. Rather than being stuck in an all-or-nothing mentality, it can integrate emotional and rational thought and connect with others with compassion.

Please note that **we all have the WISE MIND in us**. It's just that when dealing with anxiety and many other mental health conditions, we tend to lean on our Emotional Mind, which, unfortunately, doesn't give us the best results.

One of the most effective ways to cultivate your Wise Mind is to develop one of the core skills in DBT—**mindfulness**.

The Brain-Altering Power of Mindfulness

Mindfulness is one of the most effective ways to re-train how you think. And no, this is not woo-woo science.

Studies have shown that mindfulness (particularly mindful meditation) can literally change the structure and function of your brain.[18,19,20] This is important for anyone with a mental health condition because mindfulness causes us to be less reactive to unpleasant internal events and more contemplative, which leads to positive psychological results.[21]

Top 5 Ways to Be More Mindful

Mindfulness is being in the moment. It's awareness of what is inside and outside you at any given time. In addition to having a daily meditation habit, the following will also help you cultivate mindfulness.

1. **Focus on your breathing.** One of the ways you can calm the chaos inside and outside you is to pay close attention to your breathing. Close your eyes and breath in for a count of four, hold that breath for a count of four, release your breath for a count of four, stay still for another count of four—and then do it all over again for a total of 5 minutes. This is called Square Breathing or Box Breathing.

   Tip: After you've mastered Square Breathing, you can try the [4-7-8 Breathing](#) exercises on page 98.

2. **Use your five senses.** We don't notice it, but our senses are simultaneously working 24/7. To be more mindful, practice using and focusing on one sense at a time.

   What are you seeing? Take note of a color. Marvel at it, and then close your eyes.
   What are you hearing? Focus your whole attention on that sound.
   What are you smelling? Inhale deeply. What scent is it? What memory is it evoking?
   What are you touching? Reach out and touch something. Is the texture smooth or rough? Hard or soft? Can you trace a pattern?
   What are you tasting? Did you just have coffee? Is it lingering in your taste buds?

   Tip: Try the [5-4-3-2-1 Grounding Technique](#) exercise on page 99.

3. **Break down and understand your emotions.** Often, we get anxious because of a tidal wave of emotions. We get so caught up that we can't distinguish one emotion from the other, so we feel confused and overwhelmed.

    So, the next time you feel anxious (or any strong emotion), don't fight it; accept it. That's right, accept the tidal wave.

    After that, just be curious and explore your emotions. WHAT exactly are you feeling? WHY are you feeling this way? Remember, you're not your emotions. Your emotions are just an offshoot of something else.

4. **Take multiple 5-minute MINDLESS breaks.** It sounds simple, but when was the last time you took a break and did absolutely nothing? Often, if we ever take a break, we rush to get a cup of coffee and then gulp it down to get back to work. Or we may take a break, but our minds are stuck to what we were doing... thinking, planning, imagining our next steps.

    So, this time, take a 5-min break, go somewhere and think and do nothing as best you can.

    Tip: Don't know what to do during your break? Do the Body Scan exercise on page 100.

5. **Meditate.** Meditation is a form of mindfulness. Many people interchange these words but the simplest description, I believe, is this: *"mindfulness is the awareness of something, while meditation is the awareness of nothing"*[22]. Also, mindfulness is a quality or character you have, while meditation is a practice.

I'm a big believer in meditation as a form of mindfulness. It helps me calm my anxious and hyperactive mind.

I like to schedule 10 minutes to meditate in the morning. This centers me so that I don't get into a frantic state of mind. I then do another 10 minutes of meditation before bed to help me wind down. I find a few apps on the market helpful, such as Simple Habit, Headspace, and Calm. I recommend testing out different apps to see which works best for you.

Top 5 Ways to Make Meditation a Daily Habit

If you're new to meditation or have trouble making it a routine, here are some tips to help you succeed.

1. Create a consistent schedule. To build a new habit, you must be consistent in cultivating it. I advise that you practice mindfulness at the start of your day. You can do it in bed after you open your eyes or go to a place in your home where you can have at least 10 minutes of quiet before interacting with anyone. You're making 'waking up' your 'trigger' to meditate this way.

2. Keep it simple at first. Don't have any 'goal'. There's nothing specific you need to focus on or think about. Meditation can be as simple as taking a hot cup of your favorite beverage in the morning, going to a quiet place, and then focusing on the sensation of drinking.

   For example, as you sip, take note of the warm steam touching your face, the delicious smell of your dink, the liquid touching your lips, the sensation of swallowing, and feeling that warm liquid go down your throat.

3. Meditate for as long, or as short, as you like. There's no exact length of time required for meditation, and it's really more about making it a habit and

engaging in actual meditation. Starting at 5 minutes and slowly working up to 15 minutes is great if you're a beginner.

And don't worry that 15 minutes is too short to make any impact. A 2018 study showed that meditating for just 13 minutes daily for eight consecutive weeks lowered negative moods, improved attention, and working memory, and decreased anxiety.[23]

4. **Forgive yourself repeatedly.** Many people find meditation difficult because it's actually hard to quiet the mind. We're so used to this internal chaos!

However, compassion and forgiveness are crucial when integrating a new self-care practice like meditation, so note the following.

- Forgive yourself when you forget to practice.
- Don't punish yourself for getting caught up in everyday busyness.
- When meditating, forgive yourself if your mind starts to wander incessantly.
- Don't punish yourself when you don't meditate regularly.
- Don't spend too much time contemplating what you didn't do.

5. **Make meditation fun!** Let's face it, sitting, standing, or pacing for *x* minutes can get boring. So why not spruce up the moment?

For example, treat yourself to some meditation music and play it in the background during your practice. (I personally like nature sounds.) You can also use a guided meditation app (like the ones I mentioned above), find some on YouTube, or buy guided meditation audiotapes. I also really like lighting scented candles with wooden wicks. I close my eyes, listen to the sound of the wooden wick, and imagine a log fire burning.

Mindfulness and meditation are developed through constant practice. And as with any new skill, it helps to start practicing them *when you don't need it.*

You're introducing (or advancing) something new in your life, so practice under easier conditions. This way, you'll be able to adopt them in your life faster, and they'll become 'automatic' when you need them the most.

WORKBOOK: WEEK 4 – Mindfulness

Exercise: 4-7-8 Breathing Technique

This advanced breathing technique will help you slow down your mind, and it will help you bring balance to your mind and body and help reduce stress and anxiety.

Find a comfortable position.

INHALE for 4 counts through your nose.

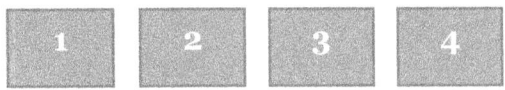

HOLD YOU BREATH for 7 counts...

EXHALE for 8 counts through your mouth.

Do this for 4 times.

Remember, consistency is important! So please do breathing practice 2x daily for 4 weeks.

Exercise: 5-4-3-2-1 Grounding Technique

5-4-3-2-1
Grounding technique

A calming technique that connects you with the present by exploring the five senses.

Instructions: Sitting or standing, take a deep breath in, and complete the following questions.

5 — 5 things you can see

4 — 4 things you can touch

3 — 3 things you can hear

2 — 2 things you can smell

1 — 1 thing you can taste

Exercise: Mindfulness Body Scan

This mindfulness exercise will help calm your nerves, focus your thoughts, and center your being.

1. Sit or lie down, whatever is most comfortable for you.

2. Close your eyes.

3. Do the [Square Breathing exercise](#) (page 59) for 4 cycles.

4. Starting with the top of your head, become aware of your scalp.

5. Notice any areas of tension. Breathe in and as you breathe out... soften and relax that part.

6. Next, become aware of your forehead.

7. Notice any areas of tension. Breathe in and as you breathe out... soften and relax that part.

8. Continue down until you've covered your whole body.

WORKBOOK: WEEK 5 – WISE MIND

Exercise: WISE MIND

The Wise Mind will come naturally to you as you develop mindfulness. This exercise makes use of a Breathing technique to arrive at Wise Mind.

1. Find a comfortable position.
2. Using the Square Breathing technique:
    a. Breathe in while saying the word "Wise" to yourself. Focus all your attention on that word.
    b. Hold your breath.
    c. Exhale while saying the word "Mind" to yourself. Focus all your attention on that word.
3. Continue until you sense that you've successfully arrived at Wise Mind.

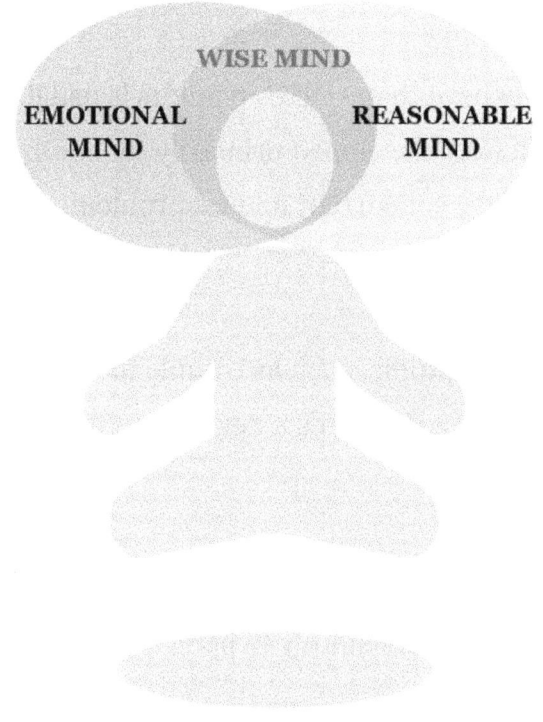

Chapter 4: ADD & ADHD

"For all the hoopla you read and hear about the overdiagnosis of ADD and the overuse of medication-indeed, serious problems in certain places—the more costly problem is the opposite: millions of people, especially adults, have ADD but don't know about it and therefore get no help at all."
- Edward M. Hallowell, M.D.

Delivered from Distraction: Getting the Most out of Life with Attention Deficit Disorder

What is ADHD?
Attention Deficit Hyperactivity Disorder (ADHD) affects millions of adults. According to a 2016 study, 2.8% of adults *worldwide* are affected by this condition.[24]

Despite this, scientists believe that ADHD in adults is usually underdiagnosed since diagnostic criteria were developed primarily for children and because adults with ADHD frequently have concurrent mental problems that may mask ADHD symptoms.

Many attention-related symptoms, such as trouble focusing, hyperactivity, and impulsive conduct, describe ADHD. It's a developmental condition, which means it lasts a lifetime.

Some people have ADHD, but it is inattentive, so they do not exhibit hyperactivity or impulsive behavior. Others are simply hyperactive-impulsive rather than inattentive, though this is less common. Many suffer from both inattention and impulsivity, as well as hyperactivity.

It is critical to highlight a misperception concerning ADHD among those who believe they have it or have been diagnosed with it. Everyone appears to believe they have ADHD, and while many are on the spectrum at some point, if you have occasional inattention that does not affect your functioning and you are not very concerned about it, you probably do not qualify for that diagnosis.

Many people believe they have ADHD when they cannot sit down and read a book for more than an hour or when they are unable to focus during a discussion. ADHD should be distinguished from simply being uninterested in what is happening at the time. Understandably, this can be even more confusing today—thanks to social media

Today's society promotes a lot of inattention. There is a lot of material out there, and there is a lot of research that shows that the more time you spend on social media, the more likely you are to display indicators of ADHD.

Although social media does not cause ADHD, the more you use it, the more inattentive you will become. For example, when you switch on CNN or any other all-news channel, there is a stock ticker at the bottom and a scrolling text bar with all the headlines and a weather ticker. Everything appears to be a breaking story, which is absurd! It's a lot of stimulation for anyone.

Work, school, kids, emails, appointments, projects, deadlines, family, friends—they are all fighting for our attention. And with continuous notifications from our phones, this has gotten much worse.

So, we are all bombarded with information from all angles, but it is different when you have ADHD symptoms.

Due to the emotional dysregulation in adults with ADHD, they find it more difficult to deal with frustration. They're less patient, and their minds may be confused and muddled, making planning and organizing difficult.

Where Things Get Difficult

Depression is the most prevalent co-occurring disorder among people with ADHD. As you might expect, when a child with ADHD performs poorly in school, they develop anxiety and feel bad about themselves. As a result, they start to develop symptoms, such as fidgeting, constantly talking, or interrupting others, which get them into trouble.

Inattentive ADHD, on the other hand, is far more difficult to detect. It manifests as a lack of concentration, simple mistakes, difficulty keeping focus, not listening when spoken to, not following through on directions, and failing to complete assignments.

And because inattentive ADHD is difficult to diagnose, many people never receive a diagnosis or do not receive one until they are far into adulthood.

Anxiety is often secondary to ADHD as it can make people feel inept, leading to performance anxiety, feelings of inadequacy, and clinical anxiety.

Furthermore, a subset of children and adults with ADHD is at a **higher risk of substance abuse and alcoholism.**[25,26]

Finally, individuals with ADHD are at a **higher risk of suicide ideation** since they are predisposed to a variety of psychological issues and dealing with other learning impairments. Due to the complexities and prevalence of mental diseases such as depression among persons with ADHD, this area of inquiry is severely under-researched.

Differentiating ADHD symptoms from learning problems and mental diseases might present several difficulties. A healthcare expert should be consulted to establish an individual's exact needs.

How to Cope with ADHD

People with adult ADHD often dislike schedules, so they may choose to work in more entrepreneurial occupations where they can wake up and start working whenever they want—even if that means working at night. (I began my own business because I wanted to be able to work my own hours.)

However, this situation may aggravate ADHD in some people who need the structure to focus better. It is more difficult to control symptoms when you need to schedule your life around your ADHD and are continually awake and tired due to not sleeping each night properly. As a result, your next day is disrupted, making you less productive and focused.

 By the way, are you enjoying the book so far? If so, please share your thoughts and leave a quick review. Your feedback is appreciated. Thank you!

So, even though you may want to be free with your schedule. It's important to still have structure to cope with ADHD.

For instance, if you're prone to losing your keys or wallet as you walk out the door, you should develop a habit of placing them in your jeans or backpack the night before if that's what you can't leave home without. If you frequently forget tasks, you may want to develop the habit of keeping To-Do lists.

Another way to manage ADHD is to nurture the DBT core skill called Interpersonal Effectiveness.

Interpersonal Effectiveness

Interpersonal Effectiveness refers to skills that foster healthy relationships.

Getting along with others while asserting your needs is essential to maintaining healthy relationships. To achieve this, you need to find that balance between taking care of yourself, your needs, and others.

Interpersonal Effectiveness in DBT means learning these three skills: Objective Effectiveness, Relationship Effectiveness, and Self-Respect Effectiveness.

Objective Effectiveness is about getting what you want out of a situation. The exercise D.E.A.R.M.A.N. on page 399 will help you dissect a situation where you are trying to get something you want, like a resolution with a loved one.

Relationship Effectiveness is also about getting what you want out of a situation with someone you care about, but it also helps you see the other person's perspective. And in doing so, you may come to a compromise. The exercise G.I.V.E on page 322 will help you develop this trait.

Self-Respect Effectiveness keeps your needs, ideals, and morals in balance when facing conflict. In an emotional scenario, it's crucial to remind yourself that you have principles that you want to adhere to, even if someone you care about disagrees with you. This skill allows you to concentrate on facts, which is very useful during emotionally charged situations. The exercise F.A.S.T on page 488 will help you with this.

WORKBOOK: Week 6 – Interpersonal Effectiveness

Exercise: D.E.A.R.M.A.N.

The D.E.A.R.M.A.N. exercise helps you develop the skill of asking for something respectfully and effectively, which builds and maintains relationships, regardless of the outcome of your request.

Describe the situation simply. Stick to the facts. Say exactly what you're reacting to.
Example: You said you would be home for dinner by 7 PM.

Your turn: _____

Express your thoughts or feelings about the situation. Use "I" statements.
Example: I feel taken for granted when you don't tell me you'll be late.

Your turn: _____

Assert your position respectfully but not in an aggressive manner.
Example: I would really like it if you call me when you're going to be late for dinner.

Your turn: _____

Reinforce (reward) when you get what you want or need.

    Example: Thank you, babe. I would really feel so much better if you did that.

    Your turn: _____

Mindful. Stay focused. Don't worry about the past or the future. Just stay on topic.

    Example: I would like to hear that you understand where I'm coming from.

    Your turn: _____

Appear confident. Show confident verbal and non-verbal cues. Do not apologize.

    Example: (Sit or stand up straight. Maintain eye contact. Use a confident tone of voice.) I hope I'm getting across to you because my feelings won't change.

    Your turn: _____

Negotiate - If the outcome you want doesn't appear to be within reach, negotiate.

    Example: How about you just text me if you're running late?

    Your turn: _____

Exercise: G.I.V.E.

Relationships aren't only about getting what we need. They're also about considering the needs and wants of the other person. The G.I.V.E exercise will help you achieve relationship effectiveness by fostering positive interactions.

Gentle. Approach with gentleness. Don't attack, threaten or express judgment during your interactions. The best communication happens when neither party feels defensive.

> **What's your request?**
>

Interested. Listen to the other person without interrupting. Expressions of interest can be verbal (e.g., ok, uh-huh, etc.) or non-verbal (e.g., keeping eye contact, not fidgeting or looking at your phone, etc.)

> **What's YOUR way of showing interest?**
>

Validate. Confirm you hear the other person by echoing their thoughts and emotions back to them. You might say, *"I understand this is frustrating for you too. I'm not happy you feel that way at all."*

What do you want to say back?

Easy Manner. Throughout the conversation, present yourself as relaxed and comfortable. Act light-hearted and have an easy attitude. (Message to the other person: you're not difficult to deal with.)

How do you convey friendliness to others?

Exercise: F.A.S.T.

Sometimes, in relationships, you might betray your own values and beliefs to receive approval or get what you want. The F.A.S.T. exercise below will help you achieve self-respect effectiveness.

Fair. Be reasonable. Respect your rights and that of others. Avoid being emotional and dramatic outbursts. Stick to the facts.

> **What's a better way of saying, "You're not hearing me!"**
>
>

(No) **A**pologies. Don't apologize for making a request, voicing an opinion, or disagreeing. The only time to apologize is if you've done something wrong.

> **What's a better way of saying, "I'm sorry I feel this way."**
>
>

Stick to your values. Stand up for what you believe in. Don't compromise your values just to be liked or to get what you want.

List down 3 things you will not compromise on.
1.)
2.)
3.)

Be Truthful. Be honest and don't lie, exaggerate or act helpless to get what you want.

Think about an incident in the past where you may not have been truthful.
What you said/did....
What you should have said/done...

Chapter 5: Phobias

> *"Usually, the term phobia refers to the psychological fear of the human mind from something that poses a threat. But when a species starts using the term fear against a biological portion of itself, there is nothing more demeaning than this."*
> *- Abhijit Naskar, The Islamophobic Civilization: Voyage of Acceptance*

A phobia is a persistent, uncontrollable fear of a specific object, place, or activity. It's usually characterized by the rapid onset of intense fear, and it usually lasts over six months.

According to the National Institute of Mental Health (NIMH), about 10% of people in the U.S. have specific phobias, 7.1% have social phobias, and 0.9% have agoraphobia.[27]

Where do phobias originate?

Many individuals believe that phobias are a natural part of our evolutionary process as a species. To survive, we needed to be afraid of some things. If our forebears came across anything dangerous, such as a spider or snake, it's understandable that they would be afraid of being bitten, poisoned, or even killed.

So, evolution has given us this built-in readiness to be afraid for our own protection. Still, some phobias may develop due to a negative experience. For instance, being bitten by a dog at a very young age may develop cynophobia (fear of dogs).

However, left untreated, phobias can be harmful. For example, fear of injections (trypanophobia) can prevent an individual from seeking much-needed medical treatment. People afraid of germs (mysophobia) may develop abnormal cleaning behaviors, such as excessive hand washing or acute concern about germs or pathogens, leading to OCD.

Distress Tolerance

One way to manage phobias is to develop *distress tolerance*, one of the core DBT skills.

Distress tolerance skills help people cope with overwhelming negative emotions. With a low threshold for distress, individuals may become overwhelmed even with relatively mild stress, resulting in negative behaviors.

DBT teaches us that pain will occur at times, but the best course is to learn to accept and cope with discomfort.

Distress tolerance requires **Radical Acceptance** as a core component. When a person cannot change the situation, they must experience it and accept it as reality without judgment. Complete acceptance makes us less prone to persistent and intense negative feelings.

Radical Acceptance involves recognizing and accepting the situation AS IS instead of trying to change it. Remember accepting is not the same as liking or condoning something. When you accept the problems you cannot control, you will feel less anxiety, anger, and sadness.

Despite the simplicity of the idea of Radical Acceptance, it can be tricky in practice, particularly when faced with circumstances that we feel are simply completely unfair or unjustified. Still, if you have no power to change these circumstances, then you must accept them AS IS—no matter how painful they may be.

For example, if you experience trauma, it could devastate you. But if you stay in that state of devastation, you cannot move on. In contrast, if you accept the event as is, knowing that there's nothing you can do to change what happened, you can move forward on a healing path.

Dwelling on negative things, even if it is someone else's fault, can be debilitating. As such, you need to constantly work at accepting the situation.

Tip: The exercise Turning the Mind (page 116) will help you develop radical acceptance of any situation.

When it comes to my father, I've practiced radical acceptance. My dad is a hoarder, and I have learned to accept him for who he is. I cannot change who he is, but I can change how I react to him and what I can do. I moved out to gain my own mental clarity and space.

It didn't happen overnight. I had to work at it. But in the end, accepting him and the situation is what healed me.

WORKBOOK: Week 7 – Distress Tolerance
Exercise: Turning the Mind

Turning the Mind to acceptance needs constant practice. When we don't get our way, we tend to reject the situation instead of trying to accept it. This exercise is all about trying, over and over and over again, to go in the direction of acceptance.

Exercise: Radical Acceptance Worksheet

Sometimes you run into a problem that is simply out of your control. It can be easy to think, '*this isn't fair*', even though that way does not help. Radical acceptance refers to a healthier way of thinking. Instead of focusing on what you want to be different, you will recognize and accept the problem or situation AS IS.

Radical acceptance is not the same as accepting or condoning something. Accepting problems out of your control will lead to less anxiety, anger, and sadness when dealing with them.

SITUATION - Describe a stressful or negative situation.
Example: I wasn't selected for a job I feel I was the best candidate for.

TYPICAL THINKING - Write down your thoughts and feelings.
Example: This isn't fair! I did and said everything right. They can't do this to me.

RADICAL ACCEPTANCE - **Write down a statement of acceptance.**

Example: This is frustrating, but I ACCEPT they felt someone else would be a good fit.

Exercise: Self-Sooth with 5 Senses

Self-Soothe with 5 Senses

Find a pleasurable way to engage each of your five senses. Doing so will distract you from what is making you feel anxious.
(i.e., Go for a walk somewhere and pay attention to what you see)

Exercise: A.C.C.E.P.T.S.

Negative emotions will usually pass or at least lessen in intensity over time. To help speed up this process, it can help if you can DISTRACT YOURSELF until the emotions subside. This is what the following exercise is all about.

ACTIVITIES: Engage in activities that require thought and concentration.

Example: gardening, baking, exercising, talking to my best friend
Your list:
_____
_____

CONTRIBUTING: Focus on someone other than yourself. Volunteer or do a good deed.

Example: create a care package for someone, call mom
Your list:
_____
_____

COMPARISONS: Look at your situation compared to something worse. Remember a time when you were in (more) pain.

Example: when my father died
Your list:
_____
_____

EMOTIONS: Do something that will create the opposite emotion you feel right now.

    Example: swimming, dancing, watching funny YouTube videos

Your list:

_____

_____

PUSHING AWAY: Push negative thoughts out of your mind. Refuse to think about a situation until a better time.

    Example: square breathing, watch a romantic-comedy film

Your list:

_____

_____

THOUGHTS: Replace negative, worrying thoughts with activities that keep your mind occupied.

    Example: say a prayer, solve a Sudoku puzzle

Your list:

_____

_____

SENSATIONS: Find safe physical sensations to distract you from negative emotions.

    Example: Five Senses exercise (page 79)

Your list:

_____

_____

Chapter 6: PTSD & Panic Disorders

"PTSD: It's not the person refusing to let go of the past, but the past refusing to let go of the person. When we feel weak, we drop our heads on the shoulders of others." - Anonymous

Living with PTSD can be a daily battle. A reader, RB, has this to say about her battle with PTSD after childhood trauma.

"For most of my adult life, I have woken up with a sore jaw and tight muscles. This is a direct outcome of the trauma that occurred in the middle of the night.

My mother was a severe alcoholic, and she would become quite volatile with her boyfriend of the week. She would have loud, violent fights with him and whoever was around. If there wasn't anyone to fight with, she would call her brother or mother and fight over the phone.

This would wake us kids often and because I was the oldest, I comforted my younger siblings all through the night. My mother was a functional alcoholic, so she would act like nothing was wrong in the mornings before work and school.

Those tight muscles I deal with every morning are my body's way of protecting myself while I sleep. Years later, I guess it's something my body and brain can't shake. Sometimes I can still hear her yelling and breaking glass in my dreams. I don't know what 'restful sleep' is. I don't think I've ever had them."

What is PTSD?

An individual suffering from Post-Traumatic Stress Disorder (PTSD) shows disturbing behaviors after experiencing a traumatic event, such as a natural disaster, combat, or assault. People with PTSD experience intense fear, helplessness, or terror in response to the event that threatened their safety.

PTSD sufferers avoid reliving the event, avoid any reminder of the situation, and are hypervigilant. There is a general numbing feeling over them, and persistent signs of extreme emotions such as irritability, complete distrust of others, and angry outbursts are present. They also report feeling disconnected from their lives and losing control.

PTSD symptoms normally appear within three months of the stressful event; however, symptoms can appear later. To be diagnosed as a PTSD patient, the symptoms must last for more than one month and be severe enough to interfere with daily life, such as work, relationships with friends and family, behaviour in social gatherings, etc. Symptoms must also be unconnected to medication, substance abuse, or another illness.

PTSD symptoms are wide and varied, so professionals have broken them into four main categories. (PTSD requires at least one or two symptoms from each of these four categories to coincide.)

1. **Intrusion symptoms** include flashbacks of the event that occur at times when you unconsciously wish they did not. This can manifest as nightmares or as unexpected ideas.

2. **Avoidance symptoms** are when you evade anything that reminds you of the trauma. For example, people who have been in serious vehicle accidents may never want to drive again.

3. **Negative thoughts or moods associated with the trauma.** Someone who believes they are not going to live very long, for example, has no idea why they believe this; they simply believe that something bad will happen to them in the future.

4. **Being on edge or hyper-reactive** is when someone is on edge or hyper-reactive. They may experience bouts of rage or have problems sleeping because they need to constantly check locks.

PTSD used to be classified as an anxiety disorder. However, with the new diagnostic and statistical manual published in 2013, PTSD was moved to the category of trauma and stress-related disorders. This is significant because PTSD is now classified as more than anxiety.

Some people feel invalidated by this issue of qualifying trauma. Does this mean their traumatic experience isn't 'bad enough' to be diagnosed as PTSD? This is not the intent of the diagnosis.

Specific incidents are excluded as traumatic experiences for PTSD because not all things you experience have a traumatic effect on the symptoms defined for PTSD. However, that doesn't mean that your trauma doesn't make you depressed, ruin your self-esteem, or lead to anxiety. This simply means that your reaction to the trauma is different from what we see in people with PTSD.

On brain scans, we've seen that people with PTSD have changes in areas of the brain like the amygdala and hippocampus that people without PTSD don't have.

The amygdala, which is responsible for some mating functions, memory and storage purposes, and potential threat assessment, become overstimulated. The opposite happens to the hippocampus, which is responsible for helping store long-term memories and acting as a processor between short-term and long-term memory. The conversion of short-term memory into long-term memory is called memory consolidation.

Cortisol can also be released due to hippocampus damage, resulting in risk factors like obesity, alcohol abuse, and other stress-related conditions.

In response to threats, the part of the brain responsible for triggering a fight-or-flight reaction may respond excessively, sometimes in disproportionate ways to the threat itself. The part of the brain responsible for calming this (over)reaction is not functioning correctly.

Studies show that PTSD makes the brain process and store traumatic memories differently from a normal brain. Because of this, a person with PTSD will experience any number of the following: intrusive memories of the event, nightmares, avoidance behaviors, dissociative flashbacks, an exaggerated startle response, hypervigilance, and may engage in risk-taking behavior.

People with PTSD may also attempt more risky behaviors to test if they can get a positive result from a traumatic situation. Gambling, risky sexual activity, driving, or extreme sports can be outlets for PTSD. If you find yourself partaking in risky behavior after a traumatic event, it's time to take a step back and perhaps consult a professional.

C-PTSD

If PTSD is a condition resulting from a specific trauma, Complex PTSD (C-PTSD) results from *repeated trauma*.

Usually, the trauma starts in childhood and can be physical, emotional, or sexual. Neglect or abuse can also cause C-PTSD because it happens during one of the most vulnerable developmental years. Traumatic experiences shape your personality. It's like you have a fracture. People suffering from this can spend years trying to mend the fracture.

When compared to a person with PTSD who may check locks, have flashbacks, refuse to drive, or jump every time they hear a loud noise, C-PTSD may manifest more behaviorally. It can lead to relationship difficulties, low self-esteem, anger issues, and mood instability.

C-PTSD patients may develop depression or anxiety because of these problems, but at the core of the problem is a fracture that occurs because of a traumatic emotional event that happened during one's formative years. So, the baggage from all that trauma is hardwired. How you respond to the world is influenced by this hardwiring.

A person with PTSD may experience changes in their personality, but not to the same extent as those with C-PTSD. Negative thoughts can linger, not necessarily to depression, but negatively affect your outlook. Other symptoms may be memory problems, being irritable all the time, having much shame, and having problems sleeping.

Trauma-based disorders are often complicated by depression, so how can we treat them? If you have significant depression or anxiety symptoms, you can take medication, but treatment for the underlying trauma requires psychotherapy.

One of the therapies for PTSD and C-PTSD is [Eye Movement Desensitization and Reprocessing (EMDR)](). As part of this therapy, patients are encouraged to talk about the trauma they encountered while moving their eyes in response to stimuli in the room. Crossing the midline of your brain is accomplished by moving your eyes back and forth. As you move from side to side, your brain reprocesses how the event has affected you emotionally. This is a very basic explanation of the therapy.

DBT techniques have also been successfully used for PTSD and C-PTSD patients. [28,29]

As DBT was developed by Marsha M. Linehan, Ph.D., for people who suffer from borderline personality disorder (BPD), it can also be used as a form of trauma-based therapy. (BPD is thought to have its roots in childhood trauma and has many characteristics as PTSD and C-PTSD.)

The DBT approach for trauma-based patients focuses on the DBT skill called Emotion Regulation. This approach is considered helpful because the patient is taught coping skills *before* addressing the trauma(s) that brought on PTSD or C-PTSD. It's an interesting approach because it doesn't re-traumatize the patient. There's no need to re-live anything, only how to cope and get out of state one is feeling.

Emotion Regulation

The goal of Emotion Regulation is to understand our emotions and develop the skills we need to manage them, rather than letting our emotions manage us. The objective is to effectively handle negative emotions AND develop positive emotions simultaneously.

As mentioned throughout this book, negative emotions are not bad and shouldn't be ignored. Negative feelings are a natural part of our lives. We just need to acknowledge and accept them as they are. And in doing so, we reduce our vulnerability to them.

When we reduce our vulnerability to negative emotions, we lower our emotional suffering and increase our ability to experience positive emotions.

When you feel something, you usually exhibit a corresponding behavior. When you're very angry, you might have a fight or argument with someone. When you're feeling extreme sadness, you might withdraw from friends.

During these moments, it will help you take a step back and imagine doing the OPPOSITE of what you would normally do or what you think you will do. Doing this will help you change your emotion. (Related **Opposite Action** exercise on page 131.)

For example, instead of yelling, try talking calmly and politely whenever you are angry. If you withdraw when you're sad, make it a point to visit a friend instead the next time you feel this way.

Also, when facing an overwhelming emotion, make it a habit to look at the facts at the moment to help reduce the intensity of these extreme emotions. (Related **Check the Facts** exercise on page 388.) Are you sure the emotions you're having are based on the realities of the situation?

Lastly, let's not underestimate the mind-body connection when it comes to emotional processing.[30] Simply put, we must take care of our bodies to improve our minds. And in doing so, we're better able to regulate our emotions. (Related **PLEASE** exercise on page 308.)

Changing Your Focus from Negative to Positive

Humans tend to focus more on the negative than the positive. A single criticism is more likely to get our attention than ten compliments!

If you notice yourself focusing on the negative aspects of an experience, try to stop and focus on the positive by focusing on the positive aspects of life daily and acknowledging the things that go right, even if things are not perfect. Don't let small problems ruin the moment.

Adding one or two positive activities won't change your life overnight, but the happiness they generate will add up over time. I recommend taking some time, like 15-20 minutes, and writing down all the activities and things that bring joy to your life.

Write it all down on paper or on your notepad app. Then narrow it down to the Top 3 activities and spend at least 20 minutes each day doing one of these activities. For instance, if your Top 3 activities are jogging, reading, and talking with friends, choose one of these, say jogging, and commit 20 minutes to it each day and take steps to make it happen.

For example, you can write down this goal:
For the next seven days, I'll jog for 20 minutes.

Then go out and do it! After seven days, see how you feel. If you feel better, continue doing it. If you don't, consider switching to one of the other activities and repeating the process. Ideally, your activities should stimulate your mind and body simultaneously for that mind-body connection.

The following are some simple positive activities you can start immediately. Of course, this is not an exhaustive list. It's just to give you some ideas and a starting point.

- Eat a good, leisurely meal.
- See a movie.
- Take a tour of a local attraction.
- Enjoy a picnic.
- Take a walk.
- Enjoy a relaxing night at home.
- Visit with family or friends.
- Take up a new hobby.
- Listen to music.
- Have a dance party.
- Bake something.
- Learn a new language.
- Read a book.
- Spend time with your family.
- Take on a new challenge (with friends!).
- Phone a friend.
- Write a letter (your grandma would love it!).
- Break a sweat!
- Start a gratitude journal.
- Do a craft.
- Enjoy some sunshine.
- Take a break from social media.
- Try some yoga.

WORKBOOK: Week 8 – Emotion Regulation
Exercise: Opposite Action for Overwhelming Emotions

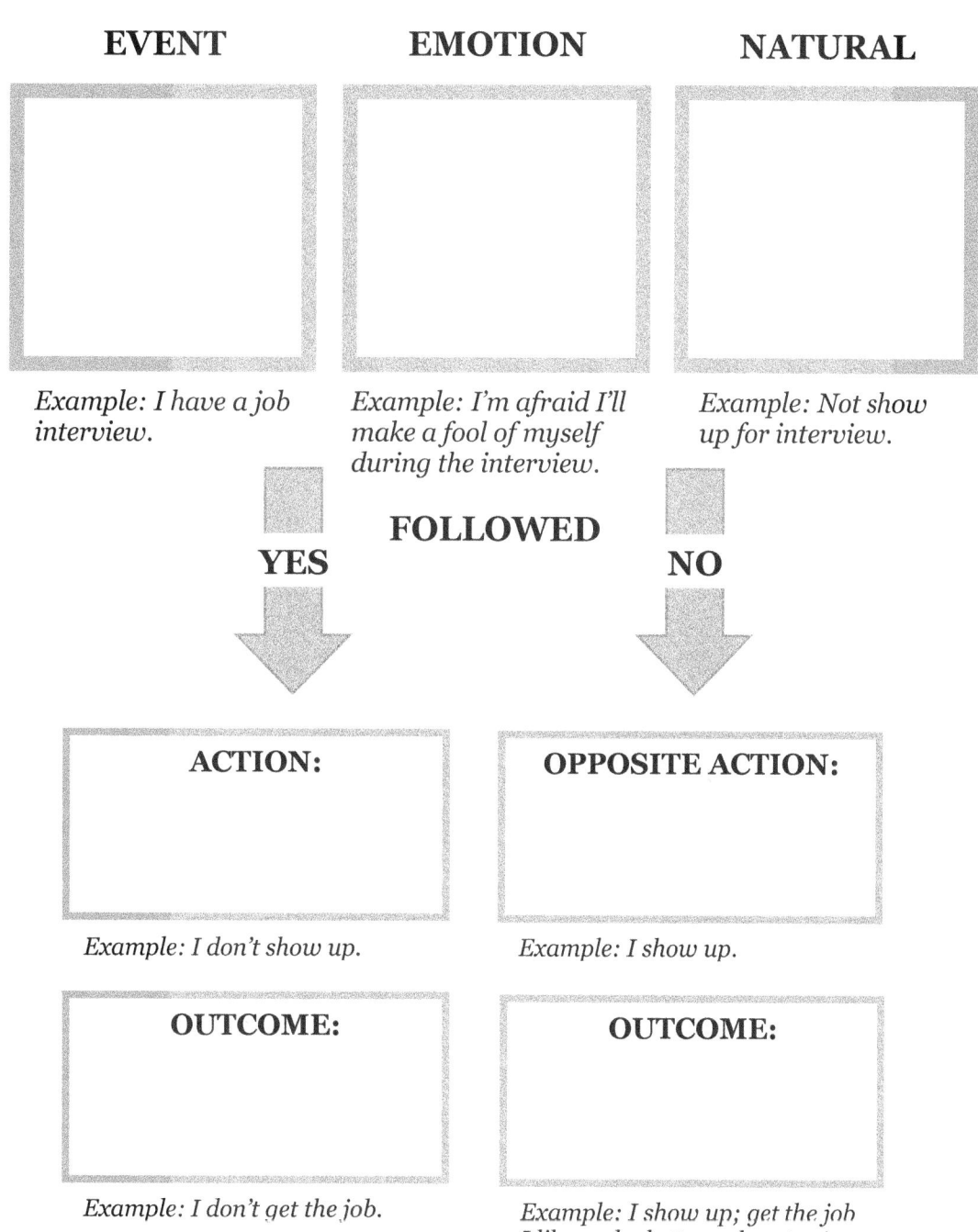

Exercise: Check the Facts

Check The Facts
Emotion Regulation Skill

Helping me make sense of a situation where I may have overreacted

Maybe you can look back on your life and think of a few situations where you overreacted. Or you might notice that something once felt like a big deal when it was really unimportant. You can *check the facts* in the moment to reduce the intensity of these extreme emotions. Ask yourself the following questions to check the facts:

What event triggered my emotion?

What interpretations or assumptions am I making about the event?

Does my emotion and its intensity match the *facts* of the situation? Or does it just match my assumptions of the situation?

Exercise: P.L.E.A.S.E.

Your body and mind are closely linked, and the health of one directly affects the other. An unhealthy body will make it difficult to manage your emotions. The acronym P.L.E.A.S.E. can be used to help you remember important aspects of this connection.

Ways I Can Treat **P**hysical Illness (hunger, fatigue)

Ways I can **E**at Healthy

Ways I can **A**void Mood-Altering Drugs (Caffeine, Alcohol)

Ways I Can Make Sure I **S**leep Well

Ways I Can Make Sure I **E**xercise

Chapter 7: OCD & Compulsive Behaviors

> *"It's like having mental hiccups. Mostly, we can function despite the 'hiccups,' but we're exhausted attempting to carry on as if they didn't exist."*
>
> *- Sheila Cavanaugh*

I've always had some form of OCD, but it didn't become severe until my sophomore year of high school. Before I could leave for school, I had to complete a 'morning ritual'.

As a result, I was frequently late for class, which affected my studies. To avoid having to conduct the morning ritual, I would stay up late at night, generally until 3 or 4 a.m. on weekends, watching TV and eating unhealthy snacks. I was avoiding going to bed so that I didn't have to perform the ritual the next day.

Other common obsessions include seeing blood and being terrified that I will become infected with a disease if I simply see or come into contact with it. This made utilizing a public restroom difficult at times. I would avoid stepping on lines when walking on the sidewalk because it may bring bad luck. In addition, I would tap or check items a specific number of times until the feeling was 'just right', or something horrible would happen.

Fortunately, my OCD was considered relatively minor, and it has substantially improved since then. Other books I've read about treating OCD include *Jeffery M. Schwarz'* book *Brain Lock*[31], which I highly recommend.

In this book, the author treats people with far more severe OCD than I do. One patient, for example, showered for hours, once up to seven hours, because he felt dirty.

Another patient was a man who was so afraid of battery acid that he avoided places where there had been a car accident because he was afraid something would be 'contaminated', and he would go home, change, and throw away his clothes before moving on.

What is OCD?

Obsessive-compulsive disorder (OCD) is characterized by obsessions and compulsions. The Anxiety and Depression Association of America (ADAA) estimates that 2.2. million adults (or 1% of the US population) are affected by OCD.[32]

An obsession is a recurring, persistent, unwelcome, and unnoticed thought, picture, or urge that interferes with interpersonal, social, or vocational functioning. People suffering from OCD believe their thoughts are illogical or excessive, yet they do not believe they have control over them.

Compulsive behaviors or mental acts are things a person repeats to decrease anxiety. Rituals are frequently associated with the obsession, such as repeated handwashing for someone preoccupied with contamination or repeated prayers for someone obsessed with religion.

Following g are some of the most common OCD compulsions.

- Checking rituals, such as checking that the door is locked.
- Counting rituals, such as counting steps or tiles on ceilings.
- Scrubbing and washing until the skin are raw.
- Chanting or praying.

- Touching, rubbing, or tapping (e.g., feeling the texture of the material in a store, touching people, walls, doors, or oneself).
- Hoarding items for fear of throwing away something important.
- Organizing (e.g., arranging and rearranging items on a desk, shelf, or furniture in perfect order; vacuuming the carpet in one direction).
- Rigid performance such as getting dressed in a specific pattern.
- Aggressive urges (i.e., a desire to throw things or hit things).

When an individual's thoughts, ideas, and impulses consume them to the point that they interfere with their life or well-being, they are diagnosed with OCD.

These routines are irrational and strange to OCD sufferers, but they feel forced to perform them to relieve anxiety or prevent awful thoughts. Obsessions and compulsions can cause tremendous misery and embarrassment for those who suffer from them, and they may go to great measures to conceal them.

OCD Causes

Genetics: People with close relatives who got OCD as teenagers (mom, dad, siblings) are more likely to develop OCD. Several genes involved in serotonin transport or response have been connected to the development of OCD. Defects in other genes involved in brain transmission may also contribute to the illness. OCD does not occur in all people who have the linked variants, and some of the variants do not result in OCD.

Brain Structure: Based on differences in the frontal cortex between OCD and non-OCD test subjects, researchers are beginning to pinpoint brain areas that may be affected by OCD. Whether the illness involves alterations in chemical messengers (neurotransmitters) such as serotonin and dopamine is being investigated. A problem controlling the activity and interaction of different brain areas is also thought to contribute to the illness.

A person suffering from OCD finds it difficult to pay attention to events that do not immediately influence them. As a result, they do not automatically retain the events the way we do.

For example, my brain may recognize that I had done something similar, such as locking the front door in the morning. This is known as *implicit learning*. Despite not being actively or expressly focused on shutting the door, I had the impression that I had done so despite having no recollection of it. However, those with OCD may have this difficulty; thus, they may stare at a light switch for a long time and still feel that the switch is off.

People with OCD frequently can't be sure they did something inappropriate because they can't recall *not* doing it. For example, they may be afraid of unintentionally having sex with someone they just met at the bar. Later, they explore their memory for evidence to be absolutely positive that they hadn't molested or abused someone. Unable to find it, they become increasingly terrified and decide that they must have molested someone because they cannot recall not having done so.

Brain imaging evidence suggests that when patients have intrusive obsessions, specific brain areas become more active. These areas are linked to the limbic system, which is thought to be where intense emotions are created. This is why people obsess over things that put them at risk, harm, or shame.

OCD symptoms appear when the limbic system and the prefrontal cortex are dysfunctional. As a result of both of these disorders coexisting, we place an undue emphasis on our thoughts.

When you have episodic memory, you can relive prior experiences in your mind. While I don't recall whether or not I locked the door to my house this morning, this anxiety isn't as important to me as it would be to someone with OCD, who can be extremely anxious about their safety and fearful of making a mistake and being blamed.

Some patients describe their bad thoughts as vivid visuals. When people are terrified, they can sometimes "see" what happens.

If they check their memory repeatedly, they may lose their memory of what they did and did not do, as it becomes more difficult to distinguish between episodes.

Environment: Aside from genetic considerations, researchers investigate environmental factors connected with OCD, such as pregnancy problems and stressful life experiences. A conclusive link between any of them and this condition has yet to be established. An individual's chance of getting OCD may be determined by genetic and environmental variables.

All of these factors appear to impact the existence of OCD, though more research is needed. In all likelihood, one's OCD is caused by a parent who suffers from OCD and grew up in a strict environment where everything had to be neat and done precisely.

OCD Misconceptions

People easily quip, '*I'm so OCD*', while discussing their eccentric cleanliness, yet these sentiments are quite disrespectful to people who suffer from OCD. Many varieties of OCD have been depicted in popular culture as oddities rather than serious disorders, including characters based on stereotypical OCD features and entire TV shows that exploit people suffering from hoarding behaviors. Many individuals are unaware of how incapacitating this can be.

Furthermore, the caricature of an OCD patient as an extreme "neat freak" fails to convey that, as we've already demonstrated, the condition can emerge in various ways.

Hopefully, knowing these facts can help you understand that this disorder is more than just a quirky personality attribute.

If you have a drug use disorder and one or more of the numerous varieties of OCD, a dual diagnosis treatment program can help you recover.

In a Dual Diagnosis Disorder Inpatient Unit or Outpatient Clinic, professionals will treat both the OCD and the underlying depression that many people suffer from. They also address your substance use medically and provide therapy, education, and support to help you stay away from drugs and alcohol while focusing on your treatment plan for the things that make you who you are.

OCD Categories

According to specialists, OCD types fall into six different categories.

1. Organization

This is possibly the most well-known variety of OCD, and it involves obsessions with objects being in exactly the right spot or being symmetrical. For example, someone may feel compelled to keep all wall hangings level, all labels on pantry cans facing outward, or everything on their workstation totally clean. If the person does not meet the compulsions to have things just so, they may experience unhappiness or fear that the lack of organization will cause them or their loved ones harm

2. Contamination

Those suffering from an obsession or compulsion related to contamination will typically find themselves or their surroundings being washed to a dangerous extent. For example, they may purchase a large quantity of individually wrapped hand soaps, open each packet once, then buy a new one every time they wash their hands.

People with such behaviors tend to be extremely fearful of being infected by bacteria on surfaces. Therefore, those who suffer from this OCD type may go to great lengths to avoid:

- Contact with others.
- Public washrooms.
- Restaurants.
- Handles and doorknobs.

- Medical facilities.
- Enjoying the outdoors.

Mental Contamination

Mental Contamination is much the same as physical contamination, except instead of germs in the physical world, it is internal uncleanliness that is the source of the individual's obsession.

Uncleanliness is often caused by psychological trauma. The sufferer may spend hours and hours washing their bodies if, for example, they are ridiculed or emotionally traumatized by someone. So, a fear of physical illness does not cause compulsions, but emotional damage does.

3. Checking

Checking is an obsession in which a person is preoccupied with the possibility of causing damage or injury by being careless. They may need to double-check something or even look at it for a while before feeling more comfortable. Compulsions might include checking any of the following:

- Window and door locks.
- Water faucets.
- Appliances.
- Wallets.
- Pockets.
- Lights.
- Electrical plugs and sockets.

A checking compulsion might also be manifested in the following conditions.

- Frequently seeking reassurance from friends and/or family members that they're not offended by something the OCD sufferer said.
- Constantly researching symptoms of a disease.
- Concentrating on details to ensure they don't forget anything
- Obsessively reviewing documents before submitting them to ensure nothing offensive has been inadvertently inserted.

4. Hoarding

Hoarding is characterized by:

- Trouble getting rid of old, unusable items.
- A tendency to collect too many useless things.
- Difficulty finding time to organize hoarded objects.

Hoarders will usually have cluttered homes with old and useless items, so they are typically unable to use more than a few square feet of space.

A person with hoarding tendencies may have difficulty disposing of discarded newspapers, plastic bags, and even decayed food.

For several reasons, it is arguably the most dangerous type of OCD. One major threat of an unclean environment is the potential for contracting several illnesses, some of which are deadly.

Hoarders' homes may also be challenging to navigate for reasons other than hygienic ones. The accumulation of materials in hoarders' homes may contribute to a risk for falls, become a fire hazard, and/or prevent the individual from getting out of a burning house in the event of a fire.

Hoarding Types

Following are the three different hoarding types:

1. **Sentimental Hoarding** is when a hoarder attaches a great deal of significance to each item they keep, making it difficult to get rid of it. They may begin to believe that it might be impossible to keep the memory associated with the object if they discard it.

2. **Deprivation Hoarding** is when a hoarder cannot throw away items because they anticipate the possibility that they will need them someday. One example of deprivation hoarding is to wear only one pair of shoes but own fifteen others—just in case.

3. **Preventing Harm to Others Hoarding** is when an individual holds on to broken glass or even human waste that might harm others. Although these types of fears are irrational, their motive is to protect other people at the risk of their own safety.

5. Ruminations

Rumination is a series of prolonged thoughts on an entirely unproductive topic.

Different from intrusive thoughts, ruminations aren't really objectionable. Some examples are thoughts such as fears of harming someone, religious preoccupations, or intense thoughts of perfection. Instead of suppressing these thoughts, these OCD sufferers may spend hours upon hours every day indulging in them.

6. Intrusive Thoughts

An individual suffering from intrusive thoughts is usually disturbed by them; unlike someone suffering from ruminations

Intrusive thoughts are usually distressing or disgusting ideas that enter people's heads seemingly at random. These obsessions can include hurting a loved one, inflicting harm to a stranger, or even believing that simply thinking about something increases the likelihood of it happening.

A person may need to perform an action to silence intrusive thoughts, such as speaking something aloud or mentally repeating something. People who have intrusive obsessions may have aggressive or dangerous thoughts, but they do not agree with or act on them. In fact, these notions are so diametrically opposed to how people feel that often, they're bothered why their minds even generated the thoughts in the first place.

DBT and OCD

Research has shown that DBT is a viable treatment for OCD.[33,34,35]

The DBT skill Mindfulness focuses on being present in the moment, which can help when trying to interrupt or redirect repetitive thoughts and actions.

As an OCD sufferer, thoughts would come back stronger the more I tried to ignore them. By applying the DBT principle of Radical Acceptance, I let my thoughts pass through my mind without judgment, as if I were an observer. I say to myself, *"The OCD is passing through"*.

Before DBT, I would get very worried and anxious. I used to entertain every thought, including ideas of self-harm. Now, I have the tools to NOT act upon an intrusive thought just because it comes to me.

Instead of giving in to the compulsion, I engage in other activities. A busy and active lifestyle helps me a lot. I've noticed that my OCD gets worse when I become aware of it or when I'm stressed or anxious. To keep my mind focused and engaged, I work out, do yoga, walk, meditate, etc. Additionally, I feel less stressed and have more energy when I sleep well, eat well, and exercise.

One of the best tips I took away was to be aware of my obsessions and compulsions. Taking note of when I'm obsessed versus when I want to compel myself is important for me to differentiate. *Brain Lock*[31] suggests diverting attention from OCD thoughts by focusing on another task for 15 seconds to a minute.

For example, if I needed to check if the tap was turned off, I would simply take a deep breath, regroup, and walk away. I've also reduced my checking OCD by training myself to check things only once. For instance, if I feel I must check if I locked the door, I would carefully and slowly (mindfully) check that door is locked ONCE and then move on. This is very different from how I was before when I had to check it 10-15 times—and I'd still feel compelled to check it again to be sure.

Once I started to radically accept that I had OCD, I could free myself from the notion that something was wrong with me, and it gave me hope and made my OCD a lot more manageable. Now, I just say, *"It's not me; it's the OCD."*

The DBT skill [Interpersonal Effectiveness](#) also helped me a lot. Part of my Checking OCD was to constantly seek external reassurance. I was always asking people around me if I offended them. It's very tiring to keep on explaining yourself, but I couldn't help it!

At the same time, I was suffering alone. I was confused and embarrassed about my condition that I didn't communicate my problems to others. No one knew how I was feeling inside. As a result, just like many other OCD sufferers, I isolated myself, and my life revolved around my rituals, which worsened my condition.

Thanks to the DBT interpersonal effectiveness skills I learned, I was able to slowly build positive relationships in my life.

The DBT skill Distress Tolerance was instrumental to my healing too. As you've probably deduced by now, my OCD focuses on Organization, Contamination, and Checking. Whenever these would kick in, I would self-soothe (page **Error! Bookmark not defined.**), distract myself (page 468), or do both to get myself out of that situation or way of thinking.

Finally, the DBT skill Emotion Regulation assisted me in coping with my obsessions by teaching me how to comprehend my emotions. By understanding the emotions I had while my OCD was kicking in, I managed them to a point where I lessened my emotional suffering.

For example, I was always under great emotional stress and suffering whenever I could not perform my morning ritual before school. If I didn't do them, I would be sweating bullets all day for fear that something bad would happen, which would worsen my anxiety disorder.

The exercise Check the Facts (page 388), in particular, helped me a lot. Whenever I was in fear because I didn't do my routine, this exercise helped me see that my emotions DID NOT fit the facts of the situation. With constant practice, I was eventually able to drastically lessen my feelings of fear because my mind could list down the facts or truths of the situation.

The Importance of Stress Management

OCD is a challenging condition to manage. Trust me, I know. This problem is also readily aggravated when you are under a lot of stress, so in addition to the DBT skills I've adopted, I've also taken active steps to lessen potential stressors in your life. Following are my tips on how you can do this.

1. **Communicate with family and friends and ask for their help.** You need to be honest and open with your loved ones about your OCD. I know it's not easy, but you need to tell them about your situation and ask them to be kind and patient with you.

    Remember, these are the people you surround yourself with, so they have a big impact on how stressful, or not, your life can be. And with their love and support, you'll be much able to cope with your OCD.

2. **Practice gratitude.** Learning to be more grateful has helped me better control my emotions with this condition. When I realized how much worse some people's OCD was than mine, I appreciated what I had.

    Although I wish I didn't have this condition, I am grateful to have excellent health, a home over my head, and the opportunity to grow up in a first-world country. Within human history and among people growing up in true poverty or war, I am within the top 5% of fortunate people. So I know I have a lot to be thankful for.

    This is not to deny that OCD is a crippling disorder, but knowing that it can be treated, managed, and improved helped me work on myself to achieve a better life.

3. **Declutter your space.** Another benefitting my emotions and mental health is decluttering my space. I knew I didn't want to wind up a hoarder like my dad, so I set a goal of owning as few things as possible.

When I relocated from Korea to HK for graduate school, I tossed away many items, including clothes that I had only worn a couple of times. So many possessions just added to the stress of moving!

I've steadily reduced my belongings over the years to maintain my environment nice, orderly, and uncluttered. And I've since realized that decluttering my physical space improved my mental space.

4. Create a 'stress list'. You may not realize it, but there might be certain people or situations that are guaranteed to stress you out. For example, seeing a particular sibling, extra work tasks on Fridays, a person who has a habit of crossing your boundaries, and so on might be your 'stressors' and exacerbate your OCD. By creating such a list, you can prepare yourself better on how to address them.

For instance, if 'extra work tasks on Fridays' is your stressor, prepare by either ensuring you leave work earlier on Fridays or having a ready list of sentences you can use to say no to the extra workload.

5. TAKE CARE OF YOUR BODY. One of the most important things I've learned during my OCD journey is that what I do with my body matters.

For example, I make sure I get **consistent, good-quality sleep**. (According to the National Sleep Foundation, that's at least seven hours.[36]) Sleep affects cortisol, the stress hormone, so I do my best to get at least seven hours of shut-eye by ensuring I stop work at a certain time, stop checking my digital devices at a certain time, go to bed a certain time, and wake up a certain time.

Another thing I do is **get active**. I have a consistent yoga, meditation, and workout routine. All these lower my adrenaline and cortisol levels and increase my body's release of endorphins, the mood-elevating hormone.

I also **eat REAL FOOD** now. One of the ways I dealt with my OCD was to eat unhealthy snacks. For years, I didn't realize that all those chemicals were stressing my body and potentially making my OCD worse!

For example, a 2009 study published in the British Journal of Psychiatry indicated that processed foods may support the development of mental health problems.[37] Research has also shown that people who eat a 'Western diet' (i.e., high on sugar) are 35% more likely to develop depression.[38]

So, I'm more vigilant with what I eat and make sure I only eat food that truly nourishes my body.

WORKBOOK: WEEK 9-12 - DBT for Your Healing

WEEK 9 – Mindfulness

To recap, please go back to the **Mindfulness** exercises on page 98. On this page is another exercise to help you cultivate mindfulness in your life: **The Spiral Staircase**.

1. Find a comfortable position. Stand up, sit down or lie down.

2. Imagine a spiral staircase within you.

3. Now, starting at the top, slowly descend the staircase, going deeper and deeper within yourself with each step.

4. Take note of what you're feeling with each step.

5. There is no rush. Do not push yourself any further than you want to go.

6. Take note of the silence.

7. Concentrate your attention on the center of your being as you reach it.

WEEK 10 – Interpersonal Effectiveness

To recap, please go back to the **Interpersonal Effectiveness** exercises on page 107.

One of the important Interpersonal Effectiveness skills to develop is **Objective Effectiveness**, which is **your ability to ask and get what you want from others or in any given situation**.

Often, we get in our own way and don't dare to ask for what we want because of certain 'myths' or ideas in our heads. For example, you don't want to go against your friends because you think they won't like you anymore if you say 'no'. This is a myth. True friends will still like you even if you say 'no' to them every now and then.

So the following exercise is called **Challenging Myths**. For each myth, write a challenging statement that makes sense to you.

Example:
Myth: I don't deserve to have what I want or require.
Challenge:
Everyone deserves to be happy. I deserve to be happy. And to be happy means, I get my way or get to do what I want to do.

Your Turn...
Myth: I don't deserve to have what I want or require.
Challenge:

_____

_____

Myth: If I ask for something, I'm a needy person.

Challenge:

_____

_____

Myth: Before I make a request, I need to know whether or not the person will say yes.

Challenge:

_____

_____

Myth: People will get angry with me if I say 'no'.

Challenge:

_____

_____

Myth: If someone tells me 'no', they don't like me.

Challenge:

_____

_____

Myth: Asking for something is selfish.

Challenge:

_____

_____

Myth: If I can't solve something or need help, I must be incompetent.

Challenge:

_____

_____

Myth: It's not important if I don't have what I want or need; I don't really care.

Challenge:

_____

_____

Myth: No one cares about what I want or need.

Challenge:

_____

_____

WEEK 11 – Distress Tolerance

To recap, please go back to the Distress Tolerance exercises on page 116. Another exercise to help you when overcome with extreme emotions is this: **TIPP**.

Temperature: Calm down by subjecting your face to cold temperature. You can run the tap and splash your face with cold water, stick your head for a few seconds in the fridge, or simply step outside during cold weather.

Intense Exercise: Calm down your body by engaging in strenuous exercise. Sometimes, just a quick 7-minute routine will do. If not, just go on until you feel your emotions subsiding.

Paced Breathing: Thoughts and emotions racing? Slow down by breathing in slowly, and then exhaling even slower (e.g., breathe in for 4 seconds, exhale for 5 seconds).

Paired Muscle Relaxation: Do this at the same time you do Paced Breathing above. As you breathe in, slowly tense your body muscles (not to the point of cramping!), and then as you breathe out, release all that muscle tension and say to yourself, 'RELAX'.

WEEK 12 – Emotion Regulation

To recap, please go back to the Emotion Regulation exercises on page 131.

One of the ways to cultivate your Emotion Regulation skills is to reduce your vulnerability to negative feelings by increasing your arsenal of positive feelings. The following exercise is called **Building Positive Emotions**, and it will help you define what makes you positive and happy and encourage you to do them more often.

Build Positive Experiences NOW

List 10 things that make you happy. It can be *any* event such as riding your bicycle, taking care of your plants, singing, etc.

1.)
2.)
3.)
4.)
5.)
6.)
7.)
8.)
9.)
10.)

Select one (ANY one) from the above list and then commit to doing it each day. It doesn't matter what you choose and how long you want to do it. The goal is to do it EVERY SINGLE DAY.

Example:
I choose: yoga
I will practice yoga every day for 30 minutes in the morning.

Your turn:

I choose: _____

I will _____ every day for _____.

Be Mindful of Positive Experiences

Whenever you do the event you chose above, give it your FULL ATTENTION. No multi-tasking, and don't do anything else. In fact, if possible, STOP what you're doing and just absorb the moment. Just experience the positive event.

Today, I felt happy when I:
(Example: Spent time in the kitchen cooking my favorite childhood dish.)

_____
_____
_____
_____

These are the words that describe that event for me:
(Example: relaxed, grateful, in the zone, happy, nostalgic, carefree)

_____
_____
_____
_____

Chapter 8: Supplements and Medications

Disclaimer

Medication and supplements, like any other illness, can have a role. I am not a doctor, and the material in this chapter is based only on anecdotal evidence. Although vitamins and medication can assist, remember that eating a well-balanced, whole-food diet is also crucial for keeping your body and mind healthy and having enough fuel for the day.

Before beginning any supplements or medications on your own, please see your doctor or healthcare expert.

Supplements

Supplements that Help with Anxiety

GABA: Gamma-aminobutyric acid is a neurotransmitter in the central nervous system that operates as an amino acid in the body. GABA inhibits nerve transmission, suppressing neural activity and providing a soothing effect.

Low GABA levels in your body increase the symptoms of persistent anxiety disorders, post-traumatic stress disorder (PTSD), and depression. A lack of GABA activity has been linked to more severe symptoms, whereas a sufficient level of GABA may help calm symptoms and make them more bearable for you.

Melatonin is a sleep aid, and it should not be used on a long-term basis but just when your anxiety keeps you awake. In addition to its antidepressant properties, melatonin may also be used to treat anxiety, sleep difficulties, and circadian rhythm issues.

Melatonin is used as a first-line treatment for patients suffering from insomnia, parasomnia, or irregular circadian rhythms.

Magnesium is a mineral that helps relax muscles and is best taken at night. Due to soil depletion around the world, most individuals are magnesium deficient.

Magnesium may help lower anxiety and tension in the brain. The hypothalamus, a brain region that regulates pituitary and adrenal gland function, is considered to be affected, and these glands regulate your stress response. Leafy greens, nuts, seeds, dark chocolate, avocados, tofu, salmon, dry beans, whole grains, wheat germ, and wheat and oat bran are all high in magnesium.

Men should get 400-420 mg of magnesium each day. Adult women should take 310-320 mg of magnesium per day. (Note: Reduce your dose if you develop diarrhea.)

5-HTP: 5-Hydroxytryptophan is an amino acid that your body naturally produces. 5-HTP supplements are thought to treat depression by increasing serotonin levels. (Note: Do not use an SSRI/SNRI, or you can run into a condition called serotonin syndrome, which can be dangerous.)

Vitamin D, also known as the sunshine vitamin, helps with depression and anxiety. Vitamin D is vital for mood regulation and preventing depression. People suffering from depression who took vitamin D supplements reported an improvement in their symptoms.[39]

Vitamin D is best absorbed by basking in the sun for 20-30 minutes per day. If it isn't an option, supplements will suffice. Adults should consume 600–800 IU per day.

Vitamin C can also enhance your mood by lowering cortisol, a stress hormone created by your body when you are stressed. Vitamin C is also a powerful brain booster! Several studies have suggested that vitamin C may aid in the treatment of oxidative stress-related cognitive disorders such as anxiety.[40] Citrus fruits and vegetables are the best sources of vitamin C. If your diet is low in these foods, a supplement can help. Adults should consume 65-90 mg per day and not exceed 2000 mg per day.

B Complex boosts energy and enhances mood. It also improves your capacity to concentrate and recall information. There is some evidence that multivitamins can help with anxiety symptoms.

According to one study, young adults who took a multivitamin including B vitamins, vitamin C, calcium, magnesium, and zinc for 30 days experienced significantly fewer anxiety symptoms than those who took a placebo.[41]

Furthermore, a meta-analysis of eight trials discovered that taking a multivitamin and multi-mineral supplements for at least 28 days reduced perceived stress and anxiety in healthy individuals.[42] Moreover, high-dose B vitamin supplementation may be more advantageous than low-dose B vitamin supplementation.

Omega 3 fatty acids, particularly DHA, have been related to a lower incidence of depression. DHA aids in creating serotonin, which is crucial for mood regulation. Because omega-3 fats have potent anti-inflammatory qualities, they may aid people who suffer from anxiety. Omega 3 fatty acids can be found in fish and seafood and nuts and seeds.

An analysis of 19 studies found that omega-3 fatty acid treatment reduced anxiety symptoms significantly compared to controls. Over 2,000 milligrams of omega-3s per day were proven to have considerable anti-anxiety effects.[43]

CBD (cannabinoid) is a non-hallucinogenic component of marijuana that has soothing properties. It is not legal everywhere in the world. CBD may also benefit persons suffering from other types of anxiety, such as social anxiety disorder (SAD) and post-traumatic stress disorder (PTSD). It can also be used to treat anxiety-related insomnia.

CBD was researched for its impact on those suffering from depression in 2011. They were given either 400 milligrams (mg) of CBD or a placebo. The CBD consumers reported a drop in their anxiety levels overall.

CBD has also been demonstrated in multiple studies to reduce PTSD symptoms such as nightmares.

Medications
Medications Used for Anxiety, Stress, and Worry

Anti-depressants: It's widely known that depression and anxiety often go hand in hand. There are two kinds of anti-depressants: **SSRIs** and **SNRIs**. Both of these classes take approximately three weeks to start working, and often patients must try different brands and doses of these drugs before settling on one that works for them. Some of these drugs have significant side effects such as headaches, weight gain, and irritability.

Working with your doctor to choose the right medication for you can be a long and frustrating process. Lastly, it's important to remember that medications alone will not fix your anxiety.

SSRI (Selective Serotonin Reuptake Inhibitors) acts on the chemical serotonin to regulate mood and emotion. SSRIs are anti-depressants.

Examples of SSRIs are:
- Citalopram (Celexa)
- Escitalopram (Lexapro)
- Fluoxetine (Prozac)
- Paroxetine (Paxil)
- Sertraline (Zoloft)
- Vortioxetine (Trintellix)

SNRI (Serotonin and Norepinephrine Reuptake Inhibitors) act on the brain chemicals serotonin and norepinephrine to regulate anxiety, mood, and emotion. SNRIs are anti-depressants, but they are also anti-anxiety medications. Additionally, they have been used for chronic pain.

Examples of SNRI are:
- Desvenlafaxine (Pristiq)
- Duloxetine (Cymbalta)
- Levomilnacipran (Fetzima)
- Venlafaxine (Effexor XR)

Anti-anxiety medications are used for people prone to anxiety attacks or panic attacks. Some of the medications used are for when a person is in an acute state of panic or is about to embark on something that may induce a panic attack, such as during a flight or when public speaking).

Examples of Anti-Anxiety Medications are:

- Benzodiazepines (Ativan, Valium, Klonopin, Xanax)
- Buspirone (Buspar)

Medications Used for ADD & ADHD

Stimulants

This drug class has been used to treat ADHD for years, and these drugs work in most cases of ADD/ADHD. Examples of short-acting stimulants include Adderall, Ritalin, Dexedrine, and Focalin. Long-acting stimulants last longer and are more often used. Some of these include Methylphenidate, Adderall XR, and Vyvanse.

Non-Stimulants

Sometimes stimulants do not work for ADHD or cause unpleasant side effects. This class of drugs can help with impulse control, focus, and concentration. Examples of these drugs include Clonidine, Guanfacine, and Viloxazine.

Anti-Depressants

As described above, anti-depressants can help with depression and anxiety, common among people with ADD and ADHD.

Medications Used for Phobias

Medications used for phobias are not usually part of initial treatments. Phobias are treated mainly with therapy; however, medications may be introduced in severe cases.

When medications are introduced for phobias, they will be an anti-depressant. Most SSRIs are excellent for the treatment of social phobias.

MAO inhibitors are sometimes introduced but require careful monitoring due to interactions with other drugs.

Beta-blockers may occasionally be used to block the stimulating effects of adrenaline: increased heart rate and blood pressure, and shaking caused by anxiety.

Occasionally doctors will do short-term therapy using sedative-hypnotic drugs such as Xanax or Valium. These drugs can be habit-forming, so it's best to use them sparingly, if at all.

Medications Used for PTSD & Panic Disorders

Like the other disorders listed, PTSD and Panic Disorders are often treated with anti-depressants, anti-anxiety meds, beta-blockers, and MAOIs, as described above.

Another medication doctors use to help with nightmares or flashbacks is **Prazosin (Minipress)**. This can help your brain "shut off" at night and assist with insomnia and nightmares. Often this med requires dose changes, so it's important to keep a sleep journal and share your findings with your doctor.

In conjunction with these treatments, sometimes antipsychotics are used. Despite the negative connotation of the class name, these meds can help treat PTSD. Examples include Olanzapine, Quetiapine, and Risperidone.

Medications Used for OCD & Compulsive Behaviors

Anti-depressants are the most common drugs that doctors will start with when treating OCD and Compulsive Behaviors. People with OCD will often suffer from depression, so having an SSRI on board can help with both OCD and depression. Specifically, the following medications have been known to work well for people with OCD:

- Clomipramine (Anafranil)
- Fluoxetine (Prozac)
- Paroxetine (Paxil)
- Venlafaxine (Effexor)
- Fluvoxamine (Luvox)
- Sertraline (Zoloft)
- Citalopram (Celexa)
- Escitalopram (Lexapro)

As I have explained, medications are not a one-stop solution, and therapy is one of your best defenses to combat the symptoms associated with these anxiety disorders.

If you need support beyond CBT, DBT, supplements, and medications, the following are a few options to explore with your doctor.

Clinical trials: Test unproven therapies by joining research trials.

Deep-Brain Stimulation: Involves surgical implants of electrodes in the brain.

ECT (ElectroConvulsive Therapy): Involves receiving electric shocks from electrodes attached to your head to induce seizures, which cause your brain to release hormones like serotonin.

While medication helps in some cases, it is not a standalone solution to managing life with an anxiety disorder. I've found using anxiety management techniques, particularly DBT practices, to cope with life's stressors essential to improving my quality of life.

Again, this chapter is not meant to be a medical treatment manual, and everything is based on anecdotal evidence. Before starting any therapy, supplements, medications, or alternative remedies on your own, please speak with your doctor or healthcare professional first.

And if ever you feel you need immediate help, you should contact your local suicide hotline, call 911 if needed, or visit your local emergency department.

Conclusion

There are always ways to improve your situation, regardless of the sort of anxiety you are experiencing or the intensity of your condition. In this book, we discussed a variety of therapies and approaches for improving your thoughts and habits.

Learning to understand what triggers your anxiety, letting go of what no longer serves you, and leaning on resources are all foundations to reducing your anxiety and the symptoms that come with it.

Too frequently, we tend to view worry as something to be avoided at all costs. The truth is that a little anxiety protects us against things that can damage us, and we need it to survive. Plus, there's positive anxiety, such as falling in love, the start of college, our first jobs, our wedding day, and so on!

Managing anxiety and stress is critical to staying healthy, and we must take a step back to realize when worry is normal and when it is stress that must be addressed.

People suffering from anxiety disorders should realize that the goal is efficient stress management rather than complete removal.

You will be better prepared to deal with stress if you take the following steps.

- Consume nutritious foods.
- Get enough sleep and rest.
- Exercise.
- Consume caffeine and alcohol in moderation.
- Set attainable goals and expectations.
- Learn to relax, whatever that means for you.

- And, of course, learn the DBT skills of Mindfulness, Interpersonal Effectiveness, Distress Tolerance, and Emotion Regulation we covered in this book.

You've put a lot of effort into reading this book. Some of it may have been more difficult than you anticipated. But know that all of these will work to help you.

Managing anxiety, or any mental health condition, is a lifelong challenge. So, please do continue to practice the DBT skills you learned here. Don't just go and re-read the chapters and perform the exercises whenever anxiety hits you. You need to make an effort to practice these DBT skills daily so that they become natural to you.

Taking care of yourself is not a linear process. Sometimes, you will come across problems that might seem more than you can handle on your own. There will be occasions when your anxiety worsens, and you will have frightening thoughts.

My advice to you is: **be kind to yourself, remember that you are not alone, and keep in mind that your life is worth living!**

THANK YOU for taking the time to read this book. I hope that my journey to self-healing inspires you to move forward with yours.

I wish you nothing but a happy life.

"Smile, breathe, and go slowly."
- Thich Nhat Hanh

Review Request

If you enjoyed this book or found it useful I'd like to ask you for a quick favor:

Please share your thoughts and leave a quick review.

Your feedback matters and helps me make improvements to provide the best content possible.

Reviews are incredibly helpful to both readers and authors like me, so any help would be greatly appreciated.

You can leave a review here by scanning the QR code:

http://tinyurl.com/dbtskills-bundle-review

Also, please join my ARC team to get early access to my preleases.

https://barretthuang.com/arc-team/

THANK YOU!

Glossary

Acute Stress Disorder
A condition characterized by a powerful and unpleasant reaction that develops in the weeks following a traumatic event.

Attention Deficit Hyperactivity Disorder (ADHD)
A long-lasting disorder that affects a person's capacity to focus, sit still, and control behavior.

Borderline Personality Disorder (BPD)
A condition characterized by a person's inability to regulate emotions.

Cognitive Behavior Therapy (CBT)
A form of psychological treatment aims to reduce symptoms of various mental health conditions, primarily depression and anxiety disorders.

Complex PTSD (C-PTSD)
A condition in which you have some PTSD symptoms and some extra symptoms, such as difficulties controlling your emotions, feeling enraged, or being distrustful of the world.

Dialectical Behavior Therapy (BDT)
A modified type of cognitive-behavior therapy that's been specially adapted for people who feel emotions intensely.

Eye Movement Desensitization and Reprocessing (EMDR)
A form of psychotherapy developed by Francine Shapiro in the 1980s. A person receiving EMDR treatment is asked to recall troubling experiences while doing bilateral stimulation, such as side-to-side eye movement.

Generalized Anxiety Disorder (GAD)
A condition characterized by persistent worrying or anxiety about several areas that are out of proportion to the impact of the events.

Learned Helplessness
: A phenomenon in which people believe they cannot change their situation after repeatedly experiencing a traumatic event.

Learned Optimism
: The practice of learning to recognize and fight negative ideas and replacing them with positive ones.

Obsessive-Compulsive Disorder (OCD)
: A condition in which people have recurring, unwanted thoughts, ideas, or sensations (obsessions) that make them feel driven to do something repetitively (compulsions).

Obsessive-Compulsive Disorder (OCD)
: A condition wherein a person has uncontrollable, recurring thoughts (obsessions) and/or behaviors (compulsions) that they feel compelled to repeat.

Panic Attack
: A brief period of extreme fear that results in strong physical symptoms despite the absence of any real danger or apparent cause.

Panic Disorder
: An anxiety disorder characterized by sudden and recurring bouts of great fear, which may go with physical symptoms such as chest pains, heart tremors, panting, vertigo, or gastrointestinal problems.

Phobia
: Anxiety or aversion to something excessive or unjustified.

Post-Traumatic Stress Disorder (PTSD)
: A disorder that progresses in some people after witnessing a shocking, frightening, or dangerous event.

Social Anxiety Disorder
: A condition characterized by an intense and persistent fear of being observed and judged by others.

References

1 LaFreniere, L. S., & Newman, M. G. (2020). Exposing worry's deceit: Percentage of untrue worries in generalized anxiety disorder treatment. *Behavior Therapy, 51*(3), 413–423. https://doi.org/10.1016/j.beth.2019.07.003

2 Linehan, M. (2021). Building a Life Worth Living: A Memoir. Random House.

3 Mayo Foundation for Medical Education and Research. (2021, July 8). *Chronic stress puts your health at risk*. Mayo Clinic. Retrieved April 18, 2022, from https://www.mayoclinic.org/healthy-lifestyle/stress-management/in-depth/stress/art-20046037

4 Ritschel, L. A., Lim, N. E., & Stewart, L. M. (2015). Transdiagnostic applications of DBT for adolescents and adults. *American Journal of Psychotherapy, 69*(2), 111–128. https://doi.org/10.1176/appi.psychotherapy.2015.69.2.111

5 Groth, A. (2012, July 24). *You're the average of the five people you spend the most time with*. Business Insider. Retrieved April 21, 2022, from https://www.businessinsider.com/jim-rohn-youre-the-average-of-the-five-people-you-spend-the-most-time-with-2012-7

6 Pourjali, F., & Zarnaghash, M. (2010). Relationships between assertiveness and the power of saying no with mental health among undergraduate student. *Procedia - Social and Behavioral Sciences, 9*, 137–141. https://doi.org/10.1016/j.sbspro.2010.12.126

7 Kedia, G., Mussweiler, T., & Linden, D. E. J. (2014). Brain mechanisms of social comparison and their influence on the reward system. *NeuroReport, 25*(16), 1255–1265. https://doi.org/10.1097/wnr.0000000000000255

8 Karim, F., Oyewande, A., Abdalla, L. F., Chaudhry Ehsanullah, R., & Khan, S. (2020). Social media use and its connection to Mental Health: A Systematic Review. *Cureus*. https://doi.org/10.7759/cureus.8627

9 Ouellette, C. (2020, December 23). *FOMO statistics you need to grow your business*. TrustPulse. Retrieved April 2022, from https://trustpulse.com/fomo-statistics/

10 Bressan, R. A., & Crippa, J. A. (2005). The role of dopamine in reward and pleasure behaviour - review of data from Preclinical Research. *Acta Psychiatrica Scandinavica, 111*(s427), 14–21. https://doi.org/10.1111/j.1600-0447.2005.00540.x

11 Houlis, A. M. (n.d.). *5 things successful people do when setting boundaries at work*. Fairygodboss. Retrieved April 2, 2022, from https://fairygodboss.com/career-topics/setting-boundaries-at-work

12 Marie, O. (2020, November 28). *5 things science tells us about morning routine*. Science Times. Retrieved April 2, 2022, from https://www.sciencetimes.com/articles/28438/20201128/5-things-science-tells-morning-routine.htm

13 P., S. M. E. (2006). *Learned optimism how to change your mind and your life; with a new preface*. Vintage Books.

14 Scheier, M. F., & Carver, C. S. (1992). Effects of optimism on psychological and physical well-being: Theoretical overview and empirical update. *Cognitive Therapy and Research, 16*(2), 201–228. https://doi.org/10.1007/bf01173489

15 Rasmussen, H. N., Scheier, M. F., & Greenhouse, J. B. (2009). Optimism and physical health: A meta-analytic review. *Annals of Behavioral Medicine, 37*(3), 239–256. https://doi.org/10.1007/s12160-009-9111-x

16 Allen , V. L. (2017). Learned Optimism: A Balm for Social Worker Stress. *Social Work & Christianity, 44*(4), 83–91. https://doi.org/10.34043/swc.v46i2

17 Achor, S. (2018). *The happiness advantage: How a positive brain fuels success in work and life*. Currency.

18 Davidson, R. J., & Lutz, A. (2008). Buddha's brain: Neuroplasticity and meditation [in the spotlight]. *IEEE Signal Processing Magazine, 25*(1), 176–174. https://doi.org/10.1109/msp.2008.4431873

19 Davidson, R. J., Kabat-Zinn, J., Schumacher, J., Rosenkranz, M., Muller, D., Santorelli, S. F., Urbanowski, F., Harrington, A., Bonus, K., & Sheridan, J. F. (2003). Alterations in brain and immune function produced by mindfulness meditation. *Psychosomatic Medicine, 65*(4), 564–570. https://doi.org/10.1097/01.psy.0000077505.67574.e3

20 Hölzel, B. K., Carmody, J., Vangel, M., Congleton, C., Yerramsetti, S. M., Gard, T., & Lazar, S. W. (2011). Mindfulness practice leads to increases in regional brain gray matter density. *Psychiatry Research: Neuroimaging, 191*(1), 36–43. https://doi.org/10.1016/j.pscychresns.2010.08.006

21 Hofmann, S. G., & Gómez, A. F. (2017). Mindfulness-based interventions for anxiety and depression. *Psychiatric Clinics of North America, 40*(4), 739–749. https://doi.org/10.1016/j.psc.2017.08.008

22 Shapiro, E. and D. (2017, May 23). *The difference between mindfulness and meditation*. Medium. Retrieved April 2, 2022, from https://medium.com/thrive-global/mindfulness-meditation-whats-the-difference-852f5ef7ec1a#

23 Basso, J. C., McHale, A., Ende, V., Oberlin, D. J., & Suzuki, W. A. (2019). Brief, daily meditation enhances attention, memory, mood, and emotional regulation in non-experienced meditators. *Behavioural Brain Research, 356*, 208–220. https://doi.org/10.1016/j.bbr.2018.08.023

24 Fayyad, J., Sampson, N. A., Hwang, I., Adamowski, T., Aguilar-Gaxiola, S., Al-Hamzawi, A., Andrade, L. H., Borges, G., de Girolamo, G., Florescu, S., Gureje, O., Haro, J. M., Hu, C., Karam, E. G., Lee, S., Navarro-Mateu, F., O'Neill, S., Pennell, B.-E., Piazza, M., … Kessler, R. C. (2016). The descriptive epidemiology of DSM-IV ADULT ADHD in the World Health Organization

World Mental Health Surveys. *ADHD Attention Deficit and Hyperactivity Disorders*, 9(1), 47–65. https://doi.org/10.1007/s12402-016-0208-3

25 Fuller-Thomson, E., Lewis, D. A., & Agbeyaka, S. (2021). Attention-deficit/hyperactivity disorder and alcohol and other substance use disorders in young adulthood: Findings from a Canadian Nationally Representative survey. *Alcohol and Alcoholism*. https://doi.org/10.1093/alcalc/agab048

26 Molina BSG;Pelham WE;Cheong J;Marshal MP;Gnagy EM;Curran PJ; (n.d.). Childhood attention-deficit/hyperactivity disorder (ADHD) and growth in adolescent alcohol use: The roles of functional impairments, ADHD symptom persistence, and parental knowledge. Journal of abnormal psychology. Retrieved April 30, 2022, from https://pubmed.ncbi.nlm.nih.gov/22845650/

27 U.S. Department of Health and Human Services. (n.d.). *Specific phobia*. National Institute of Mental Health. Retrieved April 2, 2022, from https://www.nimh.nih.gov/health/statistics/specific-phobia

28 Becker, C. B., & Zayfert, C. (2001). Integrating DBT-based techniques and concepts to facilitate exposure treatment for PTSD. *Cognitive and Behavioral Practice*, 8(2), 107–122. https://doi.org/10.1016/s1077-7229(01)80017-1

29 Bohus, M., Kleindienst, N., Hahn, C., Müller-Engelmann, M., Ludäscher, P., Steil, R., Fydrich, T., Kuehner, C., Resick, P. A., Stiglmayr, C., Schmahl, C., & Priebe, K. (2020). Dialectical behavior therapy for posttraumatic stress disorder (DBT-PTSD) compared with Cognitive Processing Therapy (CPT) in complex presentations of PTSD in women survivors of childhood abuse. *JAMA Psychiatry*, 77(12), 1235. https://doi.org/10.1001/jamapsychiatry.2020.2148

30 Pally, R. (1998). Emotional processing: The mind-body connection. *International Journal of Psycho-Analysis*, 79, 349-362.

31 Schwartz, J., & Beyette, B. (2016). *Brain Lock: Free Yourself From Obsessive-Compulsive Behavior: A Four-Step Self-Treatment Method To Change Your Brain Chemistry*. Harper Perennial.

32 *Facts & Statistics: Anxiety and Depression Association of America, ADAA*. Facts & Statistics | Anxiety and Depression Association of America, ADAA. (n.d.). Retrieved April 2, 2022, from https://adaa.org/understanding-anxiety/facts-statistics

33 Miller, T. W., & Kraus, R. F. (2007). Modified dialectical behavior therapy and problem solving for obsessive-compulsive personality disorder. *Journal of Contemporary Psychotherapy*, *37*(2), 79–85. https://doi.org/10.1007/s10879-006-9039-4

34 Ahovan, M., Balali, S., Abedi Shargh, N., & Doostian, Y. (2016). Efficacy of dialectical behavior therapy on clinical signs and emotion regulation in patients with obsessive-compulsive disorder. *Mediterranean Journal of Social Sciences*. https://doi.org/10.5901/mjss.2016.v7n4p412

35 Shameli, L., Mehrabizadeh Honarmand, M., Naa'mi, A., & Davodi, I. (2019). The effectiveness of emotion-focused therapy on emotion regulation styles and severity of obsessive-compulsive symptoms in women with obsessive-compulsive disorder. *Iranian Journal of Psychiatry and Clinical Psychology*, 356–369. https://doi.org/10.32598/ijpcp.24.4.456

36 Hirshkowitz, M., Whiton, K., Albert, S. M., Alessi, C., Bruni, O., DonCarlos, L., Hazen, N., Herman, J., Katz, E. S., Kheirandish-Gozal, L., Neubauer, D. N., O'Donnell, A. E., Ohayon, M., Peever, J., Rawding, R., Sachdeva, R. C., Setters, B., Vitiello, M. V., Ware, J. C., & Adams Hillard, P. J. (2015). National Sleep Foundation's sleep time duration recommendations: Methodology and results summary. *Sleep Health*, *1*(1), 40–43. https://doi.org/10.1016/j.sleh.2014.12.010

37 Akbaraly, T. N., Brunner, E. J., Ferrie, J. E., Marmot, M. G., Kivimaki, M., & Singh-Manoux, A. (2009). Dietary pattern and depressive symptoms in middle age. *British Journal of Psychiatry*, *195*(5), 408–413. https://doi.org/10.1192/bjp.bp.108.058925

38 MD, E. S. (2020, March 26). *Nutritional psychiatry: Your brain on food*. Harvard Health. Retrieved April 3, 2022, from https://www.health.harvard.edu/blog/nutritional-psychiatry-your-brain-on-food-201511168626

39 Parker, G. B., Brotchie, H., & Graham, R. K. (2017). Vitamin D and depression. *Journal of Affective Disorders*, *208*, 56–61. https://doi.org/10.1016/j.jad.2016.08.082

40 Plevin, D., & Galletly, C. (2020). The neuropsychiatric effects of vitamin C deficiency: A systematic review. *BMC Psychiatry*, *20*(1). https://doi.org/10.1186/s12888-020-02730-w

41 White, D., Cox, K., Peters, R., Pipingas, A., & Scholey, A. (2015). Effects of four-week supplementation with a multi-vitamin/mineral preparation on mood and blood biomarkers in young adults: A randomised, double-blind, placebo-controlled trial. *Nutrients*, *7*(11), 9005–9017. https://doi.org/10.3390/nu7115451

42 Long, S.-J., & Benton, D. (2013). Effects of vitamin and mineral supplementation on stress, mild psychiatric symptoms, and mood in nonclinical samples. *Psychosomatic Medicine*, *75*(2), 144–153. https://doi.org/10.1097/psy.0b013e31827d5fbd

43 Su, K.-P., Tseng, P.-T., Lin, P.-Y., Okubo, R., Chen, T.-Y., Chen, Y.-W., & Matsuoka, Y. J. (2018). Association of use of omega-3 polyunsaturated fatty acids with changes in severity of anxiety symptoms. *JAMA Network Open*, *1*(5). https://doi.org/10.1001/jamanetworkopen.2018.2327

Index

Acute stress Disorder, 78
Attention Deficit Hyperactivity Disorder (ADHD), 102
Borderline Personality Disorder (BPD), 22
CBT, 22
Checking, 135, 141
Cognitive Behavior Therapy (CBT), 17, 27
Complex PTSD (C-PTSD), 125
Contamination, 140
DBT, 22, 28
Deprivation hoarding, 143
Dialectical Behavior Therapy (DBT), 17, 27
Distress Tolerance, 27, 114, 116, 146, 154, 167
Emotion Regulation, 27, 127, 131, 146, 155, 167
Exercise: 4-7-8 Breathing Technique, 98
Exercise: 5-4-3-2-1 Grounding Technique, 99
Exercise: A.C.C.E.P.T.S., 120
Exercise: Boundary Journaling, 68
Exercise: Building Positive Emotions, 155
Exercise: Check the Facts, 132
Exercise: D.E.A.R.M.A.N., 107
Exercise: F.A.S.T., 111
Exercise: G.I.V.E., 109
Exercise: Happiness Habit, 88
Exercise: Mindfulness Body Scan, 100
Exercise: Opposite Action for Overwhelming Emotions, 131
Exercise: P.L.E.A.S.E., 133
Exercise: Radical Acceptance Worksheet, 117
Exercise: Self-Acceptance and Change, 28
Exercise: Setting YOUR Boundaries, 66
Exercise: Spiral Staircase, 150, 151
Exercise: The ABCDE Model, 86
Exercise: TIPP, 154
Exercise: Turning the Mind, 116
Exercise: WISE MIND, 101
Eye Movement Desensitization and Reprocessing (EMDR), 126
Fear of Being Offline, 46
Fear of Missing Out, 45
FoMO, 45, 47
Generalized Anxiety Disorder, 77
Generalized Anxiety Disorder (GAD), 16, 44, 169
Hoarding, 136, 142
Interpersonal Effectiveness, 27, 106, 107, 145, 151, 167
Intrusive thoughts, 143
Learned helplessness, 80, 82
Learned optimism, 79, 80, 82, 83, 86, 172
Meditation, 94, 95
Mindfulness, 27, 92, 93, 97, 98, 100, 144, 150, 167, 173
Obsessive-Compulsive Disorder (OCD), 16, 78, 135
OCD Category, 140
Organization, 140
Panic attack, 73, 77, 161
Panic disorder, 77, 79, 122, 163
Phobia, 20, 79, 113, 114, 162
Post-Traumatic Stress Disorder (PTSD), 79, 123, 157, 160
Preventing harm to others hoarding, 143
Radical Acceptance, 23, 114, 117, 144
Ruminations, 143
Sentimental hoarding, 143
Social Anxiety Disorder (SAD), 78, 160

DBT Workbook For Depression

The Complete Guide for Treating Depression & Anxiety with Dialectical Behavior Therapy | DBT Skills for Men & Women for Mindfulness, Happiness and Emotional Health

By Barrett Huang

https://barretthuang.com/

Contents

Introduction 181
   My Story 182
   Who Should Read This Book 187
   Goals of This Book 187
   Content Warning 188
   Safety 188
   Be Kind to Yourself 189
Depression 101 190
     Depression vs. Sadness 191
   What Causes Depression? 192
   Depression Signs & Symptoms 194
   What are the Different Types of Depression? 198
   Depression Recommended Treatments 201
     Medication 202
     Brain Stimulation Therapy 203
     Light therapy 205
     Exercise/Physical Activity 205
     Psychotherapy 206
Living with Depression 209
   Depression and the Brain 210
   Depression and the Body 211
   Depression and Relationships 212
   Depression in Women 214
What is Dialectical Behavior Therapy? 217
   Dialectics 218
   Why DBT for Depression? 222
   DBT Core Concepts 222
     Radical Acceptance 223

    Change 227

  DBT Core Skills 232

    Mindfulness 232

    Distress Tolerance 252

    Emotion Regulation 285

    Interpersonal Effectiveness 313

Continuing the Road to Happiness 329

  Self-Esteem: The Link Between Self-Perception and Depression 329

  Nutrition: Eat to Beat Depression 335

Conclusion 337

Appendix A – PHQ-9 Depression Self-Assessment 339

Appendix B – Journaling for Depression Relief 342

Review Request 345

References 346

Indexes 353

Introduction

"Depression is the most unpleasant thing I have ever experienced. It is that absence of being able to envisage that you will ever be cheerful again. The absence of hope."
– J.K. Rowling

The school bell rings for lunch. The class erupts into wild noise, and everybody talks all at once. I slowly stand up, hunch over to grab my backpack, and quietly leave the room.

I walk across the halls amidst all the excited chatter and chaos. I don't greet anyone, and no one greets me. I reach the cafeteria, but I don't go in for lunch. I walk on until I reach the library. Once inside, I go to my favorite dark corner, and as quietly as possible, I bring out my lunch and eat silently.

Since there are no distractions, I finish lunch in record time. However, my next class is still far off, so I fall asleep in my little dark corner. (I'm so tired and sleepy all the time.)

I get back to class, and the afternoon just goes on and on and on. The bell rings, and nearly everyone jumps out of their seats. Kids are grabbing bags, heading out the door, and making plans with each other. Just like that, the room is empty.

I grab my bag, go out the door, and slowly walk home. Once I reach home, I head straight to my room and close the door. I don't let anyone know I'm back, and no one notices me. My day is almost done. And just like yesterday, I feel invisible.

The above is how I spent most of my teenage years— in complete loneliness and isolation. Even now, I find it difficult to remember and put into words this very difficult time in my life.

As I started my journey to mental healing, I discovered everything that caused my mental health problems. Let me start at the beginning...

My Story

My parents emigrated from China to Canada in the 1980s. My sister and I were born in Toronto. English is our first language, so there was no "language barrier" to overcome. We also attended a multicultural school, so our cultural identity, at least on the surface, was not an issue. It was everything else that was the problem.

Although the intention was to provide a better future for the family, I always resented why my parents were so stuck in their old-fashioned Chinese ways. This created a chaotic situation for me because, at home, everything was Chinese, but outside, everything was Canadian. It felt like being in two different worlds but not belonging in either.

My father was a hoarder who suffered from undiagnosed Obsessive-Compulsive Disorder (OCD). One of his compulsions was to have everything he had arranged a certain way and located in a specific place. He would get upset if something wasn't where it was supposed to be. Imagine living in a house where you were afraid to touch anything and couldn't return things where they belonged. Also, since he was a hoarder, our home was always cluttered.

My mother had undiagnosed General Anxiety Disorder (GAD). She was constantly worried about something and always expected some disaster to strike at any moment. For example, despite living in a safe and secure neighborhood, she constantly worried that someone would enter our house. Imagine living in a home where you were continuously alerted that something terrible would happen at any time.

She also had a victim mindset. I heard the phrase, "*Why is this happening to me?*" way too often at home. She saw herself as the victim of circumstances, other people, or the world. She hardly ever saw her part or responsibility in situations.

Please note that I'm not sharing these stories about my parents because I blame them. In truth, I have a lot of empathy for them. And when I look back at my childhood, there was love too, and I know in my heart that they were doing their best.

Still, this does not change the reality that I grew up in a very chaotic and unstable home with parents suffering from mental health disorders. Our Chinese culture also meant that we were not in the habit of talking about our feelings. (It's seen as a sign of weakness.) Physical displays of affection were also nonexistent. These left my sister and me feeling emotionally unstable growing up.

By the time I hit my teenage years, I was already showing symptoms of OCD and GAD. (I would later be diagnosed with these disorders by a mental health professional.)

One of my compulsions was a morning ritual I had to go through before school. Do you remember the British pop girl band, the *Spice Girls*? When I was 14, I had a huge crush on Emma Bunton. One morning ritual was standing in front of her poster, talking to myself, and pretending I was courting or dating her. (Never mind that she was much older than me.) I would talk and fantasize until I felt "just right."

This particular compulsion of mine could take 10 minutes or go on for hours. As it's a compulsion, I MUST do it. I won't want to attend school if I don't reach that "just right" feeling.

Sometimes, I would skip sleep altogether to avoid this morning ritual because I knew I would have to go through the whole routine again the next day. As you can imagine, my sleeping schedule was a mess, and I would be tired and sleepy all day at school.

Another compulsion I had was not stepping on lines or cracks in the pavement. If I did, my anxiety would kick in, and I would be nervous the whole day as I waited for something bad to happen.

As a person with anxiety, that persistent sense of dread is hardwired into my psyche. Even today, I still fear that the house will burn down if I don't double-check the stove, and I sometimes check the tap 2-3 times to ensure it's completely turned off. When I leave, I sometimes triple-check that the door is locked because my mind tells me someone will break in and steal everything. (Yes, just like my mom.)

OCD and GAD disorders are very draining. And they contributed heavily to my depression.

The teenage years are supposed to be a time of change, new experiences, going out with friends, and excitement about the future. I had none of that. In fact, I didn't have any friends in a school of about 5,000 kids, so I was incredibly lonely. This loneliness made me self-isolate, and this made me sink deeper and deeper into pain and despair.

I started this section with a quote by J.K. Rowling because that's exactly how I felt for the longest time. For years, I couldn't see myself ever being cheerful again, and I had no hope for the future.

Fortunately, things started to change when I left home for college at 19. I was in a new environment and welcomed returning to my dorm room each day. Even though I was still very much alone, at least the space I came back to was not as chaotic and unstable as my home life.

In my 20s, I realized what I experienced as a child was abnormal. I needed to get away from the situation to improve my life and mindset—so I started to travel. Ironically, my first stop was China.

I was curious about the history of my parents and wanted to see where they came from. While there, I discovered the hardships my parents went through growing up. It made me realize how lucky I am to grow up in a free country. I also learned that my parents went through the Great Chinese Famine, where 30-40 million people starved to death in China, and experienced the Cultural Revolution, where another 10 million died. My parents never even had the chance to go to college. All of this helped me understand why my parents are the way they are.

It's strange to be at odds with my parents when I was constantly around them— and then to understand them once I was gone and visited where they came from. For the first time, I could see things from their perspective and developed a lot of empathy for them.

From China, I traveled to other Asian countries such as South Korea, Hong Kong, Thailand, and the Philippines. I actually stayed in South Korea for three years, teaching English as a Second Language (ESL). To this day, I consider it as one of the best decisions I've ever made. It made me independent and teaching gave me a sense of fulfillment I've never felt before.

Traveling opened my mind to different cultures and different ways of life. It also showed me how other people faced adversity. Some of the places I visited were impoverished. Yet, the people I met were so courageous and nearly everyone had a smile. They gave me hope, and I began believing I could overcome my mental hardships. I started to see some light at the end of the tunnel.

I came back to Toronto after about four years. As I figured out what to do next with my life, I also started educating myself about my mental health problems. I read many self-help books and reached the point where I felt ready and open to treatment. I met a psychologist and was officially diagnosed with OCD and GAD.

I was prescribed anti-anxiety medication and underwent psychotherapy, specifically Cognitive Behavior Therapy (CBT). After a while, I had improved to the point where I asked my doctor to lower my dosage. (For the record, I still take anti-anxiety medication, which helps me keep this disorder under control.) At some point, I noticed that CBT was no longer working for me, so I began exploring other psychotherapy treatments.

I discovered Dialectical Behavior Therapy (DBT), the treatment that I credit for enabling me to finally break free from the mental health issues preventing me from living the life I wanted.

I still experience OCD, GAD, and depression from time to time. I don't believe they will ever entirely disappear, but they no longer debilitate me. I've coped and adjusted. I'm calmer and more level-headed now, and I have the courage—and tools—to deal with life's obstacles better than before. And yes, I'll dare say it—I experience happiness now and hope. It's my sincerest wish that you achieve the same with this book.

Who Should Read This Book

This book is for everyone experiencing even the most minor symptoms of depression. You may want to read this book to understand better what you're going through, or you may already be in therapy and wish to include the exercises in this book in your treatment plan.

This book is also for anyone who knows someone struggling with depression. One of the first things we can do to help and support someone we care about is to understand their situation better. Understanding allows you to empathize, which people experiencing depression would highly appreciate.

Goals of This Book

This book seeks to help people get a better understanding of depression and to give them real-life tools to help them cope with this condition.

I was very confused about my mental health disorders. I was miserable and knew things needed to change, but I didn't even have the words to describe what I felt or thought (let alone what caused them!). So, it is my sincere hope that this book gives you clarity. Awareness and understanding are fundamental when dealing with mental health problems.

But, of course, knowing about your condition is just half the battle, and the rest is learning how to cope and, hopefully, heal. This is where the second part of the book comes in.

Dialectical Behavior Therapy (DBT) is the method that truly enabled me to deal effectively with my co-existing mental health disorders. I'll discuss this technique in detail and provide plenty of exercises to help you effectively adopt it in your life.

Content Warning

This book contains topics that may be distressing or disturbing. Some stories, topics, and incidents may prompt or trigger you. Loneliness, sadness, emotional abuse, feelings of worldliness, loss, breakups, self-harm, and death are examples of such content. Please be mindful of these and other issues that may trouble you. Reminder: please don't hesitate to ask for assistance or consult a specialist whenever you feel overwhelmed.

Safety

When dealing with depression, *safety* is essential. As mentioned, topics and stories in this book may trigger you, so it's good to take steps to *be safe* and *feel safe* while reading this book and doing the exercises provided.

How can you feel safe while reading this book? Safety means different things to different people, but the following are some ideas.

- Create a **Safe Space**. Where (or when) do you feel most safe and comfortable? This may be sitting on an old chair from your childhood in your bedroom or alone in the kitchen with a cup of coffee in the mornings. Whatever it is, consider reading this book in that safe space.
- Set a **reading boundary**. Set limits on how much you read and for how long. Take breaks as needed, and remember that it's okay to put the book down if you feel overwhelmed.

- **Self-care checklist**. Take care of your physical and emotional needs while reading. This may involve getting adequate sleep, eating healthily, and participating in activities that make you happy.

- Establish a "**Plan B**." Create a list of actions to take if you ever feel unsafe. Here are a few suggestions:
    o Stop reading.
    o Call _____.
    o Message _____.
    o Go to _____.
    o Listen to _____.
    o Watch _____.
    o Others:

    _____
    _____
    _____

Be Kind to Yourself

Whenever I look back at my adolescent years, I feel a lot of empathy. I struggled so much and went through many years of anxiety and loneliness. I anguished about so many things over which I had no control, and I had no idea how to deal with the things over which I did have influence. This resulted in a lot of anger directed towards myself, others, and life. Of course, this did not help my situation because it only worsened my mental health problems. So, I advise you to be patient, compassionate, and understanding of yourself. Kindness, I firmly believe, is the first step toward healing.

Depression 101

"Depression is the feeling of being trapped in a dark room with no windows, no doors, and no way out." - Unknown

Depression, or major depressive disorder (MDD), is a mood disorder that affects how you feel, think, and act. It's distinguished by persistent feelings of sadness, despair and loss of interest in activities one previously enjoyed. Sadly, depression is a prevalent mental disorder.

According to the World Health Organization (WHO), depression affects around 280 million people globally.[1] In the United States, an estimated 21 million adults (8.4% of the adult population) have experienced at least one major depressive episode in 2020.[2]

Depression may be "common," but there's a lot of confusion and misconceptions about this mental disorder. As I started to understand my depression disorder, I was surprised at how different factors caused and affected each other. For example, the extreme loneliness I felt in my teens contributed to the development of my depression. Then my depression made me want to withdraw even more from social interactions.

My goal with the following sections is to help you develop a deeper understanding of this illness so that you can make the most informed treatment decision possible.

Also, in my experience, understanding my depression made me more open to the help and treatments that were available to me. I hope this also applies to you.

Depression vs. Sadness

Depression and sadness are two distinct emotions. Sadness is a natural human feeling due to an event like a loss or disappointment. It's usually temporary, and people can usually pinpoint the source of their sadness.

Depression, on the other hand, is a mental health condition characterized by a chronic and pervasive sense of melancholy, hopelessness, and loss of interest or pleasure in activities. Depression, unlike sadness, can be unrelated to a specific event and can continue for weeks, months, or even years.

SADNESS	DEPRESSION
A typical human emotion	A mental health disorder
Typically happens in response to an unpleasant event	Happens as a result of genetics, life events, medication, and others
Enables people to function and do daily activities normally	Interferes with daily activities, relationships, and work
Temporary	Constant
Usually goes away with time	Requires intervention such as learning and adopting coping techniques, making lifestyle changes, seeking therapy or medication, etc.

Feelings of sadness are okay. After all, life is full of ups and downs. However, when you don't understand why you're sad, and if you feel this way for long periods that it affects your daily life, it might be depression.

What Causes Depression?

A singular motive does not cause depression; the reasons are complex and can differ for each person. Some of the possible causes of depression include:

1. **Genetics**. Although no specific gene has been linked to depression, studies have indicated that having a close family member with the condition increases your odds of developing it yourself.[3,4]

    Over the years, I've learned that my dad's mother and older brother committed suicide. Looking back at my dad, I don't remember many moments when he was truly happy. So, in my situation, I'm inclined to see my depression and other mental health problems as associated with my genetics.

2. **Brain chemistry**. Changes in the balance of chemicals in the brain, such as *serotonin, norepinephrine,* and *dopamine,* can contribute to depression. Why? One theory suggests that neurotransmitter imbalance may disrupt the communication between brain cells, leading to mood disturbances. Another theory suggests that this imbalance may lead to changes in the structure and function of brain regions involved in regulating mood.

    Serotonin is essential for mood, hunger, and sleep regulation. It's also known as the "happy" hormone. *Norepinephrine* is implicated in the "fight or flight" response of the body. It aids in the regulation of mood, attention, and arousal. Dopamine is involved in the regulation of pleasure and reward. That's why it's also known as the "feel-good" hormone.

3. **Life events**. Trauma, stress, abuse, neglect, loneliness, or significant life changes, such as a death or divorce, can trigger depression.

One of my earliest trauma memories was when I was 11 or 12. My parents were going through a difficult divorce, and my sister and I were caught in the crossfire. There was a lot of fighting, accusations, and ill feelings.

One day, my dad left for work, and my mom suddenly barged into my room, woke me up, and told me to pack a bag quickly because we were going on a trip with her. I refused to go and started crying and screaming.

For some reason, my dad returned, saw what was happening, and whisked me away to stay at a neighbor's house while they talked things out. I returned home, but I remember continuously looking over my shoulder for days. I was scared that my mother was waiting for me around the corner, ready to take me away forever.

4. **Medical conditions**. Chronic illnesses, such as cancer or heart disease, can cause depression.

5. **Substance abuse**. Alcohol and drug abuse can cause depression or worsen existing depression.

6. **Hormonal changes**. Hormonal changes during puberty, pregnancy, or menopause affect mood and may contribute to depression. For this reason, data shows that women are twice to three times more likely to experience depression than men.[5] (Please also see Depression in Women, page 214.)

7. **Medications**. Some drugs, such as birth control pills or blood pressure medication, can cause depression as a side effect.

Depression Signs & Symptoms

The symptoms of depression can vary from person to person, but some common symptoms may include the following:

1. **Constant feelings of sadness, emptiness, or hopelessness.** Depression is marked by an overall bleak outlook regarding life. You feel and believe there's nothing you can do to change or improve your situation, so you don't see how things can improve.

2. **Loss of interest or pleasure in formerly enjoyable activities.** Old hobbies and activities that used to make you happy no longer do, so you avoid them altogether.

3. **Fluctuations in appetite or weight (loss or gain).** You don't care about what you eat or drink, which may result in sudden weight loss or gain.

4. **Sleeping problems.** You might have trouble falling asleep (insomnia) or always sleep too much (hypersomnia).

5. **Loss of energy**. You often feel tired, exhausted, or utterly devoid of energy. You find even the simplest activities (e.g., getting out of bed, brushing your teeth, interacting with others, etc.) exhausting.

6. **Feelings of guilt, self-hate or self-loathing**. You might have low self-esteem and often experience feelings of worthlessness. You may also often judge and criticize yourself. You might also often experience feelings of guilt or always feel that you're "wrong."

7. **Psychomotor agitation or retardation.** You feel restless and exhibit slowed speaking or body movements. You may also have difficulties concentrating, making decisions, or remembering things.

8. **Difficulty handling emotions such as anger or irritability.** Your tolerance level for stressful situations and intense emotions is low, and you may find yourself impulsively reacting to everything and everyone.

9. **Isolation.** You don't feel connected to anyone, so you disengage from family, friends, or life and spend more time alone.

    Important: Isolation can be both a symptom of depression and a cause; for me, it was the latter. The severe loneliness I felt during my teen years led me to self-isolate, and this, in turn, caused my depression.

10. **Thoughts of self-harm, self-mutilation, or suicide ideation.** The hopelessness and deep despair that one feels when depressed may be so severe that thoughts of "ending the suffering" or "escaping the pain" takes over. (It's estimated that up to 60% of people who take their own lives suffer from major depression.[6])

Depression may also manifest in sudden physical changes or problems. This, too, can vary from person to person, but some common physical symptoms may include the following:

1. Headaches and body aches
2. Muscle tension or cramps
3. Digestive problems (e.g., stomach pain, diarrhea, constipation, etc.)
4. Skin problems (e.g., severe acne, eczema, psoriasis, etc.)

Am I suffering from depression? According to the Diagnostic and Statistical Manual of Mental Disorders (DSM-5)[7], a person must experience the following to be diagnosed with clinical depression.

1. A person must have had at least one major depressive episode that lasted at least two weeks.
2. The depressive episode must show at least five of the symptoms mentioned above.

*If you haven't been diagnosed yet but are experiencing symptoms of depression, you might want to take the **Depression Self-Assessment** exercise on page 339.*

Content Warning: the following contains distressing material.

As for me, I experienced all of the above depressive symptoms. Not all of them all the time, but I would suffer for weeks and sometimes months on end. The primary depressive symptom, *feelings of hopelessness*, is something I struggled with for years.

The issue about depression is that it's so many things at once, and each symptom impacts the other that you can quickly become trapped in a vicious spiral. For example, the loneliness and alienation I felt as an adolescent caused me to self-isolate and withdraw from everyone. I turned to internet games and junk food to escape my reality. I'd play for hours, then have a late meal before falling asleep. Exercise had never been a part of my daily regimen.

Sometimes, due to my OCD, I would skip sleep altogether because I didn't want to do my rigid morning ritual. However, OCD or not, I've always had sleep problems, which contributed to my sleepiness, low energy, and lack of focus at school.

Feelings of guilt also plagued me, and in all honesty, I still often do. In Chinese culture, there is a strong emphasis on *filial piety*, which is the idea that children should always obey their parents. Also, the son is supposed to take the reins and eventually care for the family. As a kid, I always felt I wasn't measuring up or doing enough for my family. As an adult, my sister didn't mince words that I was not "stepping up," and my parents would use a lot of emotional blackmail on me. As a result, I still often feel I'm not a good brother or son.

At the back of all this were constant feelings of sadness and hopelessness. I couldn't envision a "tomorrow" or "future" for years. I didn't have any direction in my daily life, so I didn't have any long-term goals. What's the point? I just wanted to get through each day.

My OCD didn't help either, as I had constant intrusive, unwanted thoughts (obsessions) about harming myself.

When I was living alone, there were times when I would go out on my balcony, which was on the 17th floor, and think about what would happen if I jumped. Would I break some bones? Would I become paralyzed? Would I die instantly? But then... at least it would end all of my sufferings. How would my family react if I died? Would they even care? Maybe my sister and parents would stop blaming me for everything.

This constant flow of obsessive thoughts is typical in people with OCD, and it doesn't mean we will take action. However, such thoughts drove me deeper into depression.

What are the Different Types of Depression?

There are various varieties of depression, each with its own set of symptoms and characteristics. These are a few examples of the most prevalent types:

1. **Major Depressive Disorder (MDD)** is the most prevalent type of depression. It involves persistent feelings of sadness, hopelessness, and loss of interest or pleasure in activities.

2. **Persistent Depressive Disorder (PDD)**, also known as *dysthymia*, involves symptoms of depression that persist for at least two years. Although people with PDD experience the same symptoms as MDD, they are usually less severe. Nevertheless, PDD is devastating because symptoms last for an extended period.

3. **Postpartum Depression (PPD)** is a type of depression that can affect new mothers after giving birth. It's different from the "baby blues," a common condition that causes mild mood changes and usually goes away on its own within a week or two after delivery. PPD, on the other hand, can cause severe and long-lasting depression symptoms. (Please also see Depression in Women, page 214.)

4. **Seasonal Affective Disorder (SAD)** is a type of depression related to seasonal changes. It typically occurs in the fall and winter when there is less sunlight and shorter days.

> Content Warning: the following story contains distressing material.

My friend, Ingrid*, lives in Europe, and she said, *"My first recollection of my depression was in my teens, probably around 17. I remember because we have a tradition of having a special dinner to mark the start of fall. It was one of my favorite things, and we would have "family meetings" about the menu. That year though, I didn't have any enthusiasm for it at all.*

As soon as the temperatures started dropping and the sky got darker, I felt miserable. At first, I thought I was just tired, but then the fatigue wouldn't let up. I started to stay longer and longer in bed, and when I finally gathered the strength to get up, it would get dark so soon that I'd feel even gloomier than before.

Winter came and went, and by the time spring rolled over, I was pretty much my old self again that I dismissed it. However, when the season changed to fall, I felt gloomy again. This time, my family was not so understanding.

My parents and siblings thought I was seeking attention, which made me sad and mad. I vented my frustrations about food; as a result, I gained a lot of weight over the winter months.

Even though I gained a lot of weight, I was, again, pretty much like my old self come spring, and I lost all the weight I gained as I became physically active again. Unfortunately, this made my family think I was going through a phase. They almost had me convinced... until fall came again.

---

* *Name changed for privacy.*

This time, my depression hit me hard, and I could barely get out of bed. One day, my mom saw me on the bedroom floor curled in a fetal position sobbing uncontrollably, and when she asked me what was wrong, I said, "Mom, I don't know." My mother said that hearing me say that broke her heart, and she knew something was terribly wrong.

My mom contacted a psychotherapist friend, and I was eventually diagnosed with Seasonal Affective Disorder (SAD). I don't take medication; I combine [bright light therapy](#) and [DBT](#). I also determined that stress significantly impacts my SAD, so I go almost entirely offline and refrain from checking the news during winter.

5. **Psychotic Depression** is a type of depression that showcases symptoms of depression and symptoms of psychosis. Psychosis is defined as a loss of contact with reality, which can result in delusions, hallucinations, or both. These symptoms can be severe and make it difficult for a person to function daily.

6. **Bipolar Disorder** is a mood disorder that's considered a type of depression because it involves episodes of depression. However, it's different from other types of depression because it also involves episodes of mania or hypomania.

   Mania is a period of abnormally elevated or irritable mood and increased energy. It's a particular time when a person experiences a sustained period of extreme euphoria, excitement, or irritability that is not typical of their usual behavior. The manic episodes are severe and cause serious problems at work, school, or relationships.

Hypomania is a milder form of mania. During a hypomanic episode, a person may feel unusually energetic or happy, have racing thoughts or speech, and engage in impulsive or risky behavior. Although still very disruptive, a hypomanic episode doesn't usually result in severe problems at work, school, or relationships.

Depression Recommended Treatments

Depression is one of the most prevalent mental health disorders in the world. It's even called the "common cold" of mental health disorders because of its prevalence.

Because depression is so common and yet significantly impacts a person's quality of life, there has been a lot of research and resources devoted to understanding and treating this disorder. The good news is that this has resulted in various treatments available. The bad news is that some of these treatments may be overused even though they may be ineffective, while others may not receive the attention they deserve.

Following are some of the most frequent treatments for depression. As you learn more about them, please note that **since depression is a complicated disorder with multiple causes, no single treatment works for everyone**.

When I started to see a mental health professional, I was prescribed anti-anxiety medication for my GAD. This helped manage some of my symptoms, but I needed psychotherapy to get better truly. I also found physical activities extremely helpful, so I added a fitness routine to my schedule. So, I guess I'm trying to say to please be open-minded and curious. Mental health problems are multifaceted; naturally, you may require a multifaceted approach to treatment as well.

Medication

Depression has been long believed to be caused by a chemical imbalance in the brain. For this reason, antidepressants are prevalent in the market. The most commonly prescribed medication for depression is selective serotonin reuptake inhibitors or SSRIs. They work by increasing *serotonin* levels in the brain, which can help regulate mood. Examples of SSRIs include fluoxetine (Prozac), sertraline (Zoloft), and escitalopram (Lexapro).

Serotonin and norepinephrine reuptake inhibitors (SNRIs) work similarly to SSRIs but also increase levels of *norepinephrine* in the brain. Examples of SNRIs include venlafaxine (Effexor) and duloxetine (Cymbalta).

Next, we have tricyclic antidepressants (TCAs). These medications were some of the earliest antidepressants developed, and they work by increasing levels of serotonin and norepinephrine in the brain. However, they are less commonly prescribed today due to their side effects (e.g., dry mouth, blurred vision, dizziness, increased heart rate, nausea, etc.). Examples of TCAs include amitriptyline (Elavil) and nortriptyline (Pamelor).

Monoamine oxidase inhibitors (MAOIs) are antidepressants that block the enzyme *monoamine oxidase*, which breaks down serotonin and norepinephrine in the brain. They are also less commonly prescribed today due to their side effects and interactions with certain foods and medications. Examples of MAOIs include phenelzine (Nardil) and tranylcypromine (Parnate).

Note: Antidepressants can take several weeks to work and may cause various side effects. If you're taking or thinking of taking medication, please work closely with a healthcare provider to monitor the medication's effectiveness and manage any side effects.

Nearly 85% of people who suffer from depression believe their condition results from abnormal brain chemistry.[8] However, recent research published in the 2022 issue of *Molecular Psychiatry* suggests this may not be true after all.[9]

This recent discovery suggests that prescribed medications may not be the best course of treatment or should not be the first thing to try for depression. However, please remember that depression is multifaceted, so you shouldn't discount this option altogether. The best recourse is to speak to a mental health expert about which treatments are best for you.

Very Important: If you're taking antidepressants and wish to stop to explore other treatments, please DO NOT do so without assistance from your doctor or a medical health expert. Stopping antidepressant medication alone can be dangerous, leading to potential side effects and severe health risks.[10]

For example, you may experience withdrawal symptoms, mood changes, a relapse or worsening of your condition, increased feelings of self-harm and suicide, and others. This does not mean you cannot stop taking antidepressants once you've begun. The key is slowly reducing your dosage (a.k.a. tapering) and closely monitoring any changes you may experience. And this is best done under the guidance of a mental health professional.

Brain Stimulation Therapy

Brain stimulation therapy uses electrical impulses or magnetic fields to stimulate specific brain areas. The reasoning behind this therapy is based on the idea that certain brain areas are involved in regulating different bodily functions and behaviors. When these areas are not functioning correctly, it can lead to various symptoms and disorders. Brain stimulation therapy aims to improve their functioning and alleviate the associated symptoms by stimulating these areas with electrical or magnetic fields.

Following are some examples of brain stimulation therapies for depression.

Transcranial Magnetic Stimulation (TMS)

TMS is a non-invasive therapy where magnetic fields are generated by a coil placed on the scalp, which produces small electrical currents that can activate or inhibit the brain cells beneath it.

During a TMS session, the patient sits comfortably in a chair while the coil is placed on their scalp. The coil produces a series of brief magnetic pulses that pass through the skull and stimulate the brain cells beneath it. The stimulation can target specific brain areas associated with particular symptoms or disorders.

Vagus Nerve Stimulation (VNS)

VNS is a type of therapy that uses electrical impulses to stimulate the vagus nerve, which connects the brain to various organs in the body, including the heart, lungs, and digestive system.

During VNS therapy, a small device is implanted under the skin in the chest and connected to the vagus nerve. The device delivers regular electrical impulses to the nerve, which aids in regulating many bodily functions and activities. VNS is used to treat depression because it's believed to affect neurotransmitters in the brain and modulate the activity of various regions involved in regulating mood and pain.

Electroconvulsive Therapy (ECT)

ECT is a treatment in which an electric current is passed through the brain to cause a short seizure to alleviate symptoms associated with depression.

During an ECT session, the patient is given anesthesia to minimize discomfort and prevent muscle spasms. Electrodes are placed on the scalp, and a controlled electrical current is passed through the brain, inducing a seizure that lasts for a few seconds.

ECT is usually only advised for severe cases of depression. Although it's seen as an effective treatment option, it can also have side effects, such as temporary memory loss and confusion.

Light therapy

Light therapy, also known as bright light therapy, is a treatment that involves exposure to a bright light source. Research has shown that it can effectively treat [Seasonal Affective Disorder](#) (page 198) and other types of depression.[11,12].

During light therapy, an individual sits in front of a light box that emits a bright, white light for a prescribed amount each day, usually in the morning. The light mimics natural outdoor light, which can help regulate the body's circadian rhythm and boost mood. Although light treatment is generally considered safe, some people may experience side effects such as headaches, eye strain, or nausea.

Exercise/Physical Activity

Studies show exercise as an effective treatment for depression.[13,14,15] Here are some of the reasons why.

- Exercise has been found to increase the release of endorphins and other feel-good chemicals in the brain, which can help to reduce feelings of sadness, anxiety, and stress. These chemicals act as natural

antidepressants, improving mood, reducing tension, and promoting relaxation.
- Physical activities can help to reduce the levels of inflammatory markers in the body. (Research suggests that inflammation may play a role in the development of depression).
- Exercise may help boost self-esteem and self-confidence, which can be especially good for persons with feelings of worthlessness or low self-esteem.
- Exercise routines can provide a sense of structure, which can be helpful for individuals with depression who may struggle with motivation and energy levels.
- Physical activity can distract from negative thoughts and feelings, enabling people to focus on something positive and enjoyable.

Psychotherapy

Psychotherapy, or *talk therapy*, involves consulting with a mental health professional to explore and address underlying issues contributing to depression.

The efficacy of psychotherapy in treating depression can vary depending on the individual and the type of therapy used. However, it's considered a highly effective treatment option for depression[16,17] in part because it provides a safe and supportive environment in which individuals can explore their thoughts and feelings. In one study, psychotherapy was found effective in treating depression with an average effect size of 0.70, which indicates a moderate to significant treatment effect.[18]

During a session, the therapist and patient engage in a dialogue to explore the patient's thoughts, feelings, and behaviors. The therapist then uses various techniques to help the patient gain insight into their issues, develop coping strategies, and make positive changes in their life.

Following are some of the types of psychotherapy used to treat depression.

Emotion-Focused Therapy (EFT)

EFT is a form of psychotherapy that focuses on helping individuals understand and regulate their emotions. The goal is to help people understand the emotional experiences that underpin their beliefs, behaviors, and relationships. Standard techniques used in EFT include guided imagery, role-playing, and emotion-focused journaling.

Interpersonal Psychotherapy (IPT)

IPT focuses on addressing interpersonal issues and improving interpersonal relationships. The goal is to help people identify and resolve problems related to their relationships with others, which may be contributing to their mental health problems.

During an IPT session, the therapist works with the individual to identify problematic interpersonal patterns and behaviors, such as difficulty communicating or maintaining healthy boundaries. The therapist then helps the individual develop new skills and strategies for improving their relationships and addressing interpersonal problems. Standard techniques used in IPT include role-playing, communication exercises, and problem-solving strategies.

Cognitive Behavior Therapy (CBT)

CBT aims to recognize and change problematic thought patterns and behaviors. The objective is to help individuals develop more positive and adaptive ways of thinking and behaving, leading to improvements in mental health.

During a session, the therapist works with the individual to identify negative or unhelpful thoughts and beliefs and challenge and reframe them more positively. The therapist may also work with the individual to develop coping strategies and behavioral techniques for managing symptoms of mental health conditions. Standard techniques used in CBT include cognitive restructuring, exposure therapy, and behavioral activation.

Dialectical Behavior Therapy (DBT)

DBT is a form of psychotherapy that combines elements of CBT and mindfulness practices. The goal is to help individuals understand their current circumstances, learn mindfulness, develop coping strategies for dealing with difficult situations, manage intense emotions, and learn skills to improve relationships. DBT is what we will cover in great detail in this book.

Over the years, I have tried various therapies and found DBT the most helpful. I believe it effectively combines different types of therapies, and the techniques involved are relatable and doable in real life. With DBT, I finally became the well-adjusted adult I am today. I hope it helps you as much as it has helped me.

Living with Depression

"Depression is like a heaviness that you can't ever escape. It crushes down on you, making even the smallest things like tying your shoes or chewing on toast seem like a twenty-mile hike uphill." – Unknown

Whenever I get asked about how it feels to suffer from depression, I get a bit tongue-tied.

How do you tell someone that even simple things like getting out of bed or brushing their teeth take so much energy and concentration? How do you describe to someone this constant lack of interest in doing anything at all? How do you explain this unrelenting darkness that hangs over you and that you have absolutely no way—or desire—to see beyond it? How do you make someone understand that you don't want to "participate"?

I knew my OCD was behind my obsessions (constant intrusive, unwanted thoughts) around self-harm and death. But even though I didn't want to take my own life, I had zero interest in life. (That's the depression talking.)

My anxiety disorder didn't help, either. For example, when my fears and worries kick in that I can't function properly, I'd start to feel a sense of worthlessness. Thoughts like, *"Why can't I just do this?"*, *"Why am I always panicking?"* or *"Why am I always sweating and trembling?"* made me criticize myself harshly, lowering my self-esteem. These thoughts pushed me further down the depression hole.

Understanding how the depression *caused* and *affected* so many facets of my life was the first step in my recovery. I hope the following sections do the same for you.

Depression and the Brain

As previously discussed, depression is widely believed to be caused by abnormalities in brain chemistry. However, during depressive episodes, *further changes* happen to our brains.

Brain Shrinkage

Shrinkage is one of the most prevalent alterations in a depressed person's brain, particularly in the hippocampus, thalamus, frontal cortex, and prefrontal cortex. The gravity of brain shrinkage is determined by the duration and degree of one's depression.

Research shows that people with depression lose gray matter volume (GMV).[19] This loss happens because *cortisol* prevents brain cells from growing. The graver the episode, the more GMV one loses. Since most of our nerve cells are in our GMV, slowed brain cell formation could negatively impact our ability to think and reason.

While high cortisol levels cause certain brain parts to shrink, the amygdala grows. Because the amygdala regulates emotions, this could result in difficulty sleeping, mood swings, and other issues.

Brain Inflammation

Research shows that depression is linked to cerebral inflammation.[20] Experts don't know if depression causes brain inflammation or if it's the other way around, but researchers believe the two are linked.

Inflammation in the brain can lead to changes in the way that neurons communicate with each other. Changes in neurotransmitter levels, such as *serotonin* and *dopamine*, which are important in mood regulation, may also occur.

When neurons and neurotransmitters die, the brain will likely shrink and lose its ability to change as a person ages. (This is called *neuroplasticity*.) Since new neurons and neurotransmitters have a more challenging time growing, a person suffering from depression may develop cognitive problems.

Limited Oxygen Intake

People suffering from MDD may take in less oxygen.[21] It's believed that depression changes how you breathe, leading to a lack of oxygen (*hypoxia*).

Hypoxia can impair cognitive performance. This can result in decision-making problems, losing motor skills, and experiencing bouts of forgetfulness.

Depression and the Body

Depression is a mental health disorder that can harm our physical health.

If you remember, one of the symptoms of depression is fluctuations in appetite or weight. Overeating can lead to weight gain and obesity-related conditions like type 2 diabetes. Undereating can make your body go into starvation mode, leading to low blood pressure, fertility troubles, heart problems, etc.

Research has also shown a connection between depression and the immune system.[22,23] This may be because depression can increase inflammation in the body, impairing the immune system's ability to fight off infections.

In addition, depression can change how the immune system functions. For example, depression has been linked to lower production of T cells and natural killer cells, which are important for fighting infections and cancer. Depression has also been associated with increased production of pro-inflammatory cytokines, which can contribute to chronic inflammation and other health problems.

Depression and Relationships

Depression can negatively impact your relationships.[24] As I mentioned before, my alienation at school made me withdraw from society even more. So, not only did I miss out on opportunities to meet new people and form new relationships, but it also made things worse with my family, with whom I already had issues.

People suffering from depression have *difficulty expressing their thoughts and feelings*, which can lead to a breakdown in communication with loved ones. In the Chinese culture, we don't have emotional expression; we have emotional suppression, so I was already used to NOT discussing problems with my family. However, when I left home and started to make friends and even get into relationships, it was tough to discuss, let alone try to describe, what I felt. This led to a lot of failed relationships.

The depressive symptom of *lack of interest in doing anything* is also detrimental to relationships. Of course, people who care about us want to spend meaningful time with us. Suppose all we want to do is stay in bed because we don't have the energy or the interest to do anything. In that case, this can be interpreted as a lack of interest in them. Who wants to be in a relationship where your partner is not invested in you or interested in the things you like?

There are also a lot of *negative thinking patterns* with depression, which can cause individuals to interpret their partner's words or behavior negatively. This can lead to misunderstandings and further strain on the relationship.

> Content Warning: the following story contains distressing material.

This is what Dennis[†], a reader, had to say: *"I didn't know I was depressed until it was too late. I lost my job six years ago. First, I was just a grumpy person to be around with. Then there was a lot of anger, which I directed to everyone around me. I wouldn't get physical with anyone. I was the passive-aggressive type.*
I would apply for jobs but wouldn't get them, so I lost my sense of humor along the way, and the grumpiness and anger were replaced by self-doubt, which I dared not admit to anyone.

After that, I lost interest in trying to get a job altogether. It cost too much energy, and looking back, I guess I was trying to escape failure. If I didn't apply for anything, no one could say "No" to me, right?

I started to avoid people because I didn't want to be asked how the "job hunting" was going. My wife was the sole breadwinner by this time, and my self-esteem just went down the drain. I felt enormous guilt but at the same time... I wouldn't do anything about it. We started to get into many fights; our sex life became nonexistent, and we hardly even looked at each other.

One day, my wife told me she was taking the kids and staying with her parents for a while. I knew she was going to ask for a divorce sooner or later. I would.

[†] Named changed for privacy.

The first week they were gone, I couldn't eat or sleep. At this point, I felt there was nothing left to live for anymore, and I started to have "bad thoughts." When I found myself planning the exact steps to carry out my "bad thoughts," I knew it was time to talk to someone. Either that, or I would do what I shouldn't do. So, I called my sister. She's a medical doctor, and she was the one who booked my first consultation with a psychiatrist friend she knew.

I was diagnosed with MDD, and thankfully, I'm better now. Sadly, I still lost my family. The good thing is I'm on good terms with my ex-wife. She even joined one of my sessions, and that was the first time I heard how my depression made her feel that she carried everything and everyone on her shoulders. My negative thoughts and behavior were also starting to bring her down, and that's when she knew she had to go. I don't blame her one bit.

Depression in Women

Although the above story is from a male perspective, research shows that women are more likely to develop depression than men.[25] Following are some of the risk factors that have been researched that may explain this.

Hormones

Women experience hormonal changes throughout life, including puberty, menstruation, pregnancy, and menopause. Men also experience hormonal changes during puberty but don't go through menstruation, pregnancy, and menopause. That alone increases the chances of women developing depression more than men. Why is this relevant? Hormonal changes affect brain chemistry and mood, affecting the risk of developing depression.

Societal and Cultural Factors

Biology isn't the only thing that increases the development of depression in women. Females often face social and cultural stressors that men don't face.

Gender inequality at work. Women often get paid less than men for the same work. In the US, data from the Pew Research Center reveals that in 2022, *"women earned an average of 82% of what men earned."*[26]. Women are also more likely to be a victim of violence in the workplace.[27] However, it's important to note that men are less likely to report such experiences than women.

Gender inequality at home. Working women feel more pressure to focus on their responsibilities at home than working men. This means that despite a full workload, women still care for many things at home. Working or not, women also care for others (e.g., parents, extended family, etc.) more than men.

Differences in Coping Mechanisms

Men and women may also differ in coping mechanisms for stress and adversity. Women may be more likely to ruminate and internalize stress. In contrast, men are likelier to adopt a more problem-solving, distracting coping style to help them through difficult times.[28]

Rumination, or the tendency to focus on negative thoughts and feelings, has been linked to developing and maintaining depression.[29,30]

Chapter Highlights:

- **Depression and the brain.** One of the causes of MDD is abnormalities in brain chemistry. This section discusses how the brain is physically altered during depressive episodes.
- **Depression and the body.** Depression is detrimental to physical health. It can weaken the immune system and cause various health problems.
- **Depression and relationships.** This section explores how MDD can negatively affect even the healthiest of relationships.
- **Depression in women.** Depression is twice more likely to occur in women than in men. This section discusses the various factors that influence this.

What is Dialectical Behavior Therapy?

"You don't have to be perfect to begin the healing process. You just have to be willing to start." - Unknown

Dialectical Behavior Therapy (DBT) is a type of therapy that combines cognitive-behavioral techniques (CBT) with mindfulness practices. Psychologist Dr. Marsha Linehan initially developed it in the late 1980s to treat individuals with borderline personality disorder (BPD).

As far as psychotherapies go, DBT is actually considered "new." However, it's been so effective that today, it's used to treat various mental health conditions, including depression.

When I first learned about DBT, I was fascinated by the fact that Dr. Linehan suffered from BPD. It made me wonder if DBT is so effective as a mental health treatment because the person who developed it herself suffered from a mental health condition.

Dr. Linehan was born in 1943 in Tulsa, Oklahoma, and experienced significant emotional turmoil as a child and adolescent. In the 1960s, she was admitted to the *Institute of Living*, a psychiatric clinic, because of "extreme social withdrawal" symptoms. At the clinic, she constantly engaged in self-harming behaviors and demonstrated suicidal behavior.

In the 1960s, BPD was not yet officially diagnosable as a disorder. (It would be in the 1980s.) As such, Dr. Linehan was misdiagnosed with schizophrenia, subjected to electroconvulsive therapy, and prescribed antipsychotic medication. Of course, since she did NOT have schizophrenia, these methods did not work to treat her symptoms. After two years, Dr. Linehan was released from the Institute of Living but was still unwell.

Despite her challenges, Dr. Linehan earned her Ph.D. in clinical psychology from Loyola University Chicago and began her career as a researcher and clinician. She later became interested in working with individuals with BPD. During this time, she noticed that traditional therapies were ineffective in treating their symptoms. In response, Dr. Linehan began to develop DBT, which incorporates *mindfulness practices* and *skills training* to help individuals regulate their emotions and improve their relationships.

Another thing that was ground breaking about Dr. Linehan's therapy was the application of *dialectics*.

Dialectics

Dialectics is a word that comes from the ancient Greek philosopher Heraclitus. He believed that change is constant and that reality comprises opposing forces always working together. In psychology, dialectics is a way of thinking and solving problems that involve recognizing and balancing different ideas or points of view.

So, dialectics is the art of balancing opposing viewpoints to resolve conflict. In DBT, the dialectical approach involves balancing acceptance of the present moment with a desire for change and growth to cope or heal from mental health problems.

The following are a few exercises[31] to help you get used to dialectical thinking. Please remember that dialectics is an exercise in seeing all sides. Experiencing problems or crises doesn't mean we're stuck in this state. At the same time, seeing another side of our problems doesn't invalidate how difficult or painful the situation is to you.

Worksheet: Wrong AND Right

When going through something painful or difficult, it's easy to focus on what's wrong while ignoring the other side of the debate, which is what is going right. Asking what's going right or good, no matter how minor, provides a different perspective and balance.

What's wrong?	What's going right?
Example: My best friend of nearly a decade has just stopped talking to me, and I don't know why. I feel so confused, betrayed, and alone.	*Example: I have other friends who continue to love and support me.*
Your turn:	Your turn:

Worksheet: The Silver Lining

It may not feel or appear this way when you have a significant problem or crisis, but not many things in life are *all good* or *all bad*. Consider whether there is a silver lining in what you're going through. Problems, even tragedies, can reveal opportunities.

The Situation	The Silvering Lining
Example: After 26 years of marriage, my partner and I decided to get a divorce.	*Example: I've always wanted to pursue art. I used to be good with painting but gave it up when the kids came along. Now the kids are pursuing their dreams, maybe now's the chance for me to pursue mine.*
Your turn:	Your turn:

Why DBT for Depression?

Although initially developed for people with BPD, DBT has been found to be highly effective in treating other mental health disorders.[32,33,34] This is not surprising given that DBT was originally established with an emphasis on *emotion regulation*, which is directly linked to one's ability to manage the mood changes associated with depression.

Another reason DBT is particularly beneficial, in my opinion, is that it's not all "theory." The exercises really helped me learn and use the skills in my daily life. You're physically working your way through your mental health issues. I was literally working through my mental health struggles as I tried the exercises.

DBT Core Concepts

In DBT, we need to recognise and balance two opposing viewpoints: Acceptance and Change.

Radical Acceptance

Acceptance refers to acknowledging and embracing one's emotions and experiences without judgment. It involves letting go of the idea that some emotions are "good" or "bad" and instead recognizing that all emotions are valid and serve a purpose.

The statement that "all emotions are valid and serve a purpose" has been very healing to me.

One of the main problems with mental health problems is that people, intentionally or unintentionally, frequently invalidate us. People can "see" my OCD so that they can understand it somehow. However, when it comes to my anxiety and depression, I've received comments like "just get over it," "toughen up," "why can't you just be more positive?", "stop feeling sorry for yourself; it's not that bad," and many others. I'd heard these comments so often that I started to feel bad and sometimes even doubted my emotions. With DBT, I learned that my emotions and experiences are valid and that I should accept them for what they are.

In DBT, Dr. Linehan uses the term **Radical Acceptance** because it involves fully and completely accepting reality as it is in the present moment, without judgment or resistance. It's the practice of accepting what we cannot change and letting go of the struggle to control or resist it.

People with mental health disorders struggle with difficult or distressing emotions, experiences, or circumstances. However, instead of fighting or trying to escape these realities, Radical Acceptance encourages us to embrace them fully and find a way to move forward positively.

I'll be the first to say that Radical Acceptance can be difficult, especially in particularly painful or challenging situations. Sometimes, I like to use this analogy: the bad stomach ache.

When we have a terrible tummy problem, what do we physically do? We bend over and clutch our stomachs. We may ask ourselves: *What did I eat? What did I drink? How did I get this?* We might even blame someone for our troubles: *If only Tim had not forced that spicy dish on me!* We might blame ourselves: *Why did I have to drink/eat so late last night?!* Next, we might start to worry: *What if this doesn't clear by tomorrow? I have a critical presentation in the morning.* If you suffer from an anxiety disorder like me, your thoughts might even go so far as... *what if this is cancer*?

In all of the above statements and scenarios, we are, in effect, *nurturing* our stomach ache (the problem). When we give our problems so much attention, we *stay* in that state of mind and prolong our suffering.

Radical Acceptance helps you to let go of your emotional suffering and focus on taking action to improve your situation.

So in the above "bad stomach ache" example, you forego all your contemplations and ruminations and go straight to making things better for yourself (e.g., take an antacid, drink plenty of water, rest, drink ginger tea, etc.)

There are also a few misconceptions about Radical Acceptance. I hope the following helps clarify this concept for you.

Radical Acceptance IS NOT	Radical Acceptance IS
NOT agreement, approval, or consent. You're not okay with the situation; you accept that the situation is happening or has happened.	
NOT giving up or giving in. You're not saying you don't want things to improve. Accepting NOW doesn't mean you want the situation to stay that way.	
NOT inaction. You're not saying you're okay with whatever life throws at you. You accept what happened because it's in the past; *taking action* belongs to the future.	*Accepting that a situation exists.*
NOT avoidance. You're not avoiding or ignoring your emotions or problems. You acknowledge and accept them to find ways to address them effectively.	
NOT about others. Your reality is yours alone, so you don't accept for others, only for yourself.	

Worksheet: Radical Acceptance

Radical Acceptance is reality acceptance. So for your first exercise, please write your current reality inside the circle below. Just write down whatever comes to mind. Remember, all your emotions and experiences are valid.

Examples: (1) *I'm lonely.* (2) *I'm so tired.* (3) *I'm not interested in anything.* (4) *No, I don't want to "participate."* (5) *I'm grieving.*

Change

Change is the opposing viewpoint in DBT. It's the part that balances Acceptance and refers to the active process of developing new skills and behaviors to feel better and improve your situation.

If you think change is hard, you're right. Humans are hardwired to resist change. One of the primary reasons is that change often requires us to step out of our comfort zones and confront the unknown. We may also worry about losing what we have or fear we cannot handle "new."

Another reason we may resist change is that it requires effort and energy. Change often involves breaking old habits, learning new skills, and developing new ways of thinking. This can be difficult and time-consuming and requires a willingness to be patient and persistent.

Lastly, humans are social creatures who often rely on the support of others. When we try to change our lives, we may face resistance from others who are not ready or willing to see us change or change with us. This can make us feel isolated or unsupported, undermining our motivation to change.

So, if you resist change, that's okay; that's a normal reaction.

At the start, I, too, had issues with "change" regarding my mental health problems. It made me feel that I was somehow the one at fault and to blame for my circumstances. But DBT taught me that I need to change because the "methods" I was using to deal with my mental health problems weren't working or weren't working as well as they used to. And why should I keep using them if they're not or no longer working?

Imagine having a favorite sweater. It's gotten two sizes too small and doesn't keep you warm anymore. Why grab it every time it gets cold?

Worksheet: Desire to Change

Start cultivating a change mindset by writing down a few thoughts on how change can benefit your life. Please don't overthink this. Just write down whatever comes to mind inside the circle below.

Examples: (1) I'm ready for "new." (2) I'm ready for "different." (3) I'm ready for "better." (4) It's time to be happy again. (5) I'm ready for more people in my life.

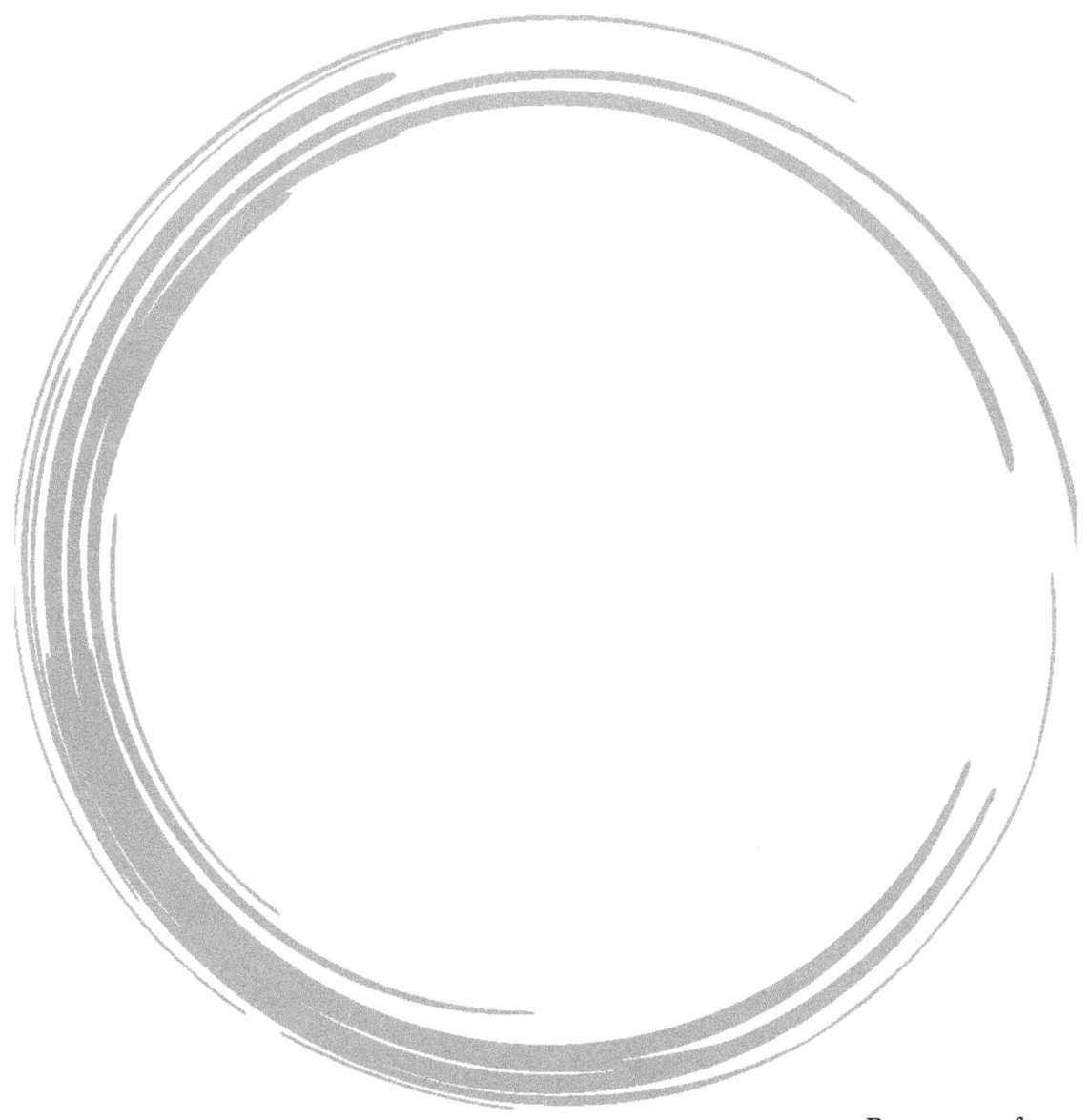

Worksheet: Acceptance and Change

Let's bring Radical Acceptance and Desire to Change together.

RADICAL ACCEPTANCE: Write statements accepting your reality today.

DESIRE TO CHANGE: Write statements expressing your desire to change or how change can benefit your life.

DECLARATION: Acknowledge today and what you want for tomorrow.

RADICAL ACCEPTANCE:	DECLARATION:	DESIRE TO CHANGE:
I'm lonely.	"I accept who I am today. Life has its ups and downs and I can't control everything that happens. So, I choose not to fight against the things I can't change.	I'm ready for "new."
I'm so tired.		I'm ready for "different."
I'm not interested in anything.		I'm ready for "better."
I don't want to "participate."	I also accept that I'm not living my best life now. I don't feel happy or fulfilled living this way. So I'm opening myself to change. I'm going to give myself the opportunity to grow and find happiness and inner peace."	It's time to be happy again.
I'm in pain.		I want to smile again.
I don't have hope.		I want friends.

Now, it is your turn!

RADICAL ACCEPTANCE: DECLARATION: **DESIRE TO CHANGE:**

DBT Core Skills

DBT comprises four core skills: *Mindfulness, Distress Tolerance, Emotion Regulation,* and *Interpersonal Effectiveness*.

Acceptance is enabled by Mindfulness and Distress Tolerance skills, whereas **Change** is accomplished through Emotion Regulation and Interpersonal Effectiveness skills.

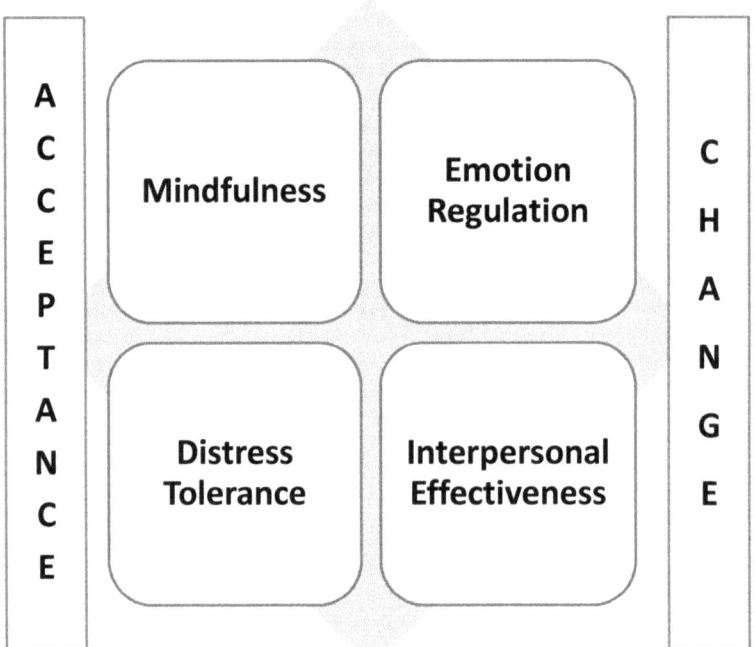

Mindfulness

> "Mindfulness is simply being aware of what is happening right now without wishing it were different; enjoying the pleasant without holding on when it changes (which it will); being with the unpleasant without fearing it will always be this way (which it won't)." - James Baraz

Mindfulness is being fully present in the present moment, fully aware of your surroundings, thoughts, and feelings. It involves paying attention to your experiences without judgment and with a sense of curiosity and openness.

It's the practice of being fully engaged in the moment. You're not in the past or in the future. You're just in NOW.

Mindfulness is a core component of DBT because it helps us develop greater awareness of our thoughts, feelings, and behaviors. It also cultivates greater acceptance and non-judgment of our experiences. Practicing mindfulness allows us to observe our thoughts and emotions without getting caught up in them.

As you learn more about DBT and this book, you will also realize that mindfulness is the basis for all the other skills you will learn.

Mindfulness was not unknown to me, but I never practiced it. I didn't think I could do it, let alone think of it as a way to get better. I thought, *"How can I practice "mindfulness" when my mind is too troubled by the mental health problems I already have?"*

Of course, with DBT, I realized that I had it backwards. Mindfulness is a way to quiet my mind to get a grip on whatever's happening. For this reason, I like to call mindfulness a "mental pause." It's that ability to take a moment to focus and be aware of yourself and your surroundings. Today, mindfulness is part of my daily life.

Often, people think that mindfulness and meditation are the same. They may be related, but they have some essential differences.

Mindfulness is a quality or character trait. A mindful person is someone who can easily be present in the moment. They're aware of their thoughts, feelings, and sensations without judgment. They can observe external stimuli and their internal experiences without getting caught up in them or reacting impulsively.

Meditation is a practice that involves setting aside time to intentionally focus on a particular object or activity, such as the breath or a mantra. Meditation aims to train the mind to be more focused and attentive and to develop greater awareness of one's thoughts and feelings.

So, meditation is a tool for developing mindfulness, but mindfulness is something that we can cultivate and practice in all aspects of our lives.

The Breath

At first glance, "breathing" may seem so basic. After all, we've been doing it since the day we were born. However, it's important to note that most people, especially those suffering from mental health disorders or medical conditions, are "shallow breathers."

Shallow breathing (a.k.a. chest breathing) takes fast, short breaths that only fill a tiny area of the lungs. This form of breathing frequently involves using the chest muscles rather than the diaphragm, the primary breathing muscle. Shallow breathing can negatively affect our health and well-being. It can reduce oxygen intake and increase stress and fatigue. This is why when we have a mental health episode, it's easy to end up hyperventilating or experience shortness of breath.

So, our usual breathing pattern does NOT promote mindfulness. We need to learn how to breathe deeper and with more intention. We do this through breathing exercises.

Breathing exercises can effectively cultivate mindfulness because they require you to focus on your breath, which can help quiet your mind and bring your awareness to the present moment. Focusing on your breath will make you less likely to focus on distracting thoughts or worries.

Here are a few ways in which breathing exercises can help you be more mindful:

1. **Breath awareness.** Focusing on your breath can help you become more aware of the physical sensations in your body and the present moment. As you inhale and exhale, notice how the air moves in and out of your nostrils, the rise and fall of your chest and belly, and your body sensations as you breathe.

2. **Centering.** Deep breathing exercises can help you feel more centered and grounded, which can help you feel calmer and more focused. Taking slow, deliberate, deep breaths can slow your heart rate and reduce stress and anxiety.

3. **Attention training.** When you focus on your breath, you're training your attention to be present in the moment. This can help you develop greater awareness and concentration, which can help you be more mindful in other areas of your life.

4. **Emotional regulation.** Breathing exercises can help you regulate your emotions by slowing your breathing and calming your nervous system.[35] By regulating your breath, you can reduce distress, anxiety, and overwhelm and

cultivate feelings of calm and relaxation. (We'll cover Emotion Regulation in detail on page 285.)

On the following pages are several exercises that will help you develop the core DBT skill of mindfulness. We'll start with breathing exercises (beginner to advanced) and end with various types of meditation practices.

Note: During your breathing exercises, try to observe your breath. Please note how it feels in your nose, throat, chest, and stomach. If your thoughts wander (and they will!), gently bring them back to your breath. If it helps you focus, use the phrases "breathing in" and "breathing out" as you do the exercises.

Worksheet: Belly Breathing

Belly Breathing (a.k.a. diaphragmatic breathing) promotes relaxation and stress reduction. It's a great beginner exercise for shallow breathers. The following are the steps for belly breathing.

1. Sit down comfortably or lie down on your bed.
2. Put one hand on your belly and the other on your chest.
3. Inhale gently through your nose, allowing your belly to expand like a balloon. (Your chest should remain relatively still.)
4. Exhale slowly through your mouth, letting your belly deflate like a balloon. (Try to let all the air out of your lungs.)
5. Continue to breathe this way, focusing on the sensation of your belly rising and falling like gentle ocean waves with each breath.

Ensure that you're breathing deeply from your diaphragm rather than shallowly from your chest. You can also practice this technique with closed eyes, visualizing a peaceful scene to enhance relaxation. Gradually increase the duration of your belly breaths as you become more comfortable with the technique.

Worksheet: Equal Breathing (Sama Vritti)

This breathing technique is about equal inhalations and exhalations to improve focus and promote calmness.

1. Lie on your bed or mat, or find a comfortable seated position.
2. Close your eyes and take a few deep breaths to relax your body.
3. **Inhale** slowly and deeply through your nose for a count of four

4. **Exhale** slowly and thoroughly through your nose for a count of four.

| 1 | 2 | 3 | 4 |

5. Continue inhaling and exhaling through your nose for a few more cycles, maintaining an even count for each inhale and exhale.

As you become more comfortable with the practice, you can gradually increase the length of your inhales and exhales to a count of five, six, or more.

Worksheet: Box Breathing

In the previous exercises, you were inhaling and expelling your breaths. This time, we'll add holding your breath to the exercise.

1. Lie on your bed or mat, or find a comfortable seated position.
2. Close your eyes and take a few deep breaths to relax your body.
3. **Inhale** through your nose for four counts. Imagine drawing air all the way into your belly.

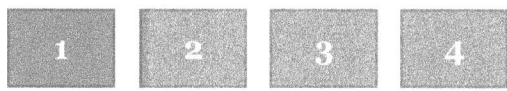

4. **Hold** your breath for four counts.

5. **Exhale** gently and completely through your mouth for four counts, releasing all the air from your lungs.

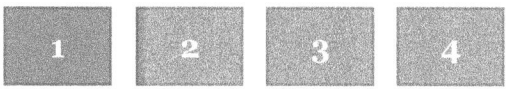

6. **Hold** your breath for four counts before starting the next inhale.

Repeat this pattern for several minutes, gradually increasing the duration of each breath and holding as you become more comfortable with the technique. The goal is to create a slow, steady breathing rhythm that helps calm your mind and body.

Worksheet: 4-7-8 Breathing

4-7-8 Breathing is an advanced breathing technique that promotes deep relaxation. In this exercise, you'll hold and exhale your breath longer than your inhalations. This controlled breathing technique is also believed to decrease symptoms of depression and anxiety.[36]

1. Lie on your bed or mat, or find a comfortable seated position.
2. Close your eyes and take a few deep breaths to relax your body.
3. INHALE for 4 counts through your nose.

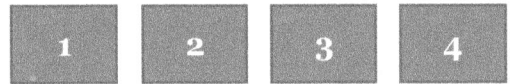

4. HOLD YOUR BREATH for 7 counts...

5. EXHALE for 8 counts through your mouth.

6. Do steps 3-5 for at least four cycles.

When you're finished, release your hand and sit quietly, noticing any sensations in your body and mind.

Worksheet: Nadi Shodhana (Alternate Nostril Breathing)

Nadi Shodhana is a yogic breathing technique that aims to balance the flow of energy (*prana*) in the body and calm the mind. The purpose of this breathing practice is to purify and balance the *nadis*, which are the subtle energy channels in the body according to yoga philosophy.

1. Sit in a comfortable seated position, either on the floor or in a chair, with your spine straight and your shoulders relaxed.
2. Place your left hand on your left knee, palm facing up, and bring your right hand to your face.
3. With your right hand, bring your index finger and middle finger to rest between your eyebrows, and use your thumb to close your right nostril.
4. Inhale deeply through your left nostril for a count of four, then use your ring finger to close your left nostril.
5. Hold your breath for a count of four.
6. Release your right nostril and exhale slowly for a count of eight.
7. Inhale deeply through your right nostril for a count of four, then use your thumb to close your right nostril.
8. Hold your breath for a count of four.
9. Release your left nostril and exhale slowly for a count of eight.
10. This completes one cycle of Nadi Shodhana. Repeat steps 4-9 for several more rounds, alternating nostrils with each cycle.

As you become more comfortable with the practice, you can gradually increase the duration of each breath and hold.

When you're finished, release your hand and sit quietly, noticing any sensations in your body and mind.

Worksheet: Mindful Breathing Reflection

It would be best if you made time for breathing exercises to develop mindfulness. To get the most out of the previous exercises, it also helps to do a bit of reflection. Following are a few questions for you.

1. **WHAT** is the best time for you to do breathing exercises?

    Example: In the morning, just after I wake up and before I go to work.

    Answer: _____

2. **WHERE** is the best place for you to do breathing exercises?

    Example: at my attic, I created a small "ME" space there

    Answer: _____

3. **WHICH** breathing exercise was easy, and why?

    Example: Belly Breathing because I didn't have to think about breath counts.

    Answer: _____

4. **WHICH** breathing exercise was challenging, and why?

    Example: Nadi Shodhana because I needed to get used to the technique of alternate nostril breathing.

    Answer: _____

5. **AFTER** a breathing exercise, reflect on how you felt? For example, were you more relaxed, less stressed, or less anxious?

    Answer:

    _____
    _____
    _____
    _____

Worksheet: Meditation 101

Meditation is a mindfulness practice to help you focus on the present moment without judgment or distraction. For beginners, here is a step-by-step instruction for basic meditation.

1. Choose a quiet, comfortable area where you will not be bothered. Place your feet flat on the floor and sit on a cushion or chair with your back straight. Place your hands on your knees or your lap for support.
2. Set a 5-10 minute timer. This will assist you in remaining focused and committed to your practice.
3. Take a few deep breaths and close your eyes. Exhale slowly through your lips and inhale slowly through your nose.
4. Begin to concentrate on your breathing. Take note of the sensation of air passing in and out of your nose and the rise and fall of your belly. Allow your breathing to be as natural and effortless as possible.
5. When your mind wanders (which it will!), gently bring it back to your breath. To stay focused, employ a mental anchor, such as the words "inhale" or "exhale."
6. Any ideas or sensations that arise should be noted, but they should not be allowed to consume you. Merely observe them without judgment or distraction, then return your focus to breathing.
7. Take a few deep breaths and slowly open your eyes when your timer goes off. Reflect on how you're feeling, and take note of any changes (mental, emotional, or physical).

Worksheet: Loving Kindness Meditation

Loving Kindness Meditation (LKM) is a time to promote kindness and compassion to yourself and others. Here is a step-by-step guide:

1. Lie on your bed or mat, or find a comfortable seated position.
2. Let yourself relax by taking a few deep breaths.
3. Once you feel centered, start focusing on a feeling of inner love and kindness. Next, silently offer a simple statement of kindness to yourself.

   Examples:
   May I be content.
   May I be happy today.
   I'll remember that I'm a good person.
   I'm doing my best.
   I'm a good person

   What statements of love and kindness do you want to say to yourself?

   _____
   _____
   _____
   _____
   _____

4. As you channel kindness to yourself, imagine being encircled by a warm, loving glow. Feel the love and compassion you're offering yourself; you deserve it.

5. Next, think of someone you care about and want to extend love and kindness to.

   I want to extend love and kindness to:
   Example: my youngest brother

   _____

I want to say:

Example: I know you're also going through tough times now. I wish you peace of mind.

_____
_____
_____

6. Think of someone you feel *neutral* about and want to extend love and kindness to.

   I want to extend love and kindness to:

   Example: my elderly next-door neighbor

   _____

   I want to say:

   Example: May you be healthy and pain-free.

   _____
   _____
   _____

7. Think of someone you may *dislike* and extend thoughts of love and kindness to them. (Note: It's okay to skip this step if you're not ready.)

   I want to extend love and kindness to:

   Example: my ex

   _____

   I want to say:

   Example: I wish you contentment.

   _____
   _____
   _____

8. As you do steps 5-7, feel love and compassion pouring towards them as you offer your statements of love and kindness.

9. If you're ready, extend love and kindness to all beings, including animals and plants. Consider warm, loving light pouring from you to yourself and others. If you're new to LKM, you might find it weird to extend love and kindness to all plants and animals. That's okay. You don't have to if you don't want to. However, please note that animals and plants are also living things, and extending love and kindness to them is just a way of expressing gratitude.

Examples:
I extend love and kindness to my pet cat Mia. I don't think she knows how much she helps me.
To my 15-year-old Lady Palm plant. THANK YOU for brightening my space.

_____
_____
_____
_____
_____

10. When you're done, open your eyes slowly and take a few deep breaths. Take some time to reflect on how you're feeling.

Even if it's only for a few minutes, try practicing Loving Kindness meditation daily. Over time, you'll grow in your love, compassion, and empathy for yourself and others.

Worksheet: Walking Meditation

Meditation is not always about keeping still. Mindfulness is about being present in the moment—any moment. So the following is an exercise on how to be mindful while doing the simple act of walking.

1. Find a safe and quiet place to walk, preferably a route without many distractions. It could be a garden, a park, or any other place where you can walk peacefully.
2. Take a few deep breaths and momentarily stand still to calm your body and mind.
3. Slowly put one foot in front of the other and start to walk. Keep your eyes looking forward and stand straight, but don't tense up.
4. Pay close attention to your breath or your steps as you walk. You can say "in" and "out" silently as you breathe in and out or "step" and "pause" as you take each step.
5. If your mind starts to wander, that's okay. Bring your thoughts back to your breathing or your steps. Do this over and over if necessary.
   Important: Don't judge yourself for thoughts or things that distract your attention.
6. After focusing on your breath or steps for a few minutes, start paying attention to what is happening around you. Pay attention to the sights, sounds, and smells around you. Be in the moment and avoid getting caught up in anything else.
7. After a few minutes of walking, try to be more aware of other feelings in your body, like how your arms move or how the wind feels on your skin.
8. When you're ready to end the meditation, stop strolling and stand still for a moment. Take a few deep breaths and let yourself feel centered.

Try Walking Meditation for a few minutes each day. Again, don't worry if your mind wanders or you have trouble focusing on just walking. Just keep on trying. Remember, practice makes ~~perfect~~ progress.

Worksheet: Attitude of Gratitude

Gratitude is frequently regarded as a mindfulness practice since it requires us to be fully present and aware of the positive parts of our existence. When we practice gratitude, we focus our attention on what we are thankful for, which can aid in cultivating a sense of appreciation and contentment in the present moment. Here's how to do a gratitude practice exercise.

1. Choose a peaceful and comfortable sitting area where you will not be bothered.
2. Relax your body by taking a few deep breaths.
3. Consider anything in your life for which you are grateful.

This week, I'm grateful for the following:
Examples: the bright, sunny weather that perks up my spirit

_____
_____

Today, I'm grateful for the following:
Examples: the lunch date I had with my best friend

_____
_____
_____

In the past hour, I've been grateful for the following:
Examples: a warm cup of coffee, an encouraging smile from a co-worker

_____
_____
_____

4. Next, pick one thing for which you are thankful. (It could be something from your list above or something else.) Consider WHY you are grateful for it and how it has benefited your life. Be as detailed as you can.

   Example:
   I'm thankful for a good night's sleep.
   Because: I suffer from insomnia so, it's challenging to fall and stay asleep. Last night was the first time in days that I slept the whole night. I actually woke up "energized."

   I'm thankful for:
   _____

   Because:
   _____
   _____
   _____

5. Sit still now and allow yourself to experience the emotions of thankfulness, such as joy, satisfaction, or calm.

6. Repeat step #4 for anything else for which you are grateful. You can do this practice as long as you want, concentrating on anything that makes you grateful.

   I'm thankful for the following:
   _____
   _____
   _____

Because:

_____
_____
_____

Strive to practice gratitude daily by making a mental list or writing things down in a notebook.

Distress Tolerance

> *"When you come to the end of your rope,*
> *tie a knot and hang on."* — Franklin D. Roosevelt

Distress Tolerance refers to the ability to endure and manage difficult emotions and distressing situations. We do this because if we can't tolerate or survive our depression, we might give in to impulses or behaviors that might worsen the situation.

Stress vs. Distress

Stress is a physiological response to a perceived threat or challenge, whether real or imagined. It's a normal part of the body's fight-or-flight response. It's characterized by physical, emotional, and cognitive symptoms such as increased heart rate, sweating, anxiety, and difficulty concentrating.

Distress, however, is a type of stress that occurs when the body's response to a perceived threat or challenge becomes overwhelming or prolonged. It's often described as negative or unpleasant stress (bad stress) characterized by helplessness, hopelessness, and despair.

STRESS	DISTRESS
Infrequent, short-term	Ongoing, prolonged
Motivates you to take positive action	Can be crippling or debilitating, promoting inaction
Can make you better	Can cause problems and illnesses
Something you believe you can overcome	Something you believe you cannot overcome

> Content Warning: the following contains distressing material.

This is what Kaycee[‡], a reader, had to say: *"I can't pinpoint the exact cause for my depression. My mother's side has a history of it, so maybe that's why. However, for as long as I can remember, I've always had a feeling of deep sadness and loneliness inside me.*

I think I've always felt alone because I was the middle child, and the situation at home was always full of tension. My parents often fought and got very loud and aggressive with each other. Broken plates, harsh name-calling, flying clothes out the window, even broken doors—I've seen them too often.

As my brothers grew older, I realized they were doing the same thing. They would fight and get so loud, angry, and aggressive with each other that I would go to my room and lock the door. I don't know if I was escaping them or if I was actually afraid they would go after me. Either way, I guess this was the beginning of my escaping reality.

Two years ago, I lost my business and sunk into the lowest depression I had ever felt. My impulse was to withdraw from everything and everyone. So that's exactly what I did.

I deactivated my social accounts. I didn't answer calls and text messages. I stayed indoors, and I eventually even stopped showering. I just couldn't find any desire or energy to do anything. I had to eat, but even that seemed pointless, so I consumed one meal daily. Eventually, my thoughts turned to ending it all.

[‡] *Named changed for privacy.*

One day, though, the door to my condo opened. My brothers told building security that I was "missing," so the building manager opened my door for them. When they saw me, my brothers and I stared at each other. That's the last thing I remember. I woke up in the psych ward.

In one of my therapy sessions, we uncovered a turning point in my last and most debilitating depressive episode. I shouldn't have given in to my impulse to self-isolate when my business went bust.

This is why I value DBT so much. If I'd known how to take a moment to accept my reality and tolerate my distress, maybe I wouldn't have sunk so deep.

It's important to remember that Distress Tolerance skills not only help you avoid harmful and impulsive actions but also help you build resilience and emotional strength to deal with problems and crises in the future.

You see, we cannot escape highly stressful life events. They will happen, and the secret is to learn how to survive them. The exercises that follow will help you do just that.

Worksheet: Turning the Mind

Before you can tolerate a crisis, you must first radically accept that the crisis exists. However, it's human nature to *reject* a situation when things are not going our way.

Turning the Mind is a practice that involves trying, over and over again, to move toward acceptance. Here's what to do when rejecting a situation or fighting reality.

1. **OBSERVE.** Start by noticing HOW you're rejecting something. This can be your thoughts, emotions, physical responses, etc.
   Example: In my head, I'm hearing, "WHY ME?!?" I guess that's me rejecting the situation even though it already happened. My fists are also clenched, so I'm angry right now.

   What are you observing?
   _____
   _____
   _____

2. **COMMIT.** Make a conscious decision to shift your focus away from your emotional and physical reaction(s) and move toward acceptance.
   Example: I'm choosing to turn my mind away from this emotion. This is the situation. It happened, and I cannot go back, so I won't.

   Your turn:
   _____
   _____
   _____

3. **REPEAT**. Observe and commit repeatedly until you feel yourself accepting the situation. (**Tip**: Do Wrong and Right or Silver Lining, pages 220 and 221, respectively.)

4. **PLAN**. Devise a plan to avoid rejecting unpleasant situations in the future.
    Example: Whenever something bad happens, I'll draw myself a bath with my favorite calming scents. I'll wash away my resistance and come out with acceptance.

    Your turn:
    _____
    _____
    _____

Worksheet: Grounding Using Your 5 Senses

Grounding exercises aim to disconnect you from intense emotions by connecting you to the present. This exercise will ask you to use your five senses: *sight*, *smell*, *sound*, *touch*, and *taste*.

Remember, there are no correct or incorrect answers here. Just provide what's being asked.

List FIVE (5) things you can see right now.

Example: desk plant, hand lotion, water bottle, Nespresso machine, post-it note

1.
2.
3.
4.
5.

List FOUR (4) things you can touch right now.

Example: my sweater, my hair, the chair I'm sitting on, my anti-anxiety bracelet

1.
2.
3.
4.

List THREE (3) things you can hear right now.

Example: my colleague in the next cubicle, people typing on their keyboards, food delivery guy

1.
2.
3.

List TWO (2) things you can smell right now.

Example: hand gel, office room scent

1.
2.

List ONE (1) thing you can taste right now.

Example: coffee

1.

If you're still distressed, repeat the activity or write down as many things as possible.

Worksheet: Self-Soothing Using Your 5 Senses

In the previous exercise, you learned how to use your five senses to *distract* yourself from any intense or unpleasant emotions you might be feeling—as they were happening.

The exercise below is about *planning ahead*. Write at least one thing that offers comfort or is soothing to you for each sense. This way, you know exactly what to do whenever you're in distress in the future. (**Tip**: Aim to self-soothe for at least five (5) minutes whenever you're in distress.)

- ☐ **Touch**: _____
  Example: grab my favorite sweater and wear it like an embrace

- ☐ **Smell**: _____
  Example: go to my terrace garden and smell the roses I planted last summer

- ☐ **Taste**: _____
  Example: pop a peppermint in my mouth

- ☐ **See**: _____
  Example: watch adorable cat videos on YouTube

- ☐ **Hear**: _____
  Example: listen to my favorite DANCE songs

Worksheet: The Happy Place

It can help to mentally leave the situation and imagine yourself in a calming, relaxing, and nurturing place when in distress. Here are the steps to do this:

1. Locate a quiet, comfortable spot where you can sit or lie down without being bothered.
2. Shut your eyes and exhale deeply, releasing any tension in your body.
3. Visualize a peaceful and relaxing place in your head. This could be a beach, a forest, a mountain, or any other peaceful setting. The image might be a real-life location or one that you've entirely invented in your head.
4. Begin by visualizing your environment's colors, forms, and textures. Envision the scene's details as vividly as possible.
5. Try to engage all of your senses as you continue to envision the scene. For example, if you're visualizing a restful day at the beach, imagine the feel of the sun on your skin, the gentle sound of the waves, the smell of the ocean, and the beautiful sunset.
6. While you immerse yourself in the image, pay attention to the sensations in your body. Consider any places of tension or discomfort and envision them dissolving.
7. Let yourself fully absorb the tranquility and calmness of the setting by staying with the visualization for as long as you like.
8. When you're finished, take a few deep breaths and slowly open your eyes. Reflect on the sense of calm and relaxation you just experienced and carry it with you for the remainder of your day.

Worksheet: Into the Cold

When submerged in water, the Mammalian Dive Response (MDR) is a physiological response that occurs in mammals, including humans. It promotes oxygen conservation by slowing the heart rate, redirecting blood flow to the vital organs, and releasing more oxygenated blood into the body.

In humans, the MDR kicks in when the face comes into contact with cold water. It activates our parasympathetic nervous system, the network of nerves that urges the body to slow down and relax.[37] The following exercise teaches you how to activate the MDR when in distress.

CAUTION: Exposing your face to cold water reduces your heart rate. Before performing any of these activities, please check with your doctor if you have a heart condition or are allergic to cold temperatures.

Depression can be triggered anytime, anywhere. For this reason, I encourage you to devise a plan for when you are at home or in public. I've started the table with a few ideas to jumpstart the list. Please add your ideas or what you feel will work best for you.

AT HOME	IN PUBLIC
o Take a VERY COLD shower.	o Go to the restroom and repeatedly wash your face with icy water.
o Open the freezer door and stick your face in it for a while.	o If it's winter, go outside and brave the cold.
o Fill a zip-lock bag with water and place it in the refrigerator. When in distress, grab the bag and place it over your face while holding your breath. (This deceives your brain into believing you're underwater.)	o Buy a water bottle that can keep cold water for hours. When distressed, go to the washroom and pour the cold water all over your face.

AT HOME	IN PUBLIC
o Fill a basin halfway with cold water and immerse your face in it.	o If you can access a refrigerator, store a face gel mask in it and use it as needed.

Other ideas:

Worksheet: STOP

STOP is a DBT activity that can help you gain control of your emotions and avoid acting on them.

S	**S**top. Stop! Freeze in place and remain motionless. Don't even twitch a muscle. Physically stopping prevents you from doing what your emotions demand you do. For example, I turned to junk food in my teens to deal with depression. I didn't care about what I ate or drank. Now, I understand the importance of nutrition to mental health. So, whenever I notice symptoms of depression, I freeze whenever I want to reach out for something unhealthy.
T	**T**ake a step back. Take yourself out of the situation. Take a deep breath and hold it for as long as you need to until you regain control. Don't let your emotions dictate your behavior. Remember, we rarely need to make split-second decisions over anything, so take your time before making any decisions.
O	**O**bserve. Mindfully observe what's going on inside and outside of you. Observe as if you were writing a list. (**Note**: You can observe your emotions, i.e., your feelings. However, if this isn't helpful, limit your self-observation to physical aspects.)

An example of self-observation:
I have a terrible migraine, and my head is pounding.

What are you observing about yourself?

_____
_____
_____

An example of observing your environment:
My desk plant looks dry, and my water bottle is empty. I smell coffee.

What are you observing about your environment?

_____
_____
_____

Proceed mindfully.

Okay, you've taken a break from the distressful situation, and now it's time to move forward—with caution. Ask yourself, "*How can I improve this situation?*" or "*What can I do to feel better?*" Be as detailed as you can with how you want to proceed.

Example:
I have a terrible migraine, and my head is pounding.
I'm going to (1) get up, (2) count my steps as I walk to the bathroom, (3) wash my face with very cold water, (4) open the medicine cabinet, (5) reach for and take paracetamol, (6) and lie down for a few minutes.

What do you want to do to proceed mindfully?

Worksheet: TIPP

TIPP skills help you tolerate your distress by changing your body's chemistry. Research shows that by altering your *physical* state, you also positively alter your mental and emotional states.[38,39]

T	**T**emperature. Our body temperature rises in stressful conditions. Cool your body down to counteract this physical stress response. (**Tip**: See Into the Cold, page 261.)
I	**I**ntense Exercise. During stressful situations, you may have a lot of pent-up energy. However, instead of reacting to intense emotions negatively, such as self-harming behaviors or unhealthy eating, it's better to channel that energy into something positive, such as engaging in intense physical activities (e.g., jumping jacks, running, HIIT sessions, etc.). Also, research shows that exercising is a great mood enhancer[40], so you'll feel much better after engaging in intense physical activities. When you're depressed, you might find intense exercise a difficult choice if *low energy* is one of your depressive symptoms. But remember that exercising boosts energy levels[41], so even if you don't feel like it, you'll help your disorder by exercising anyway. Here are a few tips to motivate you to move, despite what your depression is telling you.

1. **Make exercising an EASY choice.** If we perceive exercising as difficult, we might not do it despite our best intentions. So make exercising an easy choice by removing potential obstacles.

   For example, if you want to join a gym, choose one close to your home or workplace so it's easy to get there. If you prefer to workout in the mornings, lay your exercise clothes beside your bed the night before.

2. **Start with small goals.** Instead of trying to jump into an entire workout routine, start with small and achievable goals. For example, walk around the block quickly or go up and down a flight of stairs until you run out of breath.

3. **Devise a plan—or not.** Some people work best with a routine. If you're such a person, set a specific time and place for exercise. Write it down in your calendar or planner. Having a plan can help you stay accountable and motivated.

   On the other hand, if being spontaneous is more you, that's okay too. Fit in exercise whenever and wherever you can.

4. **Find a workout buddy.** Exercising with a friend or family member can make it more enjoyable and help keep you motivated. You can also hold each other accountable and provide support when needed.

5. **Choose an enjoyable activity.** Pick an activity you enjoy, whether dancing, swimming, running, or playing a sport. You're likelier to stick with the activity and find it less of a chore when you enjoy it.

6. **Focus on the benefits.** Remind yourself of the benefits of exercise, such as improved mood and energy, reduced stress, and better sleep. Focusing on these positive outcomes can help motivate you to get moving.

7. **Just do it.** Adopt a 'no excuses' attitude when it comes to exercising. For example, if you find exercising hard during the day, purchase low-cost exercise equipment that you can use at home. For example, resistance bands can help you do a quick 5–10 minute strength-training routine at home. Can't leave your office? Buy a cheap under-desk bike (also called a "desk cycle") to get some exercise while you work.

You can also use apps like *5 Minute Home Workouts* by Olson Applications, *7 Minute Workout* by Workout Apps, *FitOn Workouts* by FitOn, and others to get in some fast exercise throughout the day.

Paced Breathing.

Intense emotions tend to increase our breathing. Slow it down by deliberately and mindfully controlling your breath. (**Tip**: Do any or all of the Mindfulness breathing exercises.)

P

Paired Muscle Relaxation.

Paced Breathing can be combined with Paired Muscle Relaxation. While you take a deep breath, steadily tighten your muscles, but not so much that they cramp. When you exhale, slowly relax your tensed-up muscles.

Tip: When you're right in the middle of a crisis, do Paced Breathing + Paired Muscle Relaxation for a few minutes. (See also Body Scan Muscle Relaxation on the next page.)

Worksheet: Body Scan Muscle Relaxation

This exercise systematically combines Paced Breathing and Muscle Relaxation, promoting mental and emotional relaxation and reducing physical tension.

1. Find a quiet and comfortable place to lie on your back or sit in a chair with your feet flat.
2. Close your eyes and take a few deep breaths to relax and calm your mind.
3. Bring your attention to your body and observe any tension or discomfort.
4. **Begin at your toes.** Start the body scan at your toes, and focus on them. Tighten the muscles in your toes and hold for a few seconds, then release and relax them completely.
5. **Move up to your feet and ankles.** Move your attention up to your feet and ankles. Tighten the muscles in your feet and ankles and hold for a few seconds, then release and relax them completely.
6. **Progress to your calves and thighs.** Continue moving your attention up your body to your calves and thighs. Tighten the muscles in your calves and thighs and hold for a few seconds, then release and relax them completely.
7. **Focus on your stomach and chest**. Move your attention up to your stomach and chest. Tighten the muscles in your stomach and chest and hold for a few seconds, then release and relax them completely.
8. **Move up to your shoulders and arms.** Continue up to your shoulders and arms. Tighten the muscles in your shoulders and arms and hold for a few seconds, then release and relax them completely.
9. **End at your face and head**. Finish the body scan at your face and head. Tighten the muscles in your face and hold for a few seconds, then release and relax them completely.
10. Take a few deep breaths and notice how relaxed your whole body feels.
11. Stay relaxed for a few minutes, enjoying the feeling of relaxation throughout your body.

Worksheet: ACCEPTS

When you're depressed, what do you want to do? What's the emotional urge or impulse you have? For me, it was to self-isolate and turn to junk food. For others, it's to engage in negative self-talk (e.g., *I'm worthless, I'm ugly, I'm fat,* etc.). For others still, it's to take "depression naps" and stay in bed for hours.

One of the things I realized in my mental health journey is that my emotional urges or impulses exacerbated my mental health problems. **ACCEPTS** is a DBT exercise that has helped me NOT ACT on my emotional urges, and I hope it does the same for you.

Activities.

Create a list of activities you enjoy. Preferably, list down activities that require your undivided attention. The goal is to thoroughly immerse yourself in the activity and be "in the zone." Also, consider activities that will mentally or physically stimulate you. For instance, reading a self-help book is preferable to mindlessly scrolling through social networking sites.

Examples: paint, binge-watch your all-time favorite program on Netflix, swim laps, etc.

List down as many attention-grabbing activities as you like below.

1. _____
2. _____
3. _____
4. _____
5. _____

6. _____
7. _____
8. _____
9. _____
10. _____

Contribute.

When we're depressed, we may become self-absorbed (e.g., *Why is this happening to me?, What did I do to deserve this? Why am I like this?* etc.)

So, instead of focusing on yourself, *focus on others*. According to studies, thinking about others' needs benefits not only the people you help but also benefits you psychologically and physically, making you healthier and extending your life span.[42]

Examples: cook a meal for someone, go through your pantry or kitchen cupboards and gather canned goods to donate, do volunteer work

What do you want to contribute? List as many ideas as you can.

1. _____
2. _____
3. _____
4. _____
5. _____
6. _____
7. _____

C — Compare.

Another way to divert your attention away from your *current situation* is to compare it to past experiences. The goal here is to realize that you're stronger than you think. You survived a previous depressive episode, so you will this time too!

Example:
Two months ago, I neglected my personal hygiene. I think I only washed my hair once that month. I survived that depressive episode, and I will survive this one too.

To which past even do you want to make a comparison?

_____
_____
_____

E — Emotions.

Distract yourself from persistent sadness and despair by doing something that will illicit the opposite emotion (i.e., joy or happiness).

Examples: make a gratitude list, walk in nature, go to the mirror and smile at yourself again and again, do <u>Loving Kindness Meditation</u> (page 244)

_____
_____
_____

Push away.

PUSH AWAY whatever impulse comes to mind when you're depressed. For example, you might want to discontinue your sessions if you're undergoing therapy. You might think, *"I'm in therapy, but I'm still depressed. It isn't working. I think I should stop."*

If you give in to such impulses, you might do yourself more harm than good. So, instead of entertaining such thoughts, push them away.

Here are some suggestions for "pushing away." Feel free to add your thoughts as well.

- ☐ Go to a quiet place where you can be alone, then yell, "STOP!"
- ☐ Do The Silver Lining exercise (page 221).
- ☐ Try a visual imagery exercise like The Happy Place, page 260.
- ☐ Others:_____
  _____
  _____
  _____

T — Thoughts.

Distract yourself with "other" thoughts.

Examples:
If you're thinking of crying, sing a happy song in your head.
If you're having dinner at your parent's place, and something is depressing you, start counting the colors you can see in the room.

Your turn:

_____
_____
_____

S — Sensations.

Distract yourself by exposing your body to different physical sensations. Here are some examples. Feel free to add your thoughts as well.

- ☐ Drink an overly sweet drink.
- ☐ Chew a sourball.
- ☐ Put some pepper flakes in your mouth.
- ☐ Chew ginger candy.
- ☐ Take a VERY COLD shower.
- ☐ Others:

_____
_____
_____

Worksheet: IMPROVE

IMPROVE skills teach you how to make distressing or depressing moments better.

I	**I**magery. Mentally visualize yourself in a better place. *Examples:* *Imagine all your aches, pains, and sadness washing away from you like soap suds while showering.* *Remember a time in your life when you were truly happy and bring yourself back to that moment by trying to remember every detail about it.* Your turn: _____ _____ _____
M	**M**eaning. Try to find meaning in your emotional suffering. (See also The Silver Lining, page 221). *Examples:* *This sadness will make it easier to appreciate future moments of joy and happiness.* Your turn: _____ _____ _____

Prayer.

Turn to a greater power for strength and comfort. Research shows that praying boosts mental health by offering emotional comfort and decreasing mental health disorder symptoms.[43,44] (Note: If you're not religious, consider asking advice from someone you respect.)

Example:
Say this out loud: "Please give me the strength I need to bear this."

Your turn:

_____
_____
_____

Relaxation.

Engage in calming activities that might help you relax and clear your mind. List down at least three (3) calming activities.

Examples: walking with my dog in the woods, cooking, watching my favorite feel-good movies

1 _____

2 _____

3 _____

O — One thing at a time.

Focus on one specific activity. Don't think about anything other than what you're doing right now.

Example: I'm touching my calming bracelet. My eyes are closed, and I'm letting the smoothness of the calming beads relax me. I'm also tuning my breath with how I touch the beads. I inhale as I rub one bead and exhale as I go on to the next.

What are you doing?

_____
_____

Describe this moment in as many details as you can.

_____
_____
_____

V — Vacation.

Give yourself a break from adulthood and take a vacation. However, please note that these vacations should only be brief, and you shouldn't use them as your primary way of dealing with depression. Doing so may lead to *avoidance coping*, a negative way to deal with mental health problems.

Example:
Take the afternoon off. Go to a nearby café and get drinks, a sandwich, or a nice pastry treat. Next, visit a nearby park and treat yourself to an afternoon picnic.

Your turn:

_____
_____
_____

Encouragement.

Be your own cheerleader! This may be harder than you think because we're often our worst critics. Also, people suffering from depression may feel guilt and loathing for themselves. As such, practice this skill by imagining yourself offering advice to your best friend.

Example: Hey, you're doing the best you can. You've survived depression before, and you can do it again. You may not see it now, but it will be okay.

Your turn:

_____
_____
_____

Worksheet: Radical Acceptance When Feeling Depressed

As previously discussed, Radical Acceptance (page 223) is accepting the reality of your present situation. You accept you're suffering from depression because you want to be free of the emotional suffering it brings. You want to focus on feeling and being better.

The following worksheet will help you learn how to apply Radical Acceptance during a depressive episode.

1. **OBSERVE.** Notice how you might be fighting reality or questioning it.

> List down how you're ignoring, fighting, or rejecting your depression.
> *Example: Thinking or saying, "No, no, no. This cannot be happening again!"*
>
> _____
> _____
> _____
> _____

2. **REMEMBER.** Remind yourself that the existing situation (reality) is something that you cannot change.

> Write down your own depression acceptance statement.
> *Example: I'm depressed. I don't like it, but it is what it is.*
>
> _____
> _____
> _____
> _____

3. **RATIONALIZE.** Tell yourself that this current situation is not without reason. That is, "NOW" didn't happen by chance, and there are reasons why things transpired the way they did.

   This is how I rationalized my depression (i.e., this is how things happened): *I'm depressed now, not "just because" but because of many things in my past, such as the chaos, lack of security, and emotional instability I experienced at home. This was followed by the alienation and extreme loneliness I felt during my adolescence and the development of my OCD and anxiety disorders.*

   How did things happen?
   _____
   _____
   _____
   _____

4. **ACCEPT.** Practice acceptance of the situation with your whole being. That is, not just mentally but emotionally and physically as well.

   Accept with your mind:
   Example: Say, "This is the situation, and it is what it is."
   _____
   _____

   Accept with your heart:
   Example: Say, "I'm a good person; depression doesn't change this."
   _____
   _____

Accept with your body:

Example: Suppose you're sitting with your head bowed and between your hands. In this case, slowly and deliberately release your head, then sit or stand up straight.

_____

_____

5. **OPPOSITE ACTION.** Do the exact opposite of what your depression dictates you do.

Example:
I don't want to take a shower. So I will get up, head straight to the bathroom and take one.

Your turn:

_____

_____

_____

6. **IMAGINE ACCEPTANCE.** If you're still having trouble accepting your situation, try imagining how it would be to accept it. Paint a picture in your head of the possible positive consequences of accepting.

Examples:
If I accept, I can move on, think, and do something else.

Your turn:

_____

_____

_____

7. **ATTEND.** Pay attention to your physical reactions while considering what you need to accept. If you notice any physical resistance to your situation (e.g., folding your arms across your chest, frowning, clenching your teeth, etc.), address it.

Example: While visualizing acceptance, I can feel myself starting to clench my fists. I should do some deep breathing and open my hands wide each time I exhale.

Your turn:

_____
_____
_____

8. **ALLOW AND THEN LET GO.** Give yourself permission to feel grief, loneliness, or sadness. Remember that acceptance is not approval or being okay with the situation. So, there's no need to deny your emotions. Let them come... and then let them go.

Example:
I'm so sad and lonely and don't have anyone to talk to or share anything with. And then imagine letting these emotions go like water sliding off you.

Your turn:

_____
_____
_____

9. **ACKNOWLEDGE.** Recognize that even when things are hard, life is still worth living.

Example:
I'm not always this way; I have known happiness before. So, I will cling to the hope that I can be happy again.

Your turn:
_____
_____
_____

Emotion Regulation

> *"Emotional self-regulation is not the suppression of emotions, but the regulation of their intensity and expression."*
> — John Gottman

Emotions are reactions. They can be positive, such as happiness, love, and excitement, or negative, such as sadness, anger, and fear. Emotions are our responses to external or internal stimuli. For example, seeing a beautiful sunset may trigger feelings of contentment or happiness. In contrast, internal thoughts, like worrying about a looming deadline, may trigger feelings of anxiousness or fear.

Emotions are important to our identity because they significantly affect our daily lives. You may not notice it, but your emotions greatly dictate your actions. If you engage in an activity that makes you happy, you will most likely keep on doing that activity. If someone makes you angry, then you might reciprocate with anger or avoid that person.

It's important to remember that feeling an emotion doesn't cause problems. How you understand or interpret emotions is what determines whether the stimuli (internal or external) will become a problem or not.

As previously mentioned, depression is a mood disorder characterized by *persistent* feelings of sadness and despair. As such, people with depression are in a vicious cycle of negative emotions.

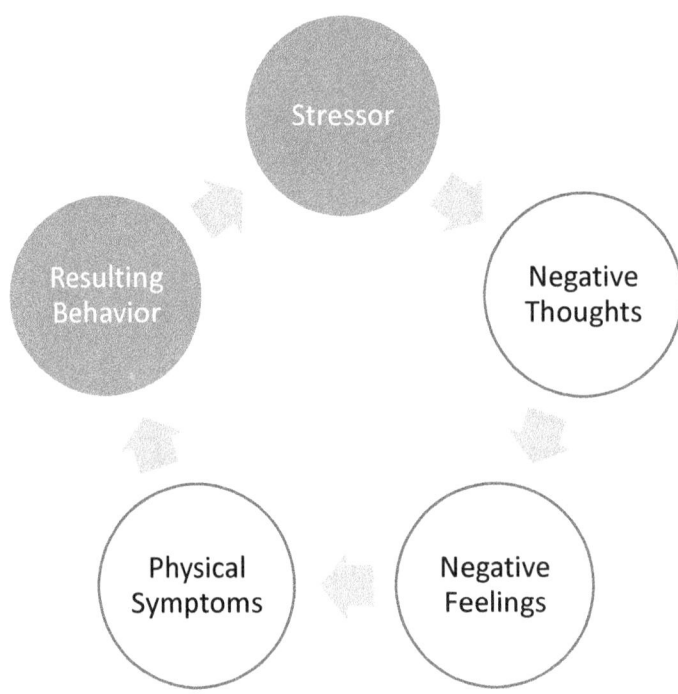

For me, the above cycle would look something like this:

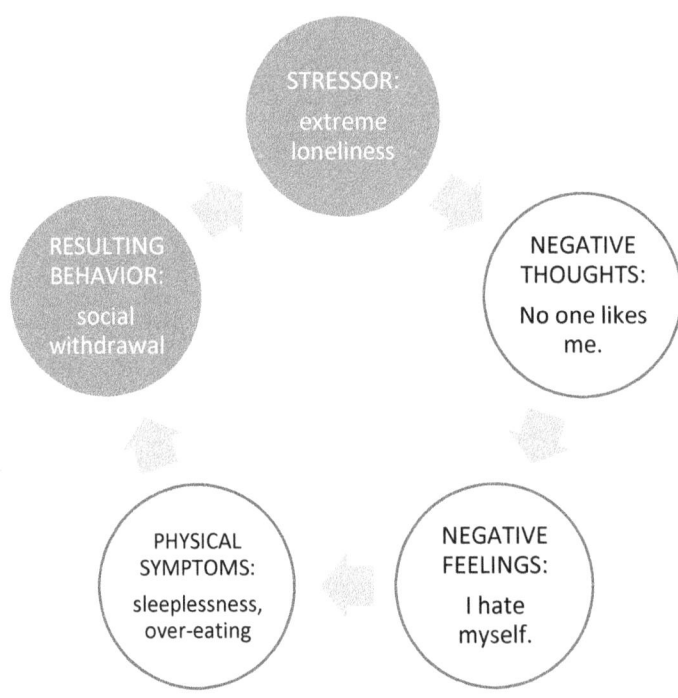

Speaking from experience, I know that breaking this cycle is hard. However, if we don't try, then the vicious cycle of depression continues, and we prolong our own suffering.

Emotion Regulation is about breaking the cycle of negative emotions, thoughts, and behavior. It's about controlling and managing your emotions instead of letting them control you.

On the following pages are various exercises that will help you decrease your emotional reactivity to your depression and increase your ability to experience and tolerate a wide range of emotions.

Worksheet: Understanding and Labeling Your Emotions

Often, our emotions are difficult to manage because we don't fully understand them. Several years ago, I was asked how depression feels and replied, *"It's like a big ball of sadness."* When asked to explain further, I felt speechless and realized I didn't know how to dig deep and describe my emotions.

If you're experiencing the same, then please do the following exercise. The more you can properly define your depression, the easier it will be to regulate the emotions contributing to it. This, in turn, will help you make more intentional choices about how to respond to your depressive stressors.

1. **Mindfulness**. Take a few minutes to sit quietly and tune in to your emotions.

2. **Specifics**. Try to label your emotions as precisely as possible. For example, see if you can narrow your sadness to any of the following:

    - ☐ disappointment
    - ☐ grief
    - ☐ loneliness
    - ☐ embarrassment
    - ☐ emptiness
    - ☐ abandonment
    - ☐ Others:

    _____
    _____
    _____

3. **Intensity levels.** Consider the intensity of the emotion you're feeling. Is it a mild emotion, like a mood, or more intense, like extreme sadness? Encircle the intensity level of your feelings below, with 1 being the least intense and 10 being the most.

| 1 | 2 | 3 | 4 | 5 | 6 | 7 | 8 | 9 | 10 |

4. **Reason.** Do your best to identify what might be causing your emotion. Is it related to a recent event, a particular thought or memory, or an ongoing situation in your life? Write down your thoughts about the situation that applies to you. (You don't need to fill out all the items below; just the one(s) directly related to the emotion you're feeling now.)

☐ Recent event / Something that recently happened:
   Example: A friend canceled our dinner plans at the last minute. I feel disappointed and alone.

   _____
   _____
   _____

☐ Thought/memory:
   Example: My mom passed away a year ago, and today I saw sunflowers, her favorite flower.

   _____
   _____
   _____

Someone I know

Example: A co-worker took credit for work I've done. I'm mad and sad.

_____
_____
_____

☐ Ongoing situation:

Example: I don't have friends.

_____
_____
_____

5. **Reflect**. Finally, take a few moments to reflect on how your emotion affects you.

☐ Any negative thoughts?

Example: I don't have friends… it's making me think I'm just not a likable person.

_____
_____
_____

☐ Any negative feelings?

Example: I don't have friends… I feel horrible and worthless.

_____
_____
_____

- ☐ Any physical symptoms?

  Example: I don't have friends... I'm so anxious about it. I have migraines all the time.

  _____
  _____
  _____

- ☐ Any emotional impulses or urges?

  Example: I don't have friends... all I want to do is stay in bed all day.

  _____
  _____
  _____

At the end of this exercise, you should understand what's causing your depression, how you're feeling about it, and how you're reacting to it.

Worksheet: The Wave

After <u>Understanding and Labeling Your Emotions</u> in the previous exercise, you'll learn how to let go of painful emotions.

Remember that letting go does not mean denying or rejecting your emotions. However, when we're sad and depressed, we may become stuck when we try to process negative emotions. Instead of just letting them go, we might hold on to them even tighter, thinking about every detail of how we feel and wondering why it's happening to us.

So after understanding and labeling your emotions, accept them, and then let them go. Here are the steps on how to do this:

1. **Radically accept.** Acknowledge your feelings with your heart, body, and mind by stating acceptance statements.
   Example: I felt lonely and depressed when my friend canceled our dinner plans. I was looking forward to it, and their decision to cancel made it seem like they didn't care. Still, the dinner is canceled, and I can't do anything about it now. It is what it is.

   _____
   _____
   _____
   _____
   _____

2. **The Wave.** Next, try to experience your feelings as a wave that's coming and going. However, imagine the waves getting weaker and weaker. For example, close your eyes and imagine "loneliness" as a wave approaching you. Don't be afraid or try to avoid it. Let it come. Let it touch you. Let it wash away. Next, imagine "loneliness" as a wave coming at you again, but this time, the wave is smaller and gentler. Just like before, let it reach you and let it wash away.

   Practice The Wave for each and every unpleasant emotion you might be feeling. If it helps, combine The Wave with any breathing exercise under [Mindfulness](#) (page 232).

Worksheet: Check the Facts

When we're depressed, it's difficult to step back and think about whether our feelings are in line with what happened. **Check the Facts** is a way to stop, think, and examine if our emotions match the facts.

Let's start with a reflective exercise. Think back to a previous situation when you may have acted too quickly in response to your emotions.

Question: What emotion do you want to fact-check?
Example: my feelings of abandonment

Your answer:

Question: What happened? What triggered this emotion?
Example: My friend canceled our dinner plans last-minute.

Your answer:

Question: What assumptions did you make about the event?
Example: They didn't care about me at all. I'm unimportant, so it's easy for them to cancel on me.

Your answer:

Question: What did you do?

Example: I got depressed. I didn't go to work for a few days and didn't answer their calls or text messages.

Your answer:

CHECK THE FACTS!

You listed your assumptions above, but <u>WHAT ELSE</u> could the situation mean? Try to think of the situation as a whole, not just from your point of view.

Question: What do you know FOR SURE?

Example: My friend canceled our dinner plans last minute.

Your answer:

Question: Are your assumptions about the event supported by FACTS?

What's your assumption?

Example assumption: My friend doesn't care about me at all. I'm unimportant, so it's easy for them to cancel on me.

Is this supported by FACTS?

Example: No. Now that I think about it, they said sorry about canceling last minute and will tell me the reason for canceling in person.

Question: Why do you think you reacted that way?

Example: My feelings of low self-esteem kicked in. I couldn't stop feeling abandoned.

Your answer:

Question: Looking back, on a scale of 0-5, did your emotion fit the facts? (0 = not at all, 5 = yes):

Example: 0

Your answer:

Question: If your emotion DID NOT fit the facts, what would you do differently?

Example: First, I would do Distress Tolerance exercises (page 252) to ease my pain. Then I'd do Check the Facts to put my emotions into perspective. Lastly, I would've gone to work and answered their calls and text messages.

Your answer:

Question: If your emotion DID fit the facts, would you do anything differently?

Example: Yes. Instead of staying home, which just prolonged my depressive episode, I should've found other, more positive ways of dealing with my emotions.

Your answer:

Note: You can use **Check the Facts** whenever you feel unpleasant emotions. It's not just a reflective exercise. Still, I recommend repeating this exercise at least twice more to develop the habit of fact-checking your emotions.

Worksheet: Opposite Action

One of the best ways to avoid acting on negative impulses or urges is to train yourself to do the opposite of what your emotions are telling you.

For example, if I could go back to my adolescent self, I would NOT socially withdraw and self-isolate because those actions only made my depression worse. Instead, I would tell my younger self to build on my self-esteem, be brave, and attempt to make friends. I've always received good marks, so I could have volunteered to tutor younger children to boost my self-esteem. I also attended a multicultural school. If I had only tried harder, I might have found other immigrant students with whom I shared more interests. But I didn't do any of those things. Instead, I gave in to what my emotions demanded.

Opposite Action is an excellent exercise to prevent you from acting on emotional impulses. It requires some pre-planning, so please take your time in accomplishing the table below.

Column A lists down unpleasant emotions. **Column B** is where you write what you usually do when experiencing these emotions. Lastly, **Column C** is where you should write down your counter-action.

Whenever you're depressed and feel the need to "act out" Column B, refer to this table and do what you wrote under Column C instead. I've filled out some of the rows to jumpstart ideas. Please feel free to add your own.

OPPOSITE ACTION		
A **Emotion** *What you are feeling.*	**B** **Emotional Impulse** *What do you usually do when you feel this way?*	**C** **Opposite Action** *Write down your opposite action here.*
Emptiness	Eat cake and ice cream to feel better	Exercise
Sadness	Cry, avoid people	Seek contact
Inferior	Negative self-talk	Practice Loving Kindness Meditation (page 244)
Loneliness	Hide, self-harm	
Fear	Stay indoors	
Hurt	Self-blame, internalize	
Vulnerable	Say "Yes" to everyone even if I don't want to	

OPPOSITE ACTION

A	B	C
Emotion	**Emotional Impulse**	**Opposite Action**
What you are feeling.	*What do you usually do when you feel this way?*	*Write down your opposite action here.*

Feel free to add more emotions and scenarios in the extra rows below.

Worksheet: Build Positive Experiences (BPE)

Build your resilience to depression by increasing positive feelings in your life. Imagine having an "emotional cup." If you fill it with as many positive emotions as possible, there's only so much room left for negative ones, right?

Build **P**ositive **E**xperiences (BPE) teaches you how to accumulate more positive, happy moments in your life.

Build Positive Experiences I

Make a list of 10 experiences that make you happy. These positive experiences should make you feel good while performing them or shortly after.

Examples: walking in nature, doing Pilates, journaling, etc.

1.

2.

3.

4.

5.

6.

7.

8.

9.

10.

Build Positive Experiences II

Pick ONE activity from the list above and commit to doing it every day. It makes no difference what you decide to do or how long you want to do it. The objective is to do the activity EVERY SINGLE DAY. (Make happiness a daily habit!)

Example: walking in nature
I will <u>take a walk</u> every day for <u>30 minutes in the morning</u>.

Your turn:
I choose: _____
I will _____ every day for _____.

Build Positive Experiences III

Make a list of 10 experiences that have the potential to provide you long-term enjoyment. You may need to plan these activities, but when they occur, they have a long-term positive impact on your life.

Examples: traveling to Europe, getting a puppy, etc.

1.
2.
3.
4.
5.
6.
7.
8.
9.
10.

Worksheet: Accumulate, Build, Cope (ABC)

ABC is similar to BPE in that the goal is to increase your resilience to depression by increasing moments of positivity and happiness. The difference is the addition of the **C** skill (Cope Ahead), which aims to prepare you for situations that may trigger a depressive episode.

Accumulate Positive Emotions.

Short-Term Positive Emotions

Create a list of **10 positive activities** you can do today to bring you joy.

Examples: 10-minute mental break, yoga, dancing, etc.

1. _____
2. _____
3. _____
4. _____
5. _____
6. _____
7. _____
8. _____
9. _____
10. _____

Long-Term Positive Emotions

Create a list of **10 positive changes** you want to make so that positive events happen more frequently in the future.

Examples: stop eating junk food TO improve my health, build my self-confidence TO make new friends

1. _____ to _____
2. _____ to _____
3. _____ to _____
4. _____ to _____
5. _____ to _____
6. _____ to _____
7. _____ to _____
8. _____ to _____
9. _____ to _____
10. _____ to _____

Build Mastery.

Excelling at something builds self-esteem and fights feelings of helplessness, sadness, and despair. List at least five things you want to learn or something you already do well but want to be better at.

Examples: baking, painting, HTML coding, etc.

1. _____
2. _____
3. _____
4. _____
5. _____

Cope Ahead.

Is there a specific situation or person that triggers your depression? If so, planning how to cope when encountering that situation or person would be beneficial.

Whatever plan you devise, rehearse it in your mind or roleplay it with someone. Practicing what you will say and do during the situation will help you cope with it better.

Question: What's the stressful event that usually triggers your depression?

Example: Sunday family gatherings

_____
_____
_____

Question: What usually happens? What are you concerned about?

Example: The chaos stresses me out. Somehow, my parents end up fighting, my sister always sides with my mom, and I'm left to side with my dad. At the end of the meal, everyone's upset. When I leave, I feel guilty, sad, and depressed for the coming days.

_____
_____
_____
_____
_____

Cope Ahead Plan

1. Rehearse the situation in your mind.
2. Plan what you plan to DO. Be as detailed as possible.

Example:
- *When the fighting starts, I will do <u>Equal Breathing</u> (page 238).*
- *When my parents start to make digs at each other, I'll do <u>Happy Place</u> (page 260).*
- *When my father asks me to side with him (again), I'll say, "Sorry, Dad, this is between you and mom." If my dad persists, I'll say, "Sorry, Dad, this is between you and mom." I will say this over and over and over until my dad leaves me alone.*
- *If I start feeling guilty, I'll say to myself, "This is not on me. This is not on me. This is not on me."*
- *When I get home, I won't even give my depression a chance. I'll do any of the activities I listed under <u>Build Positive Experiences (BPE)</u>, page 301.*

Your turn:

_____
_____
_____
_____
_____
_____
_____
_____
_____

Important: When you practice your Cope Ahead plan, it's normal to experience negative emotions because you're reliving the potential stressor as if it were happening. So, it's imperative to take a break and chill out afterward.

Make a list of things that calm you.

Examples: a cup of calming tea, journaling, hugging my dog, etc.

1. _____
2. _____
3. _____
4. _____
5. _____
6. _____
7. _____
8. _____
9. _____
10. _____

Worksheet: PLEASE

Your physical health is directly related to your emotional health and vice versa.[45] An unhealthy body makes you more vulnerable to negative emotions. In contrast, taking care of your body improves your emotional resiliency.

PL

Treat **P**hysical i**ll**ness without delay.

You must protect your health because illness lowers your resistance to negative emotions. As such, if you're feeling physically ill, don't put off seeing a doctor or taking any prescribed medications. It's also advisable to contact someone (e.g., a family member, friend, neighbor, colleague, etc.) to be with you so that you're not alone while you're sick.

If you don't want to see a doctor or are physically unable to, consider a holistic approach to treatment, such as acupuncture, aromatherapy, acupressure, yoga, etc. The goal is to get well as soon as possible.

When was the last time you were physically ill?
_____

Did you see a doctor? Y / N
Why or why not?
_____
_____
_____

Balanced Eating.

We are what we eat.[46] This means the foods we consume affect our overall health and well-being, so nourishing our bodies with food that affects us positively is essential. For example, a diet high in processed foods and sugar may contribute to feelings of anxiety and depression[47]. In contrast, a diet rich in whole foods and healthy fats may help improve mood and cognitive function[48].

So, as much as possible, eat food as close to its natural state. For example, instead of buying and consuming a jar of peanut butter, invest in a kitchen processor, buy whole peanuts, and make your own peanut butter. Plenty of websites share how to make your favorite foods from scratch, so just put Google to good use.

Important: Before making any significant changes to your diet, you should always talk to your doctor or a nutritionist. (See also Nutrition: Eat to Beat Depression, page 335.)

Avoid Unhealthy Substances.

Unhealthy substances such as alcohol and illegal drugs can make depression worse.[49] Instead, drink plain water, lemon water, green tea, healthy smoothies, etc.

What about coffee? Caffeine is a stimulant that can boost alertness and improve mood in some people. However, excessive caffeine consumption can contribute to anxiety and depression.[50] Generally, an 8-ounce (240 ml) cup of coffee has about 100 mg of caffeine. Several sites say that most healthy adults can have 400 mg of caffeine daily, the same as 4 cups (945 ml) of coffee. [51,52] As such, it's best to monitor your own reaction to coffee.

Sleep.

The American Academy of Sleep Medicine (AAS) and the Sleep Research Society (SRS) both say that adults need at least seven (7) hours of quality sleep every night.[53] Quality sleep is restful and uninterrupted, allowing one to wake up feeling refreshed and energized.

Unfortunately, sleep problems are common symptoms of depression. *Insomnia* occurs when you are unable to fall asleep or have difficulty staying asleep, or when you wake up too early and are unable to return to sleep. *Hypersomnia* occurs when you experience excessive daytime sleepiness and have difficulty staying awake during the day. If you suffer from any of these symptoms, here are some tips to help you.

1. Maintain a **consistent sleeping routine**. Even on weekends, go to bed and wake up at the same time every day.
2. Create a **relaxing sleep environment**. Ensure your bedroom is cool, dark, and quiet, and avoid screens before bedtime.
3. **Limit caffeine, alcohol, and nicotine.** These substances can interfere with sleep quality, so avoiding them in the evening or before bed is best.
4. Get **regular exercise**. Regular physical activity can help promote better sleep but avoid vigorous exercise close to bedtime.
5. **Avoid large meals and fluids before bedtime**. Eating a big meal or drinking a lot of fluids before bedtime can disrupt sleep.

6. **Wind down before bed.** Do relaxing activities before bedtime, such as taking a warm bath or reading a book.
7. **Manage stress.** Stress and anxiety can make it hard to fall asleep, so it's important to find ways to deal with stress throughout the day.
8. Use **comfortable bedding**. Purchase a comfortable mattress and pillows that support good sleep posture.
9. **Avoid napping** during the day. If you have trouble sleeping at night, avoid napping during the day.
10. Seek **professional help** if needed. If you still have difficulties sleeping despite making lifestyle changes, consult a doctor to rule out any underlying medical issues or sleep disorders like sleep apnea or narcolepsy.

Exercise.

Research has shown that exercising can make you feel happier and less sad.[54,55] One reason for this is that it can increase the release of *endorphins* in the brain. Endorphins are neurotransmitters that act as natural painkillers and mood elevators. This release of endorphins can lead to feelings of euphoria and well-being, often referred to as a "runner's high."

According to the World Health Organization, adults 18-64 should do at least 2.5 to 5 hours of moderate-intensity aerobic physical activity or 1.25 to 2.5 hours of intense aerobic physical activity weekly. This should ideally be done with muscle-strengthening activities that are moderate to highly intense 2x or more per week.

Important: **PLEASE** skills are not meant to be one-time activities. You should strive to make these activities part of your lifestyle to reap their benefits.

> *"The way we communicate with others and with ourselves ultimately determines the quality of our lives."*
> — Tony Robbins

Human beings are social creatures. It's in our nature to want to share our lives with others. As such, relationships are an integral part of human existence. And not only do we want people in our lives, but we also want to be a part of other people's lives.

Relationships make life fulfilling and meaningful. They give us a sense of belonging, provide emotional support, and contribute to our personal growth.

Great communication skills are at the heart of great relationships. Effective communication builds stronger relationships, resolves conflicts, and conveys ideas and information effectively. Bad communication, on the other hand, can lead to misunderstandings, misinterpretations, frustrations, and even the breakdown of relationships.

What is communication?

Communication is when two or more people or groups exchange information, ideas, or feelings. Communication can happen in a number of ways, such as:

1. **Verbal communication** includes spoken language, such as talking or giving a speech.
2. **Nonverbal communication** includes communication without words, such as facial expressions, body language, and tone of voice.

3. **Written communication** includes written forms of communication, such as emails, letters, and texts.
4. **Visual communication** includes communication through visual elements, such as pictures, graphs, and charts.
5. **Gestural communication** includes communication through gestures, such as waving hello or pointing.
6. **Electronic communication** includes communication through electronic devices, such as social media, video chats, and instant messaging.
7. **Touch communication** includes communication through touch, such as a handshake or a hug.

Each form of communication can be effective in different situations and with different people. Effective communication often involves using a combination of these different forms of communication to convey your message clearly and effectively.

However, as mentioned, communication is exchanging information, ideas, or feelings. It's a two-way process.

So, knowing how to communicate YOUR message effectively is just half of the equation. The other half is paying attention and understanding (correctly interpreting) the other party's message.

Researchers have found that people with depression have trouble communicating with other people.[56,57] For example, they often struggle to express themselves clearly, find the right words to describe their thoughts and feelings and speak in a monotone or flat tone. People with depression tend to be more self-critical or negative in their self-talk, making it difficult to express positive emotions and thoughts.

Nonverbal communication problems in people who suffer from depression may include a lack of eye contact, a lack of facial expression, and slumped or closed body posture. These nonverbal cues can affect how others perceive and respond to the person with depression, which can negatively impact communication and social interactions.

Note: Not everyone with depression will experience communication problems. And if they do, the severity and type of communication problems can vary from person to person. Further, communication problems are NOT exclusive to depression and often present in other mental health conditions.

In DBT, **Interpersonal Effectiveness** is about learning how to communicate effectively to get what you want and need from others in a conversation. Additionally, since communication is a two-way process, you'll learn how to build stronger relationships by actively listening to others. You'll also learn about self-respect effectiveness. Research shows that people who suffer from depression tend to be people-pleasers.[58] If you constantly put other people's wants and needs above your own, like by always saying "Yes," you'll lose your self-respect in the long run. On the other hand, you shouldn't betray your values and beliefs (e.g., manipulating, telling lies, etc.) to get what you want or to get people to like you.

Worksheet: Active Listening

Active Listening is about fully focusing on and understanding what the speaker is saying. This way, you'll be able to receive and accurately interpret other people during the communication process, preventing misunderstandings and conflict in the relationship.

Note: When you do this exercise for the first time, pick a neutral or noncontroversial topic (e.g., favorite Netflix TV series, a favorite song, etc.). The goal is to fully understand what the other person is saying, not to get into an argument.

1. **Choose a speaker.** Find someone you can talk with, such as a friend, family member, or coworker.

    Who's your speaker?
    Example: my mom

    _____

2. **Find a quiet time and place.** To minimize distractions, choose a quiet time and location where you can focus on the conversation.

    When and where are you going to have this conversation?
    Example: in the kitchen, when everybody else has left, and it's just my mom and me

    _____

3. **Face the speaker.** Face the person speaking, and maintain eye contact to show you're engaged and interested.

4. **Listen without interruption.** Allow the speaker to completely finish their thoughts before responding. Avoid interrupting, interjecting, or finishing their sentences.

5. **Show interest**. Show that you are interested in what the speaker is saying by nodding, smiling, or using verbal cues such as "*I see,*" "*Okay,*" or "*Uh-huh.*"

6. **Rephrase what you heard**. After the speaker has finished talking, rephrase what you heard to ensure you understood correctly. For example, say, "*Let me make sure I understand. You said...*"

7. **Clarify.** If you're unsure of something the speaker said, ask for clarification. For example, say, "*I don't get it. Why do you...?*"

8. **Provide feedback.** Offer feedback and ask questions to show that you have been actively listening. For example, you say, "*It sounds like you're feeling nostalgic about that song. Am I right?*"

9. **Summarize.** At the end of the conversation, summarize what was discussed to ensure that you understand the topic clearly.

Worksheet: DEARMAN

DEARMAN is about *objective effectiveness*. It's how to effectively and clearly express your needs and desires and get what you want from an interaction. You see, there's an "art" to asking. If you demand, you probably won't get what you want and may even damage your relationships. **DEARMAN** will help you ask effectively.

D	**D**escribe the situation. What do you want or need? Talk about the situation using words that are clear and to the point. Don't say what you think or feel; say what you know to be true. What's the situation? *Example: I want to ask my partner to have more patience with me. I suffer from hypersomnia and I overeat and she's pushing me too much and too hard to "change my ways."* _____ _____ _____
E	**E**xpress how you feel. Start your statements with "I." Remember that what you're talking about is how you feel and what you think. People can take "You" statements as accusations, which makes it more likely that there will be conflict in the conversation.

Example: I want to get better and will take steps to improve, but I need to do it at my own pace. I get even more stressed and depressed when I feel pressured.

Your turn:
_____
_____
_____

Assert yourself.

Convey what you want to happen without being confrontational. You don't want a fight. You want to be clearly and effectively heard.

Example: I want and appreciate your help, but I will address my sleep and eating problems my way and at my own pace.

Your turn:
_____
_____
_____

Reinforce your request.

Make it clear to the other person how crucial your request is. Also, immediately express gratitude if they give in to what you want.

Example: I know my changes may not be as drastic and the results not as fast as you want, but I would really appreciate doing this my way. I would appreciate your support.

Your turn:
_____
_____
_____

Mindfulness.

Be mindful of YOUR wants and needs. Stay on track and maintain your position whatever the other person says. When other people don't agree with you, they may object, insist, dismiss, or argue with you. Whatever they do, don't be persuaded and stay true to what you want.

Example: I hear you. But that's not what will work best for me, and what's best for me and my depression is to make the positive changes I want on my terms.

Your turn:
_____
_____
_____

Appear confident.

Don't hesitate and give the other party a chance to argue. Show confidence through verbal and non-verbal cues, but don't be intimidating. Don't raise your voice or stare the other person down. Remember to be consistent too. For example, don't maintain eye contact and immediately look away after making your request.

How do you want to show confidence?

Example: Sit or stand tall, roll your shoulders back, and maintain eye contact. Next, say, "I hope you understand because I'm not going to change my mind on this."
_____
_____
_____

Negotiate.

If the other person(s) won't give in, it's time to negotiate. This will give you both time to devise a solution that will work. You can suggest a way to move forward or ask the other person what they think should happen next.

Example: How about I make an exercise routine and schedule. It may not be as rigorous as you suggest, but it will still be progress. We can both monitor how things are in a week or so. What do you think?

Your turn:

_____
_____
_____

Worksheet: GIVE

GIVE is about relationship effectiveness. This exercise is about maintaining relationships with others by fostering positive interactions. Basically, you want the other person to feel good in the conversation so that they're more likely to grant your request.

G — Be Gentle.

Don't demand, be disrespectful or be abrasive when making a request. Also, don't say or do anything that could make the other person feel bad. Simply put—be nice!

List five ways to ask for something in a nice way.
Examples: "Is it okay if we..." or "Do you mind if..."

1. _____
2. _____
3. _____
4. _____
5. _____

I — Act Interested.

Relationships are not all about you. Communicating is about wanting to be heard and hearing what the other person says. As such, pay attention to the person(s) with whom you're conversing. (See also Active Listening, page 316.)

List five ways you convey interest.
Example: look at the other person and maintain eye contact, don't interrupt, respond to what was said, etc.

	1. _____ 2. _____ 3. _____ 4. _____ 5. _____
V	**Validate.** Show that you understand what the other person is thinking and feeling. (See also Active Listening, page 316.) List five ways you validate others. *Examples: Say, "If I understand you correctly, you mean..." or "Oh wow, I never knew that's what it meant for you."* 1. _____ 2. _____ 3. _____ 4. _____ 5. _____
E	**Show an Easy Manner.** Act in a friendly manner. Be casual so the other person thinks you're asking, not telling them what to do. People will feel more at ease and be more open to what you want if you have a friendly attitude. List 5 ways you can show friendliness. *Examples: smile, adopt a relaxed posture, make eye contact, etc.*

1. _____
2. _____
3. _____
4. _____
5. _____

Worksheet: FAST

FAST is about self-respect effectiveness. It's about protecting yourself from betraying your values and beliefs to receive approval or get what you want.

F	**Be Fair.** Be fair to yourself and other people during conversations. As you make your request, ensure it isn't anything beyond the other person's abilities to grant. Also, ensure that you ask politely. Don't make demands or make the other person feel threatened or guilty if they don't grant your request. Practice making a request fairly and reasonably. *Example: I'd like to take Friday off, please. I have an appointment with my therapist.* Your turn: _____ _____ _____
A	**No Apologies.** Don't apologize or over-apologize. There's no need to apologize for making a request, and you shouldn't say sorry if you want to say "No" to someone. Practice making a request without apologizing: *Example: I'd like to take Friday off, please. I have an appointment with my therapist.* *NOT: I'm so sorry to ask, but can I please take Friday off? I have an appointment with my therapist. I'm really sorry about not asking earlier.*

Your turn:
_____
_____
_____

Practice saying "No" to someone without apologizing:
Example: I don't want to go out drinking this weekend.
NOT: I feel bad about this, but I'm sorry, I don't want to go out drinking this weekend. Sorry!

Your turn:
_____
_____
_____

Stick to your Values.

Don't betray your values just because the other person doesn't like your request or does not agree with you. And don't betray your values if someone is nagging you to say "Yes" to something.

Practice sticking to your values when making a request:
Example: I need Friday off for my mental health. That's most important to me.

Your turn:
_____
_____
_____

Practice sticking to your values and saying "No" no matter what the other person says, does, or tries to get you to do.

Example: I understand you need more hands at work, but I need Friday off for my mental health. That's most important to me.

Your turn:

_____
_____
_____

Be Truthful.

Don't lie, dramatize or exaggerate to get what you want or to get out of something you don't want to do. Honesty is the best policy.

Practice honesty when making a request:

Example: I've been struggling and need a mental day off to take care of myself.

Your turn:

_____
_____
_____

Practice honesty when saying "No:

Example: I don't want to go out drinking this weekend.
NOT: Oh, THIS weekend? Oh man, I want to, but I can't. It's, uh... my mom's birthday! The family would hate my guts if I didn't show up.

Your turn:
_____
_____
_____

Chapter Highlights:

- **Dialectical Behavior Therapy** (DBT) is a type of therapy that combines cognitive-behavioral techniques (CBT) with mindfulness practices.
- Research shows that DBT is **highly effective in treating depression**.
- **Dialectics** is a way of thinking and solving problems that involve recognizing and balancing different ideas or points of view.
- **DBT Core Concepts**: Acceptance and Change.
- **DBT Core Skills**: Mindfulness, Distress Tolerance, Emotion Regulation and Interpersonal Effectiveness. Related worksheets for each skill featuring depression-specific situations are provided.

Continuing the Road to Happiness

Healing is a choice. It's not an easy one because it takes work to turn around and face the pain. But in the end, it's worth it."
— Marianne Williamson

Self-Esteem: The Link Between Self-Perception and Depression

Low self-esteem and depression are intimately linked, and those with poor self-esteem are at a higher risk of developing depression.[59,60]

People with poor self-esteem have a negative perception of themselves and their talents. They may feel inadequate, useless, or irrelevant. These negative ideas about yourself can make it hard to deal with stressful situations and make you feel like you have no control or hope, leading to depression.

As such, addressing poor self-esteem can be an essential component of depression treatment. Here are some suggestions for increasing self-esteem:

1. **Practice self-care.** Self-care is caring for your physical, emotional, and mental well-being. It involves deciding to prioritize your own health and happiness and taking steps to meet your own needs. Self-care aims to promote a sense of balance, reduce stress, and help you feel your best. By taking care of yourself, you can better manage the challenges and demands of everyday life.

List at least five (5) self-care activities you're doing right now.

Examples: mental breaks, short walks in nature, drinking enough water, etc.

1. _____
2. _____
3. _____
4. _____
5. _____

List at least five (5) self-care activities you plan to do from now on.
Examples: getting enough sleep, eating healthy foods, exercising, making time for hobbies, etc.

1. _____
2. _____
3. _____
4. _____
5. _____

2. **Challenge negative self-talk.** Recognize your inner critic and confront negative beliefs by challenging their authenticity and replacing them with more positive and realistic ones. Here are some suggestions for doing this:

   a.) Identify the negative thought causing you distress or making you depressed. Please write it down or say it out loud.

   Example: I'm such a lazy person. I can't even find the energy to get out of bed and brush my teeth.

   Your turn:

   _____

   _____

   _____

b.) **Challenge** your negative thought. What's the evidence supporting this thought? What evidence contradicts it? Practice dialectics and try to view the situation from a different perspective.

Example: I'm NOT a lazy person. My depression is the cause of my low energy, not me.

Your turn:

_____

_____

_____

c.) Once you've questioned the negative thought, replace it with a more positive and realistic one.

Example: I may often feel exhausted, but I still accomplish things. Last week, I spent quality time with my mom, and this week, I submitted an important work report a day ahead.

Your turn:

_____

_____

_____

d.) **Practice self-compassion.** Show kindness to yourself, just as you would a friend going through a difficult time. Remind yourself that it's okay to make mistakes and that you're doing the best you can.

e.) **Challenging negative self-talk constantly.** Repeat this exercise regularly to help train your brain to think more positively and realistically.

3. **Focus on your strengths.** Recognize your strengths, special skills, and successes. This will make you feel more capable and confident.

Despite my mental health problems, I did well in school and had good grades. Drawing was one of my special skills. While I was in Grade 6, I won an art award that I was especially proud of when I graduated elementary school. Later, I managed to get into an animation program for college in Ottawa. This was years *before* I saw a psychologist and was prescribed anti-anxiety meds, so I'm very proud of achieving this. I make it a point to remember this whenever I feel depressed.

Your turn:

_____
_____
_____

4. **Set achievable and realistic goals.** Set goals that are both attainable and practical. Divide them into smaller segments and celebrate your accomplishments along the way. By the way, a "goal" doesn't necessarily have to be big. For example, for someone suffering from depression, just "showing up" is already a major accomplishment, and you should be proud of that.

What's a goal you want to achieve?
Example: I want to sleep better to have more energy during the day.

Your turn:

_____
_____
_____

List the steps you should take to accomplish this goal.

Example: establish a sleep schedule, stop mindless phone scrolling in bed, de-clutter my bedroom, etc.

Your turn:

_____
_____
_____

5. **Surround yourself with positive people.** Spend time with people who make you feel good about yourself and who encourage and support you. According to studies, we are the average of the five individuals we spend the most time with.[61]. So be around optimistic people; their positivity will rub off on you!

    However, if you are surrounded by negative people who you cannot simply avoid (e.g., family members, friends, colleagues, etc.), make it a goal to spend less time with them. For example, skip the weekly Sunday dinners and attend every other week or once a month.

6. **Do things you like.** Participate in activities that you enjoy and make you feel good about yourself. This can range from reading a book to participating in a sport. (See also Build Positive Experiences, page 301.)

7. **Know that it's okay to prioritize YOU.** Self-care is not selfishness. When you care for yourself, you can better show up for others, including your family, friends, and colleagues. You're also more patient, compassionate, and empathetic when feeling rested, nourished, and emotionally balanced.

On an airplane, the cabin attendant always tells passengers during the pre-flight briefing to "put your oxygen mask on first before assisting others." This is before helping others. Why is this a key rule for staying alive? The reason is if you don't take care of yourself first, you won't be able to help other people with theirs. In other words, taking care of yourself allows you to show up as your best self, ultimately benefiting you and those you.

Building your self-esteem requires time and effort. Remember to be kind to yourself and concentrate on making tiny adjustments over time. Believe that you will get there, and you will!

Nutrition: Eat to Beat Depression

Nutritional psychiatry is a field of study that examines the link between what we eat and mental health. It's based on the idea that food affects our brain chemistry and can influence our mood, behavior, and cognitive function. It aims to use this knowledge to develop dietary interventions to improve mental health outcomes. This may involve promoting certain foods or nutrients or avoiding others, as well as incorporating dietary changes alongside other mental health treatments.

Nutritional psychiatry is a vast subject beyond this book's scope. So, we'll only cover a few basics here that are related to depression.

Here are some of the reasons why nutrition may be effective in depression:

1. **Nutrients influence brain function.** The brain requires nutrients such as vitamins, minerals, and vital fatty acids to function effectively. A diet deficient in these nutrients might cause brain chemistry alterations, contributing to depression.

    Example: Fruits and vegetables include essential vitamins and minerals that help with brain function and mood. Every day, try to consume various bright fruits and vegetables such as tomatoes, carrots, bell peppers, etc. As a general rule of thumb, the more color on your plate, the better.

2. **Blood sugar control.** A diet strong in refined carbs and sugar can cause blood sugar levels to soar and then plummet, resulting in weariness and mood swings. In contrast, a diet high in whole foods and complex carbs can help control blood sugar levels and provide a more consistent energy source.

Example: Healthy grains, such as brown rice, quinoa, and whole wheat bread, are high in fiber and B vitamins, which can help manage mood and blood sugar levels.

3. **Inflammation** has been related to depression, and some foods can raise inflammation while others can decrease it. Anti-inflammatory foods like fruits, vegetables, and healthy fats can help reduce inflammation and enhance mood.

    Example: Omega-3 fatty acids in fatty fish, walnuts, and flaxseeds have been demonstrated to reduce inflammation.

4. **Gut health**. The gut is considered by many as the "second brain" because it contains various neurotransmitters that influence mood and behavior. A high-fiber, fermented-food diet can help develop healthy gut flora, boosting mood.

    Example: Broccoli, peas, Brussels sprouts, and black beans are high-fiber foods. Kimchi, yogurt, and sauerkraut are examples of fermented foods.

Also, staying well-hydrated throughout the day is important. The recommended water intake for adults can vary depending on gender, body weight, physical activity level, and climate. However, a general guideline recommended by the Institute of Medicine (IOM) is that men should aim for about 3.7 liters (or about 13 cups) of total water intake per day. Women should aim for about 2.7 liters (or about 9 cups) of daily water intake.

Important: Before making any dietary changes, please consult with your doctor or healthcare provider.

Conclusion

"Healing comes from taking responsibility: to realize that it is you - and no one else - that creates your thoughts, your feelings, and your actions." — Peter Shepherd

People who suffer from depression don't feel happiness or at least find it very difficult to experience it. So, no, we cannot just "snap out of it" and "just be happy." During depressive episodes, we don't even have hope, so it's very hard to imagine being happy even though it's what we desire the most.

All I could think about for years was how to survive the day. So, I never really thought about how to make things better.

My mental health journey taught me that life doesn't just happen. As difficult as it may seem to believe, we have a lot of influence and power over how our lives turn out.

DBT is one of the tools I used to turn things around and be in control of my life instead of letting my OCD, GAD, and depression run my life. I sincerely hope you find it as helpful and effective as I have.

Here's a quick recap of what we covered in this book:

- Depression, or major depressive disorder (MDD): what it is, causes and symptoms, and currently known treatments.
- Living with Depression: Understand how MDD affects the brain and the body and how it influences relationships. Research shows that depression may be

more prevalent in women. The section Depression in Women expounds on possible reasons for this.
- Dialectic Behavior Therapy (DBT) and its core concepts fundamentals (Acceptance and Change) and its primary skills (Mindfulness, Distress Tolerance, Emotion Regulation, and Interpersonal Effectiveness). Each concept and skill is explained in detail, and numerous exercises are provided to help you apply these skills daily.
- Additional tips: how to build your self-esteem and how to use nutrition to help treat depression.

> *"Believe in yourself and all that you are. Know that there is something inside you that is greater than any obstacle."*
> *— Christian D. Larson*

Appendix A – PHQ-9 Depression Self-Assessment

The following is the **Patient Health Questionnaire-9** (PHQ-9). It's a 9-point questionnaire that psychiatrist Dr. Robert L. Spitzer and his colleagues developed.[62] The purpose of PHQ-9 is to help assess the severity of depressive symptoms. It's considered a reliable and valid measure of depression severity.

Important: Please note that the PHQ-9 is meant to help you determine if your feelings, thoughts, or behaviors are signs of depression. It is NOT meant to be a diagnosis or a replacement for a professional evaluation. After you fill out this questionnaire and figure out how to score it, please share the results with your doctor or mental health professional.

Please answer the questions below to the best of your ability.

How often have you felt the following problems in the last two weeks?
(Select your answer from the list on the right and circle it.)

	Not at all	Several days	More than half the days	Nearly every day
How often have you experienced a lack of interest or pleasure in doing things, especially activities you used to enjoy?	0	1	2	3
How often have you felt sad, down, or like there was no hope?	0	1	2	3
How often have you had sleep problems? (This can be trouble falling, staying, or sleeping too long.)	0	1	2	3
How often have you felt tired or like you didn't have much energy?	0	1	2	3
How often have you had eating issues like overeating or undereating?	0	1	2	3
How often have you had negative feelings about yourself? For example, have you often felt that you're always doing things "wrong" or often blame yourself for letting other people down?	0	1	2	3
How often have you had problems concentrating? For example, have you been having trouble focusing while reading the newspaper, watching a program, or when someone is speaking?	0	1	2	3
How often have you had problems moving or speaking? For example, have you been reacting slower that other people notice this change? Or perhaps, you're experiencing the opposite, such as being more fidgety or restless than usual?	0	1	2	3
How often have you thought about hurting yourself or dying?	0	1	2	3
Add total per column:				
Overall total:				

If you've encountered any of the symptoms listed above, how difficult has it been for you to function at work, at home, or get along with other people?

- ☐ Not difficult at all
- ☐ Somewhat difficult
- ☐ Very difficult
- ☐ Extremely difficult

Scoring:

1-9 = Low depression severity scale

Your score is low, indicating you may not suffer from depression. If you feel this is inaccurate, please learn and explore further or see a medical or mental health expert.

10-14 = Moderate depression severity range

Your score is in the moderate range, indicating that you may suffer from mild depression. As such, please seek professional advice from a medical or mental health expert as soon as possible.

15-27 = Severe depression severity range

Your score is in the high range, indicating that you may suffer from major depression. Please seek professional advice from a medical or mental health expert as soon as possible.

Appendix B – Journaling for Depression Relief

Journaling is a fantastic way to manage depression. It's a very personal activity, so there's no right or wrong way to do it. The goal is to use writing to connect with your feelings and learn more about yourself, helping you cope and heal from depression. Following are some guidelines.

1. **SET A SCHEDULE.**

    Set a journaling schedule. Find a place to sit down and write that is quiet and comfortable. Aim to set aside 15 to 20 minutes daily for your writing.

    What's the best time for you to journal?
    Example: In the morning, just after I wake up and before I go to work.

    _____

    _____

    _____

2. **USE PROMPTS.**

    Sometimes questions or prompts help start your journaling. For example, "*What's making me sad today?*" or "*What's making me happy today?*" or *"Did something trigger my feelings today?"* can help you get started and get your thoughts in order.

3. **NON-JUDGEMENTALLY.**

    Let yourself write freely and without judging what you write. Don't worry about spelling or grammar. Just write what you want to say.

4. **BE HONEST.**

    Tell the truth about how you feel. Write down any thoughts or feelings that are making you feel bad. It's important to recognize these feelings so you can get past them.

5. **GRATITUDE.**

    Take a moment to think about the things you're thankful for. Every day, write down at least three things you're grateful for. This can assist you in shifting your focus from negative to positive aspects of your life. (See also Attitude of Gratitude, page **Error! Bookmark not defined.**.)

    What are the three things you're grateful for today?

    Example: unexpected call from my brother, eating my favorite salad for lunch, snuggling with my partner, etc.

    _____
    _____
    _____

6. **SMALL GOALS.**

    Write down one or two small goals you want to achieve each day. Setting small goals can help you feel like you're progressing and gaining speed.

    What's your small goal today?

    Example: wake up earlier, take short walks after lunch, etc.

    _____
    _____
    _____

7. **REFLECT.**

    Take a minute to think about what you've written. Ask yourself, "*What do I know now that I didn't know before?*" When you think about your thoughts and emotions, you can learn more about yourself and your feelings.

    What have you discovered today?
    Example: I discovered that if I MAKE TIME, I can go for short walks after lunch. I used to think I never had the time for it. I realize now that I was just making excuses.

    _____
    _____
    _____

Review Request

If you enjoyed this book or found it useful…

I'd like to ask you for a quick favor:

Please share your thoughts and leave a quick REVIEW. Your feedback matters and helps me make improvements to provide the best books possible.

Reviews are so helpful to both readers and authors, so any help would be greatly appreciated! You can leave a review here:

http://tinyurl.com/dbtskills-bundle-review

Or by scanning the QR code below:

Also, please join my ARC team to get early access to my releases.

https://barretthuang.com/arc-team/

THANK YOU!

References

1 World Health Organization. (n.d.). *Depression*. World Health Organization. Retrieved March 1, 2023, from https://www.who.int/news-room/fact-sheets/detail/depression

2 U.S. Department of Health and Human Services. (n.d.). *Major depression*. National Institute of Mental Health. Retrieved March 1, 2023, from https://www.nimh.nih.gov/health/statistics/major-depression

3 Shadrina, M., Bondarenko, E. A., & Slominsky, P. A. (2018). Genetics factors in major depression disease. *Frontiers in Psychiatry, 9*. https://doi.org/10.3389/fpsyt.2018.00334

4 Levey, D. F., Stein, M. B., Wendt, F. R., Pathak, G. A., Zhou, H., Aslan, M., Quaden, R., Harrington, K. M., Nuñez, Y. Z., Overstreet, C., Radhakrishnan, K., Sanacora, G., McIntosh, A. M., Shi, J., Shringarpure, S. S., Concato, J., Polimanti, R., & Gelernter, J. (2021). Bi-ancestral depression GWAS in the million veteran program and meta-analysis in >1.2 million individuals highlight new therapeutic directions. *Nature Neuroscience, 24*(7), 954–963. https://doi.org/10.1038/s41593-021-00860-2

5 Brody, D. J., Pratt, L. A., & Hughes, J. (2018, February 13). *Prevalence of depression among adults aged 20 and over: United States, 2013–2016*. Centers for Disease Control and Prevention. Retrieved March 1, 2023, from https://www.cdc.gov/nchs/products/databriefs/db303.htm

6 Ng, C. W., How, C. H., & Ng, Y. P. (2017). Depression in primary care: Assessing suicide risk. *Singapore Medical Journal, 58*(2), 72–77. https://doi.org/10.11622/smedj.2017006

7 American Psychiatric Association. (2017). *Diagnostic And Statistical Manual Of Mental Disorders: DSM-5*.

8 France, C. M., Lysaker, P. H., & Robinson, R. P. (2007). The "chemical imbalance" explanation for depression: Origins, lay endorsement, and clinical implications. *Professional Psychology: Research and Practice, 38*(4), 411–420. https://doi.org/10.1037/0735-7028.38.4.411

9 Moncrieff, J., Cooper, R. E., Stockmann, T., Amendola, S., Hengartner, M. P., & Horowitz, M. A. (2022). The serotonin theory of depression: A Systematic

Umbrella Review of the evidence. *Molecular Psychiatry.* https://doi.org/10.1038/s41380-022-01661-0

10 Lewis, G., Marston, L., Duffy, L., Freemantle, N., Gilbody, S., Hunter, R., Kendrick, T., Kessler, D., Mangin, D., King, M., Lanham, P., Moore, M., Nazareth, I., Wiles, N., Bacon, F., Bird, M., Brabyn, S., Burns, A., Clarke, C. S., ... Lewis, G. (2021). Maintenance or discontinuation of antidepressants in primary care. *New England Journal of Medicine, 385*(14), 1257–1267. https://doi.org/10.1056/nejmoa2106356

11 Virk, G., Reeves, G., Rosenthal, N. E., Sher, L., & Postolache, T. T. (2009). Short exposure to light treatment improves depression scores in patients with seasonal affective disorder: A brief report. *International Journal on Disability and Human Development, 8*(3). https://doi.org/10.1515/ijdhd.2009.8.3.283

12 Simon, G. (2005). Review: Bright light therapy and dawn simulation reduce symptom severity in seasonal affective disorder. *Evidence-Based Medicine, 10*(5), 146–146. https://doi.org/10.1136/ebm.10.5.146

13 Craft, L. L., & Perna, F. M. (2004). The benefits of exercise for the clinically depressed. *The Primary Care Companion For CNS Disorders, 6*(3). https://doi.org/10.4088/pcc.v06n0301

14 Schuch, F. B., & Stubbs, B. (2019). The role of exercise in preventing and treating depression. *Current Sports Medicine Reports, 18*(8), 299–304. https://doi.org/10.1249/jsr.0000000000000620

15 Singh, B., Olds, T., Curtis, R., Dumuid, D., Virgara, R., Watson, A., Szeto, K., O'Connor, E., Ferguson, T., Eglitis, E., Miatke, A., Simpson, C. E. M., & Maher, C. (2023). Effectiveness of physical activity interventions for improving depression, anxiety and distress: An overview of systematic reviews. *British Journal of Sports Medicine.* https://doi.org/10.1136/bjsports-2022-106195

16 Saloheimo, H. P., Markowitz, J., Saloheimo, T. H., Laitinen, J. J., Sundell, J., Huttunen, M. O., A. Aro, T., Mikkonen, T. N., & O. Katila, H. (2016). Psychotherapy effectiveness for major depression: A randomized trial in a Finnish community. *BMC Psychiatry, 16*(1). https://doi.org/10.1186/s12888-016-0838-1

17 Cuijpers, P., Quero, S., Noma, H., Ciharova, M., Miguel, C., Karyotaki, E., Cipriani, A., Cristea, I. A., & Furukawa, T. A. (2021). Psychotherapies for

depression: A network meta-analysis covering efficacy, acceptability and long-term outcomes of all main treatment types. *World Psychiatry, 20*(2), 283–293. https://doi.org/10.1002/wps.20860

18 Munder, T., Flückiger, C., Leichsenring, F., Abbass, A. A., Hilsenroth, M. J., Luyten, P., Rabung, S., Steinert, C., & Wampold, B. E. (2018). Is psychotherapy effective? A re-analysis of treatments for depression. *Epidemiology and Psychiatric Sciences, 28*(03), 268–274. https://doi.org/10.1017/s2045796018000355

19 Qi, H., Ning, Y., Li, J., Guo, S., Chi, M., Gao, M., Guo, Y., Yang, Y., Peng, H., & Wu, K. (2014). Gray matter volume abnormalities in depressive patients with and without anxiety disorders. *Medicine, 93*(29). https://doi.org/10.1097/md.0000000000000345

20 MediLexicon International. (n.d.). *Severe depression linked with inflammation in the brain.* Medical News Today. Retrieved March 1, 2023, from https://www.medicalnewstoday.com/articles/288715

21 Burtscher, J., Niedermeier, M., Hüfner, K., van den Burg, E., Kopp, M., Stoop, R., Burtscher, M., Gatterer, H., & Millet, G. P. (2022). The interplay of hypoxic and mental stress: Implications for anxiety and Depressive Disorders. *Neuroscience & Biobehavioral Reviews, 138*, 104718. https://doi.org/10.1016/j.neubiorev.2022.104718

22 Lee, C.-H., & Giuliani, F. (2019). The role of inflammation in depression and fatigue. *Frontiers in Immunology, 10.* https://doi.org/10.3389/fimmu.2019.01696

23 Cañas-González, B., Fernández-Nistal, A., Ramírez, J. M., & Martínez-Fernández, V. (2020). Influence of stress and depression on the immune system in patients evaluated in an anti-aging unit. *Frontiers in Psychology, 11.* https://doi.org/10.3389/fpsyg.2020.01844

24 Whisman, M. A. (2001). The association between depression and marital dissatisfaction. *Marital and Family Processes in Depression: A Scientific Foundation for Clinical Practice.*, 3–24. https://doi.org/10.1037/10350-001

25 Salk, R. H., Hyde, J. S., & Abramson, L. Y. (2017). Gender differences in depression in representative national samples: Meta-analyses of diagnoses and symptoms. *Psychological Bulletin, 143*(8), 783–822. https://doi.org/10.1037/bul0000102

26 Greenwood, S. (2023, March 1). *The enduring grip of the gender pay gap*. Pew Research Center's Social & Demographic Trends Project. Retrieved March 1, 2023, from https://www.pewresearch.org/social-trends/2023/03/01/the-enduring-grip-of-the-gender-pay-gap/

27 Montúfar, V. (2018, December 10). *Women are most likely to be affected by violence in the workplace, but we are all victims*. PSI. Retrieved March 1, 2023, from https://www.world-psi.org/en/women-are-most-likely-be-affected-violence-workplace-we-are-all-victims

28 Johnson, D. P., & Whisman, M. A. (2013). Gender differences in rumination: A meta-analysis. *Personality and Individual Differences*, *55*(4), 367–374. https://doi.org/10.1016/j.paid.2013.03.019

29 Nolen-Hoeksema, S. (2000). The role of rumination in depressive disorders and mixed anxiety/depressive symptoms. *Journal of Abnormal Psychology*, *109*(3), 504–511. https://doi.org/10.1037/0021-843x.109.3.504

30 Treynor, W., Gonzalez, R., & Nolen-Hoeksema, S. (2003). Rumination Reconsidered: A Psychometric Analysis. *Cognitive Therapy and Research*, *27*(3), 247–259. https://doi.org/10.1023/a:1023910315561

31 Pederson, L., & Pederson, C. S. (2017). Module 1: Dialectics. In *The Expanded Dialectical Behavior Therapy Skills Training Manual: DBT for Self-Help, and Individual and Group Treatment Settings* (pp. 41–42). PESI Publishing & Media.

32 Lynch, T. R., Morse, J. Q., Mendelson, T., & Robins, C. J. (2003). Dialectical behavior therapy for depressed older adults: a randomized pilot study. *The American Journal of Geriatric Psychiatry: Official Journal of the American Association for Geriatric Psychiatry*, *11*(1), 33–45.

33 Feldman, G., Harley, R., Kerrigan, M., Jacobo, M., & Fava, M. (2009). Change in emotional processing during a dialectical behavior therapy-based Skills Group for major depressive disorder. *Behaviour Research and Therapy*, *47*(4), 316–321. https://doi.org/10.1016/j.brat.2009.01.005

34 Saito, E., Tebbett-Mock, A. A., & McGee, M. (2020). Dialectical behavior therapy decreases depressive symptoms among adolescents in an acute-care inpatient unit. *Journal of Child and Adolescent Psychopharmacology*, *30*(4), 244–249. https://doi.org/10.1089/cap.2019.0149

35 Zaccaro, A., Piarulli, A., Laurino, M., Garbella, E., Menicucci, D., Neri, B., & Gemignani, A. (2018). How breath-control can change your life: A systematic review on psycho-physiological correlates of slow breathing. *Frontiers in Human Neuroscience, 12.* https://doi.org/10.3389/fnhum.2018.00353

36 Valenza, M. C., Valenza-Peña, G., Torres-Sánchez, I., González-Jiménez, E., Conde-Valero, A., & Valenza-Demet, G. (2013). Effectiveness of controlled breathing techniques on anxiety and depression in hospitalized patients with COPD: A randomized clinical trial. *Respiratory Care, 59*(2), 209–215. https://doi.org/10.4187/respcare.02565

37 Kyriakoulis, P., Kyrios, M., Nardi, A. E., Freire, R. C., & Schier, M. (2021). The implications of the diving response in reducing panic symptoms. *Frontiers in Psychiatry, 12.* https://doi.org/10.3389/fpsyt.2021.784884

38 Ito, E., Shima, R., & Yoshioka, T. (2019). A novel role of oxytocin: Oxytocin-induced well-being in humans. *Biophysics and Physicobiology, 16,* 132–139. https://doi.org/10.2142/biophysico.16.0_132

39 *Serotonin: What is it, Function & Levels*. Cleveland Clinic. (n.d.). Retrieved March 1, 2023, from https://my.clevelandclinic.org/health/articles/22572-serotonin

40 Weir, K. (2011, December). *The exercise effect*. Monitor on Psychology. Retrieved February 1, 2023, from https://www.apa.org/monitor/2011/12/exercise

41 Puetz, T. W. (2006). Physical activity and feelings of energy and fatigue. *Sports Medicine, 36*(9), 767–780. https://doi.org/10.2165/00007256-200636090-00004

42 Dossey, L. (2018). The Helper's High. *EXPLORE, 14*(6), 393–399. https://doi.org/10.1016/j.explore.2018.10.003

43 Ellison, C. G., Bradshaw, M., Flannelly, K. J., & Galek, K. C. (2014). Prayer, attachment to god, and symptoms of anxiety-related disorders among U.S. adults. *Sociology of Religion, 75*(2), 208–233. https://doi.org/10.1093/socrel/srt079

44 Author, P. C. G. (2014, September 18). *Prayer and mental health: What does research say?* Psych Central. Retrieved April 1, 2023, from https://psychcentral.com/blog/new-study-examines-the-effects-of-prayer-on-mental-health

45 Pally, R., & Olds, D. (2018). Emotional processing: The mind-body connection. *The Mind-Brain Relationship*, 73–104. https://doi.org/10.4324/9780429482465-4

46 Seward, E. A., & Kelly, S. (2016). Dietary nitrogen alters codon bias and genome composition in parasitic microorganisms. *Genome Biology*, *17*(1). https://doi.org/10.1186/s13059-016-1087-9

47 Lane, M. M., Gamage, E., Travica, N., Dissanayaka, T., Ashtree, D. N., Gauci, S., Lotfaliany, M., O'Neil, A., Jacka, F. N., & Marx, W. (2022). Ultra-processed food consumption and mental health: A systematic review and meta-analysis of observational studies. *Nutrients*, *14*(13), 2568. https://doi.org/10.3390/nu14132568

48 Firth, J., Gangwisch, J. E., Borsini, A., Wootton, R. E., & Mayer, E. A. (2020). Food and mood: How do diet and nutrition affect mental wellbeing? *BMJ*, m2382. https://doi.org/10.1136/bmj.m2382

49 Keyes, K. M., Allel, K., Staudinger, U. M., Ornstein, K. A., & Calvo, E. (2019). Alcohol consumption predicts incidence of depressive episodes across 10 years among older adults in 19 countries. *International Review of Neurobiology*, 1–38. https://doi.org/10.1016/bs.irn.2019.09.001

50 Chattu, V. K., Aeri, B. T., & Khanna, P. (2019). Nutritional aspects of depression in adolescents - A systematic review. *International Journal of Preventive Medicine*, *10*(1), 42. https://doi.org/10.4103/ijpvm.ijpvm_400_18

51 Nawrot, P., Jordan, S., Eastwood, J., Rotstein, J., Hugenholtz, A., & Feeley, M. (2003). Effects of caffeine on human health. *Food Additives and Contaminants*, *20*(1), 1–30. https://doi.org/10.1080/0265203021000007840

52 Higdon, J. V., & Frei, B. (2006). Coffee and health: A review of recent human research. *Critical Reviews in Food Science and Nutrition*, *46*(2), 101–123. https://doi.org/10.1080/10408390500400009

53 Watson, N. F., Badr, M. S., Belenky, G., Bliwise, D. L., Buxton, O. M., Buysse, D., Dinges, D. F., Gangwisch, J., Grandner, M. A., Kushida, C., Malhotra, R. K., Martin, J. L., Patel, S. R., Quan, S., & Tasali, E. (2015). Recommended amount of sleep for a healthy adult: A joint consensus statement of the American Academy of Sleep Medicine and Sleep Research Society. *SLEEP*. https://doi.org/10.5665/sleep.4716

54 Wang, K., Yang, Y., Zhang, T., Ouyang, Y., Liu, B., & Luo, J. (2020). The relationship between physical activity and emotional intelligence in college students: The mediating role of self-efficacy. *Frontiers in Psychology, 11*. https://doi.org/10.3389/fpsyg.2020.00967

55 Li, J., Huang, Z., Si, W., & Shao, T. (2022). The effects of physical activity on positive emotions in children and adolescents: A systematic review and meta-analysis. *International Journal of Environmental Research and Public Health, 19*(21), 14185. https://doi.org/10.3390/ijerph192114185

56 Segrin, C. (1996). Interpersonal communication problems associated with depression and loneliness. *Handbook of Communication and Emotion*, 215–242. https://doi.org/10.1016/b978-012057770-5/50010-2

57 Chandrasekaran, B., Van Engen, K., Xie, Z., Beevers, C. G., & Maddox, W. T. (2014). Influence of depressive symptoms on speech perception in adverse listening conditions. *Cognition and Emotion, 29*(5), 900–909. https://doi.org/10.1080/02699931.2014.944106

58 Martínez, R., Senra, C., Fernández-Rey, J., & Merino, H. (2020). Sociotropy, autonomy and emotional symptoms in patients with major depression or generalized anxiety: The mediating role of rumination and immature defenses. *International Journal of Environmental Research and Public Health, 17*(16), 5716. https://doi.org/10.3390/ijerph17165716

59 Orth, U., & Robins, R. W. (2013). Understanding the link between low self-esteem and depression. *Current Directions in Psychological Science, 22*(6), 455–460. https://doi.org/10.1177/0963721413492763

60 Lee, J. Y., Patel, M., & Scior, K. (2023). Self-esteem and its relationship with depression and anxiety in adults with intellectual disabilities: A systematic literature review. *Journal of Intellectual Disability Research*. https://doi.org/10.1111/jir.13025

61 Groth, A. (2012, July 24). *You're the average of the five people you spend the most time with*. Business Insider. Retrieved April 21, 2022, from https://www.businessinsider.com/jim-rohn-youre-the-average-of-the-five-people-you-spend-the-most-time-with-2012-7

62 Kroenke, K., Spitzer, R. L., & Williams, J. B. (2001). The PHQ-9. *Journal of General Internal Medicine, 16*(9), 606–613. https://doi.org/10.1046/j.1525-1497.2001.016009606.x

Indexes

Acceptance and Change, 222, 338
Anger, 189, 195, 213, 285
Bipolar Disorder, 200
Borderline Personality Disorder, 217
BPD, 217, 218, 222
Brain chemistry, 192
Brain Inflammation, 210
Brain Shrinkage, 210
Brain Stimulation Therapy, 203
CBT, 186, 207, 208, 217
Cognitive Behavior Therapy, 186, 207
Communication, 192, 207, 212, 313, 314, 315, 316, 352
Compulsions, 182, 183
Content Warning, 188, 196, 199, 213, 253
DBT, 186, 188, 200, 208, 217, 218, 222, 223, 227, 232, 233, 236, 254, 263, 271, 315, 337, 338, 349
Depression, 181, 184, 186, 187, 188, 190, 191, 192, 193, 194, 195, 196, 198, 199, 200, 201, 202, 203, 204, 205, 206, 207, 209, 210, 211, 212, 213, 214, 215, 217, 222, 223, 240, 252, 253, 261, 263, 266, 271, 279, 280, 281, 282, 285, 287, 288, 291, 298, 301, 303, 305, 306, 309, 310, 314, 315, 320, 329, 331, 332, 335, 336, 337, 338, 339, 341, 342, 346, 347, 348, 350, 351, 352
Dialectical Behavior Therapy, 186, 188, 208, 217, 349
Dialectics, 218, 331
Distress, 232, 252, 254, 296, 338
Distress Tolerance, 232, 252, 254, 296, 338
Dr. Marsha Linehan, 217, 218, 223
Dysthymia, 198
ECT, 204, 205
EFT, 207
Electroconvulsive Therapy, 204
Emotion Regulation, 232, 236, 285, 287, 338
Emotion-Focused Therapy, 207
Emptiness, 194, 288
Exercise, 196, 205, 206, 266, 299, 311
GAD, 182, 183, 184, 186, 201, 337
Gender inequality, 215
General Anxiety Disorder, 182
Genetics, 192, 346
Guilt, 194, 197, 213, 306
Gut health, 336
Hopelessness, 191, 194, 195, 196, 197, 198, 252
Hormones, 214
Hypomania, 200
Inflammation, 211, 336
Interpersonal Effectiveness, 232, 313, 315, 338
Interpersonal Psychotherapy, 207
IPT, 207
Irritability, 195, 200
Isolation, 195
Journaling, 342
Life events, 192
Light therapy, 205
Limited Oxygen Intake, 211
Loss of energy, 194
Low depression, 341
Major Depressive Disorder, 190, 198, 337, 349
Mammalian Dive Response, 261
Mania, 200, 201
MDD, 190, 198, 211, 214, 337
MDR, 261
Medical conditions, 193
Medication, 193, 202
Mindfulness, 232, 233, 234, 247, 268, 288, 293, 320, 338
Moderate depression, 341

Morning Ritual, 183, 197
Nutrition, 335
Nutritional psychiatry, 335
Obsessive-Compulsive Disorder, 182
OCD, 182, 183, 184, 186, 197, 198, 209, 223, 281, 337
Patient Health Questionnaire-9, 339
PDD, 198
Persistent Depressive Disorder, 198
PHQ-9, 339, 352
Postpartum Depression, 198
PPD, 198
Psychomotor agitation, 195
Psychotherapy, 206, 347
Psychotic Depression, 200
Radical Acceptance, 223, 224, 225, 226, 230, 280
SAD, 198, 200
Sadness, 191
Safe Space, 188
Safety, 188
Schizophrenia, 217, 218
Seasonal Affective Disorder, 198, 200, 205
Self-care, 189, 329, 333
Self-esteem, 329
Self-hate, 194
Self-loathing, 194
Self-mutilation, 195
Self-Perception, 329
Severe depression, 341
Sleep, 351
Sleeping problems, 194
Stress, 252
Substance abuse, 193
Suicide ideation, 195
Talk Therapy, 206
TMS, 204
Transcranial Magnetic Stimulation, 204
Trauma, 192
Turning the Mind, 255
Vagus Nerve Stimulation, 204
VNS, 204
WHO, 190
Worksheet
  Radical Acceptance, 226
Worksheet: 4-7-8 Breathing, 240
Worksheet: Acceptance and Change, 230
Worksheet: ACCEPTS, 271
Worksheet: Accumulate, Build, Cope (ABC), 303
Worksheet: Active Listening, 316
Worksheet: Attitude of Gratitude, 249
Worksheet: Belly Breathing, 237
Worksheet: Body Scan Muscle Relaxation, 270
Worksheet: Box Breathing, 239
Worksheet: Build Positive Experiences (BPE), 301
Worksheet: Check the Facts, 294
Worksheet: DEARMAN, 318
Worksheet: Desire to Change, 229
Worksheet: Equal Breathing (Sama Vritti), 238
Worksheet: FAST, 325
Worksheet: GIVE, 322
Worksheet: Grounding Using Your 5 Senses, 257
Worksheet: IMPROVE, 276
Worksheet: Into the Cold, 261
Worksheet: Loving Kindness Meditation, 244
Worksheet: Meditation 101, 243
Worksheet: Mindful Breathing Reflection, 242
Worksheet: Nadi Shodhana (Alternate Nostril Breathing), 241
Worksheet: Opposite Action, 298
Worksheet: PLEASE, 308
Worksheet: Radical Acceptance When Feeling Depressed, 280
Worksheet: Self-Soothing Using Your 5 Senses, 259

Worksheet: STOP, 263
Worksheet: The Happy Place, 260
Worksheet: The Silver Lining, 221
Worksheet: The Wave, 292
Worksheet: TIPP, 266
Worksheet: Turning the Mind, 255
Worksheet: Understanding and Labeling Your Emotions, 288
Worksheet: Walking Meditation, 247
Worksheet: Wrong AND Right, 220
World Health Organization, 190, 311, 346

The DBT Anger Management Workbook

A Complete Dialectical Behavior Therapy Action Plan For Mastering Your Emotions & Finding Your Inner Zen | Practical DBT Skills For Men & Women

By Barrett Huang
https://barretthuang.com/

Contents

Contents.. 357

Introduction 360
   Who Should Read This Book   364
   Goals of This Book   364
   How to Use This Book   364

What is Dialectical Behavior Therapy?........................366
   DBT Fundamentals   370
      Acceptance and Change   370
   DBT Core Skills   375
      Mindfulness   375
      Distress Tolerance   382
      Emotion Regulation   386
      Interpersonal Effectiveness   394
   DBT for Anger Management   406

What is Anger? 409
   Anger 101   409
      Amygdala Hijack   410
   The Anger Cycle   411
   The 10 Different Types of Anger   415
   Male and Female Anger   417
      Brain Biology   417
      Societal Norms   417
      Premenstrual Syndrome   418
      Menopause   419

Why Are You Angry? 421
   The Source of Your Anger   421
      Worksheet: Anger Triggers 1   425
      Worksheet: Anger Triggers 2   426

Worksheet: Anger Iceberg	429
How Your Anger Grows	430
How Do You Express Your Anger?	433

The Costs of Your Anger 435

Physical Costs of Anger	435
Emotional Costs of Anger	436
Mental Costs of Anger	437
Social Costs of Anger	438
Financial Costs of Anger	438
Relationship Costs of Anger	439

REAL LIFE Tools to Effectively Manage Your Anger 443

Anger and Vulnerability	443
Top 8 Tips to Be More Vulnerable	444
Worksheet: Vulnerability List	450
Mindfulness Skills for Anger Management	454
Worksheet: Mindful Body Scanning (Anger Observation)	455
Worksheet: Mindfully Angry (Anger Description)	457
Distress Tolerance Skills for Anger Management	458
Worksheet: Radical Acceptance	459
Worksheet: STOP	465
Worksheet: ACCEPTS	468
Emotion Regulation Skills for Anger Management	472
Worksheet: BPE	473
Worksheet: PLEASE	475
Worksheet: COPE AHEAD	481
Interpersonal Effectiveness Skills for Anger Management	483
How to Set Boundaries	484
Worksheet: FAST	488
Anger and Unfairness	490

    How to Prevent Yourself from Exploding 491

    Healthy Ways to Communicate Your Anger 493

Living a Life Less Angry 495

  HANGRY is Real 495

  Get Enough Sleep! 496

  Be Accountable for Your Own Emotions 498

  Setbacks 499

  Let It Go 500

  Live a Positive Life 502

Conclusion 505

Appendix A – Miller-Patton Anger Self-Assessment 506

Review Request 511

Further Reading 512

About the Author 513

Referenc 514

Indexes 520

Introduction

"Anger is an acid that can do more harm to the vessel in which it is stored than to anything on which it is poured."
— Mark Twain

When I was 16 years old, I had a part-time job at Pizza Hut. I was happy to have that job because I was saving up for extra spending money for college.

At one point, I was working at a different location, covering for someone. I don't exactly remember why, but it was SUPER BUSY one Friday evening. There wasn't enough staff to handle the deluge of orders, so the lines kept growing, and people who had already ordered were becoming more and more impatient because their food was taking too long to arrive.

I had the great luck of being at the front taking orders. This meant I was mostly the recipient of all those impatient glares and occasional rude remarks, so I would call out to the back every now and then to follow up on orders.

I don't know what exactly triggered me. I don't remember a specific remark or anything. But I guess I was flustered because I suddenly whirled around to my colleagues at the back and SCREAMED at the top of my lungs that they should HURRY.THE.H***.UP!!! I then grabbed one of the soft drinks on the tray in front of me, threw it against Jack§ , and asked him in a VERY loud voice for everyone to hear if he was stupid or something because he was holding everyone up (not true at all).

---

§ Not his real name.

Everyone in the store became quiet. I could feel my face all red and my jaw clenching. I angrily turned back to the next customer in line, and to this day, I remember him looking at me and saying, "*Dude, chill out. It is all good.*" I proceeded as if nothing had happened, and the store slowly returned to normal.

As what often happens, I felt a deep sense of guilt, shame, and remorse after lashing out. After the shift, I looked for Jack§ to apologize, but he had already gone home. The following day I was back at the Pizza Hut store where I originally worked, and that was that. (Miraculously, no one reported me.)

No, I didn't look for Jack§ to say sorry. I wasn't brave enough for that, but every time I remember that incident, even now, 20 years later, I still cringe in shame.

I would be lying if I said that was the only time I lashed out. Looking back, **I was a very angry teen**.

I was angry at my parents. I am angry about why they bothered to migrate from China to Canada 'to have a better future' when, in my eyes, all they did was live in the past. As a result, I felt that our family never really belonged in Canada.

I was angry at the loneliness I felt every day at school because I didn't have a single friend. I am angry for being different from everyone else.

I was angry at myself because I could feel the anger underneath my skin's surface. My mind recognizes it is not right, and my heart doesn't want me to be angry—but I can't help it.

I was angry at the world. I believed life was unfair, and I didn't see many prospects ahead of me. I was not a teen excited about the future.

I wish I could tell you, dear reader, that a light bulb moment came, and I miraculously stopped being angry. But that's far from the truth.

In reality, I was suffering from a host of mental health issues for most of my adolescent life, and ANGER was one of the ways I manifested my mental health problems.

You see, my father had a hoarding disorder. He kept everything and couldn't let go of anything, so our home was one chaotic mess! He also had Obsessive-Compulsive Disorder (OCD). He always needed things to be a certain way and in a certain spot. He would get very angry and aggressive if things weren't in the right order.

On the other hand, my mother had General Anxiety Disorder (GAD). She was always worrying about... well, pretty much everything. She was always afraid something bad would happen. And since life is not all sunshine and rainbows, when something negative did happen, my mother would be the first one to blame everyone else. She was always playing the victim.

This was my home situation. This was my normal.

As I went to school and saw other kids, I noticed how different things were for other people. I started to compare, resulting in A LOT of conflict and unrest inside me. Since my parents were emotionally absent and I had no friends, there was no one to ask for help. (Truth be told, I wouldn't even know where to begin to describe things!)

Ultimately, it is no surprise that I grew up as an adult with OCD and GAD. I also suffered from depression. But underneath it all, ANGER was always present.

Mostly, my anger was just underneath the surface. Other times though, it would erupt like a volcano, and I would get aggressive towards others. This, of course, would be followed by extreme remorse, which fueled my anxiety and depression even more! I was caught in a loop of anger and misery.

I didn't begin to heal until I left home for college.

At this time, I knew deep down that something was not quite right and realized I needed help. I started seeing professionals in the mental health field, and I was prescribed anti-anxiety medication, which helped me cope a bit with everyday life. But this was just the beginning of my journey.

Again, I wish I could tell you I was on the right path to mental healing from the get-go, but I wasn't. It is true what they say: healing is not a linear process; there are many ups and downs. But this I know to be true: *every step is progress*.

I tried various types of therapy. But the one that worked for me, allowing me to cope and overcome my various mental health and anger issues, is the one I am sharing with you in this book—Dialectical Behavior Therapy (DBT).

DBT really unlocked something inside me. It is very different from the other types of therapy I tried, and I credit it for teaching me the techniques and skills I so desperately needed in life. Today, my anxiety, OCD, depression, and anger problems no longer take over my life.

My journey has inspired me to learn more about the mind and behavior. So I majored in psychology and have completed the DBT Skills certificate program of Dr. Marsha Linehan, the founder of DBT. I have also deepened my knowledge of philosophy, happiness, and self-improvement. Still, I'd like to emphasize that the contents of this book draw primarily from my personal struggles with anger and how DBT helped me cope and manage it. I sincerely hope that it helps you as you take your journey to healing.

Who Should Read This Book

This book is for anyone who's struggling with anger issues in their lives. Please note that anger in itself has a purpose. So the goal is not to completely get rid of it. However, there's a line between healthy anger and problematic anger, anger and rage, anger and out-of-control fury, anger and aggression, and so on.

Unhealthy anger is very draining, and as mentioned in the quote above, it does more damage to you (the vessel of anger) than your intended targets. In short, your anger hurts YOU more than anyone else. This book is for those who don't want to suffer the weight and burden of their anger anymore.

Goals of This Book

This book aims to teach you DBT skills for dealing with and managing anger so that it does not control your life. However, it is also critical to identify the source of your anger. Why are you angry? What (or who) are your triggers? What exactly does your rage mean? Once you understand your anger inside out, you'll find it easier to apply the DBT skills you'll learn in this book to manage your anger.

How to Use This Book

The first part of this book discusses dialectical behavior therapy (e.g., its history, what it entails, what skills are involved, etc.) so that you understand what makes this particular therapy different from other types of therapy. It is important to remember that learning is more than just knowing something. Real learning happens when you apply, use, and engage with your knowledge. As such, DBT worksheets will be provided at the start and throughout this book so that you fully adopt DBT skills in your life.

The second part of this book is all about anger. Anger is not just an emotion or feeling but a *reaction*. It is an emotional, mental, and physical reaction. To what? You'll find out as you go through the pages of this book. This part will truly be a journey within yourself.

The final part of this book is where it all comes together. It is how to use DBT skills to cope, manage, and eventually let go of out-of-control or destructive anger in your life.

Anxiety, loneliness, and anger dominated my childhood and adolescent years. As I grew older, my anger took center stage more and more. I never wanted to accept it, but it is true: it is easier to be mad than to be sad.

Fortunately, I sought help and was lucky enough to eventually find the therapy that worked for me. Today, whenever I look back, I no longer feel rage. I only feel empathy for my younger self.

So let this be my message to you before you read further:

PLEASE BE KIND TO YOURSELF

You deserve kindness, understanding, and compassion, just like everyone else. You are not your anger. Your anger is a reaction to something. And during this journey, you will figure it all out. But don't rush anything, put too much pressure on yourself, or go on this path for the sake of others. Just be kind to yourself and focus your time and energy on making yourself feel better. The rest will follow.

What is Dialectical Behavior Therapy?

"You have the power to heal your life, and you need to know that. We think so often that we are helpless, but we're not. We always have the power of our minds... claim and consciously use your power." – Louise L. Hay

Dialectical Behavior Therapy, or DBT, was developed by Dr. Marsha Linehan[1], Ph.D., in the 1980s as a result of her and her colleagues' work with patients with borderline personality disorder (BPD). Working with BPD patients who were suicidal, Linehan realized that, unlike cognitive behavior therapy (CBT), which focuses primarily on detecting negative thought patterns and changing them to positive ones (*change-focused*), it is far more effective to employ two opposing (*dialectical*) strategies: Acceptance AND Change.

But perhaps what also makes DBT so effective is that Dr. Marsha Linehan suffered from mental health issues herself.[2]

ACCEPTANCE   **CHANGE**

In the 1960s, she was sent to a clinic for "extreme social withdrawal" at just 17 years of age. According to Dr. Linehan, she engaged in various self-harming activities while in the clinic, such as cutting and burning her skin using cigarettes. As such, she was kept in isolation for her own safety.

In the 1960s, bipolar disorder (BPD) was not yet known, so she was misdiagnosed with schizophrenia and aggressively medicated for it (which, of course, did not help because that was not the mental health issue from which she suffered).

Dr. Linehan was eventually released from the clinic after 26 months, but she was far from better. However, about four years later, she had a sudden insight while praying.

She suddenly realized that she had been attempting to end her life multiple times because the gap between the person she wanted to be and the person she actually was was so huge that it filled her with hopelessness and desperation. She so badly wanted to live a better life, but she didn't know how to bridge that gap... until she realized that Change itself is not enough.

She should also ACCEPT her reality AS IS. No judgments. Her behavior, though destructive, made sense because she was suffering from the weight of her reality at the time. Dr. Linehan would later call this epiphany Radical Acceptance.

This part of DBT—Radical Acceptance—is so different from other types of therapy because all it entails is for you to acknowledge your present reality. There's no need to understand it, evaluate it, judge it, twist it, overthink it, or fight it.

RADICAL ACCEPTANCE = IT IS WHAT IT IS

When I first learned about Radical Acceptance, I was taken completely aback. So many of the other therapies I tried focused on answering, *"why are you like this?"* as the first step to healing.

Please don't get me wrong. It is important to understand yourself. But by focusing on *"why are you like this?"* first, it sort of implied that what I was doing was just "wrong". Now, many professionals will argue with this, but as someone who experienced mental health issues, I am saying that this is MY experience. This is how I felt during this phase of therapy. (And please, DO NOT let anyone invalidate your experiences! I had to learn that the hard way.)

I also noticed that the more time I spent attempting to answer the question, *"why am I like this?"* the more time I spent in that frame of mind. So, even though I knew it was a step toward recovery, I didn't feel any better while exploring it. (In all honesty, I felt worse at times since revisiting specific events in my life to better understand them merely made me relive all the feelings involved with them, which made me either angrier or even more miserable because I was full of regret.)

In contrast, with Radical Acceptance, I felt free. This is my reality now. Full stop. Now what?

Well, this brings us to the second foundation of DBT—Change.

People don't realize that most of us with mental health problems and anger issues know deep down that we should not think, say, or act the way we do. We can't help but react that way, but a little voice in our heads says, *"Well, that could be better."* But, how?! Isn't that the real question? So many people say, *"Change for the better"*. My struggle was always the HOW of things. Fortunately, DBT showed me how.

In addition to accepting her reality, Dr. Linehan realized that real change is possible by learning new behaviors.

CHANGE = LEARN NEW BEHAVIORS TO LIVE BETTER

Dr. Linehan believed that by changing how we act (or react) to situations, we can change how we feel about them in time. When I first learned this, it made perfect sense to me.

For the most part, we are the by-product of our genes (*nature*) and our environment (*nurture*). There's massive debate over which is more predominant, but I have always been a proponent of nature AND nurture. We are influenced by both. But the *nurture* part that's *conditioning,* and research shows that we can condition ourselves to do anything.[3]

So, DBT's CHANGE principles are the HOWs that you need to cope with and manage your anger issues.

DBT Fundamentals

Dialectic means seeing things from multiple perspectives. In Dialectical Behavior Therapy, Dr. Linehan defines it as "a synthesis or integration of opposites".[4] In particular, it is the synthesis of Acceptance and Change.

Acceptance and Change

Note that there are no first and second steps here. Acceptance and Change (or desire to change) can happen simultaneously. At first glance, this may seem impossible, but is it? A person can be gentle and firm at the same time; someone can exhibit the characteristics of a team player and a team leader at the same time; a person can be angry and still show compassion at the same time.

So, this is the goal of DBT: Accepting your emotions about a situation at any given moment while simultaneously Changing the behaviors that cause you further suffering.

Here's how I put this into practice: I moved away to go to college, but that doesn't mean I never went home for the holidays. My father was still a hoarder suffering from OCD, and my mother was still a woman with anxiety who treated me like a child. For many years, this caused my depression and anger problems to worsen, so I went home less and less.

However, after learning about DBT, my mindset changed. Whenever I went back home, and something unpleasant happened, Radical Acceptance would kick in. I'd just take a moment to acknowledge my anger. Change would then follow in the sense that I would NOT react the same way as I used to because now I know that if

I stay in that anger or do something that feeds that anger, I am just prolonging my own suffering.

Before DBT (teen years): Mom enters my room without knocking, re-arranges the papers on my desk, and throws stuff she thinks is useless (oh yes, THAT happened). Since there IS logic to the madness on my desk, even if she doesn't see it, I would get very angry, say hurtful words, and sometimes in a fit of rage, I would be like that *Tasmanian Devil* cartoon character and deliberately wreck my room. Since my mom loves to play the victim, a litany of all their sacrifices would come out. This, in turn, would make me angrier or fill me with remorse (sometimes both). The whole event would, of course, hang like a dark cloud over the family over the holidays, and sometimes, I'd carry it for days on end back at my college dorm. (See? I was prolonging my suffering.)

After DBT (adult years): Mom went to visit my apartment while I was out. It is normal for Asian parents to have keys to their children's homes. What was not normal was when my mom went through my kitchen cupboards and threw out what she considered unhealthy food. When I came back home and saw my cupboards cleared out of all my favorite food, I excused myself. I went to the bathroom to splash cold water all over my face and neck (a DBT technique I'll explain later), and as I looked at myself in the mirror, I made a mental note to install a lockable pantry door where I could stash all my stuff. The End.

Oh, I am not saying it was easy or that things improved overnight. However, by implementing the new behaviors I learned from DBT, many aspects of my life improved, not just my relationship with my parents but also my relationships with colleagues, friends, partners, and, most importantly, myself.

One of the things I truly appreciate about DBT is that it is not all just theory. It offers many exercises so that we can truly understand and adopt its principles. The following are the first of many DBT worksheets throughout this book. I encourage you to accomplish them not just once but over and over until the DBT way of thinking becomes second nature to you.

Worksheet: Acceptance and Change

Everything starts with Acceptance AND Change. The following is an example of how you can start applying these DBT fundamentals in your life.

SELF-ACCEPTANCE: Accept today's reality AS IS.
DESIRE TO CHANGE: Set yourself up to welcome change.
DECLARATION: Acknowledge today and what you want for tomorrow.

SELF-ACCEPTANCE

I AM ANGRY right now.

I AM DOING MY BEST. THAT'S ENOUGH.

Things are not going as planned. That's okay.

It's okay to feel this way.

My anger makes sense to me right now. avalid.

DECLARATION:

"I accept myself as who I am right now. I'm like this for a reason even though I don't know why. What I do know is that I don't feel happy or fulfilled living this way. This is not my best life. So I'm opening myself to learning new things to increase my happiness."

DESIRE TO CHANGE:

I am not as happy as I know I could be.

I AM OPEN TO CHANGE.

My ANGER is not who I am. I want to explore who I am.

I will not feel guilty for wanting to be better.

There's nothing wrong with wanting 'more'.

Now, it is your turn!

SELF-ACCEPTANCE: Write statements acknowledging your circumstances at the moment.

DESIRE TO CHANGE: Write statements that affirm your openness and willingness to change for the better.

DECLARATION: State your acceptance of today AND your desire for a better life tomorrow.

         SELF-ACCEPTANCE: **DESIRE TO CHANGE:**

                                  DECLARATION:

DBT Core Skills

DBT is composed of four primary skills: *Mindfulness*, *Distress Tolerance*, *Emotion Regulation,* and *Interpersonal Effectiveness*.

As the above image implies, Acceptance is made possible by adopting *Mindfulness* and *Distress Tolerance* skills, while Change happens by learning *Emotion Regulation* and *Interpersonal Skills.*

Mindfulness

Say Mindfulness, and most people would immediately have a vision of someone meditating on a mat with their eyes closed and their legs crossed. But there's a difference between the two: mindfulness is a state of mind, while meditation is a practice.

Mindfulness is a state of awareness. You are 'awake' and fully present in the moment (not distracted), whatever the situation, whatever you're doing. Meditation is a practice that helps you become more mindful.

In DBT, Mindfulness is split into two aspects – WHAT and HOW.

WHAT Skills

These skills deal with <u>what you need to do to be more mindful</u>.

1. **Observe**: Pay attention to what is going on inside and outside you. Take note of what you're feeling.
2. **Describe**: Explain what you see (observe) in your own words.
3. **Participate**: Be in the moment to get the most out of the experience. You probably don't even notice it anymore, but you're doing A LOT of things simultaneously. For example, you're barely awake, but you're already (1) reaching for your phone while (2) thinking about your work deadlines and (3) your first meeting of the day, while (4) worrying if the kids did their assignments. When was the last time you just focused on waking up?!

HOW Skills

These skills focus on <u>how you can be more mindful every day</u>.

4. **Non-Judgmentally**: When we are mindful of something, we don't need to label or judge it. We simply observe.
5. **One-Mindfully**: Pay attention to one thing at a time. Don't multitask when it comes to awareness.
6. **Effectively**: Evaluate what works best for you today. Things that worked for you in the past may no longer be effective for you. Learn to let go of these "old systems" and do what works for you now.

Mindfulness WHAT and HOW skills aim to educate us on how to notice and experience reality AS IS, to be less judgmental, and to effectively live in the moment.

Worksheet: Mindful Breathing

1) Pick a place where you won't be disturbed.
2) Sit down or lie on a mat or on your bed, whatever is comfortable for you.
3) Close your eyes.
4) Breathe in deeply for a count of four (4), and then exhale for a count of four (4). Do this four (4) more times. (Five rounds in total).
5) On your next inhale, Observe your breath and Describe it.
    - Are you breathing in easily?
    - Do you smell anything? If so, describe the smell. (Important: Describe the smell Non-Judgmentally. Don't give any opinion or say you like the smell or dislike it. Simply describe the smell (e.g., *fresh, floral, citrusy,* etc.)
6) As you exhale, Observe your hands and Describe them.
    - Where are your hands?
    - Are your hands closed? Semi-curled? Palms up? (Important: Remember to observe and describe One-Mindfully. Don't focus on any other part of your body. Focus solely on your hands.

You can stop here or continue this exercise.

For every inhale and exhale, pick something to Observe and Describe, and remember to do so Non-Judgmentally and One-Mindfully. If you ever find your mind wandering, that's okay. Just re-group, re-focus, and get back on track.

Wise Mind

In DBT, Mindfulness is the skill you need to arrive at Wise Mind, which is the middle ground between our emotional and rational minds.

It is said that we make most of our decisions based on emotions.[5] But acting, reacting, or behaving based on feelings alone, especially negative ones, doesn't always bring out the best in us, nor does it lead to the best situations.

The good thing is that Wise Mind is not something we need to create. We all already have it. Think of it as a muscle that we just need to use more often. With constant effort to use it, relying on Wise Mind will become natural to us.

EMOTIONAL MIND:
- feelings
- stress
- anger
- fear
- **acting based solely on emotions**
- judgmental
- opinionated
- reactive or defensive

WISE MIND
- Wise Mind is the balance between your rational and emotional minds.
- Wise Mind honors feelings but bases actions, reactions and decisions on reason or logic.

RATIONAL MIND:
- data
- statistics
- facts
- **acting/reacting based solely on logic**
- focused
- organized
- based on past experience
- non-judgmental

Worksheet: Wise Mind

The goal of **Wise Mind** is to help us make sense of our thoughts and feelings so that we can come up with a balanced (Wise) response to events.

EMOTIONAL MIND:　　　　　　　　**RATIONAL MIND:**

　　　　　　　　WISE MIND
　　　　　Do what is right while
　　　　　　soothing your
　　　　　　　emotions.

What you <u>want</u> to do　　　　　　**What you <u>should</u> do**

1. Think of an event when you regretted your action/reaction/behavior. Be as detailed as possible about the event.

    Example: I shouted at a colleague and stormed out of a meeting because of an argument over our project.

    Your turn:

    _____

    _____

2. Why did you react that way?

   Example: I was frustrated over the lack of progress in the project.

   Your turn:

   _____
   _____
   _____

3. Why do you regret your action/reaction/behavior?

   Example: It didn't help the situation at all, and my co-workers started avoiding me.

   Your turn:

   _____
   _____
   _____

4. What would you do differently?

   Example: Instead of blaming my colleague and getting angry, I would help come up with solutions. That way, the people would be more motivated about the project.

   Your turn:

   _____
   _____
   _____

Notes: Question #1 above points to a time when you were in Emotion Mind. With the benefit of hindsight, Question #4 points to Wise Mind. Think of other situations when you acted based on Emotion Mind and what you would do differently. With constant reflection, you're practicing how to use Wise Mind.

Distress Tolerance

Distress Tolerance is our ability to face and effectively handle stressful, upsetting, and difficult situations.

When faced with difficult situations, some people tend to ignore, deny or escape what's happening. This may work temporarily, but in the long run, it causes you more harm and does not equip you with the tools you need to handle future crises. Other people, me included, tend to lash out and do something without thinking of its consequences. Our goal is to feel better immediately, not realizing that we've just made the situation worse.

For example, my OCD and anxiety disorders got so bad that, at one point, I avoided stepping on cracks on the pavement. My every step needed to land perfectly. Otherwise, my day was doomed. And if God forbid, I did step on a line or crack on the floor, I would get very frustrated and angry. I would lash out. It didn't matter where I was or who was in front of me. I'd say something mean or throw a fit, and that was that.

Distress tolerance skills helped me tremendously because they taught me how to endure and handle very upsetting situations without making them worse and to accept reality (life as it is *in the moment*, not forever) even though I can't change it and it is not what I want it to be.

The following exercises (Grounding on page 383 and TIPP on page 266) are some of the first DBT distress tolerance skills I learned. I still use them today whenever I feel very upset about something. I hope they help you too.

Worksheet: Grounding Technique Using Your 5 Senses

Grounding techniques connect you to the present so you can disconnect from your worries. Using your five senses—sight, smell, sound, touch, and taste—is an excellent way to ground yourself. Do this exercise anytime you feel stressed, worried, or anxious.

Remember, there is no right or wrong answer here. Don't evaluate or judge anything. Just provide what's being asked.

List FIVE (5) things you can see right now.

Example: desk lamp, water bottle, computer speakers, board marker, keys

1.
2.
3.
4.
5.

List FOUR (4) things you can touch right now.

Example: plate, spoon, fork, apple

1.
2.
3.
4.

List THREE (3) things you can hear right now.

Example: bird, Spotify music, neighbor

1.
2.
3.

List TWO (2) things you can smell right now.

Example: cologne, coffee

1.
2.

List ONE (1) thing you can taste right now.

Example: gum

1.

If you're still feeling in distress, do the exercise again or list down AS MANY things as you can per sense.

Worksheet: TIPP

The following Distress Tolerance exercise focuses on altering your body's chemistry in order to counteract unfavorable or undesirable cravings or emotions. You'll discover that altering your physiological state will enable you to alter your emotional state more quickly.

Temperature: Anger makes your temperature rise. Counter this by cooling yourself. You can splash your face with cold water, go out in the cold, or you can put your head inside the refrigerator for a few seconds.

Intense Exercise: Release your anger by exercising intensively. If you don't have much time, apps like the *5 Minute Home Workouts* by Olson Applications can be used to get in some fast exercise throughout the day. The trick is to press on until your powerful emotions start to subside.

Paced Breathing: Notice how you tend to breathe rapidly when you're angry? Slow down your anger by taking slow, deep breaths in and out. For example, take 4 seconds to breathe in and 5 seconds to breathe out. **Tip**: Feel free to use apps such as Prana Breath or Breathe to help with this step.

Paired Muscle Relaxation: Do this while performing Paced Breathing above. When you inhale deeply, slowly contract your muscles (without tensing them to the point where they cramp), then when you exhale deeply, let all that tension go and tell yourself to relax.

Emotion Regulation

Let me start by saying that your feelings are always valid. I truly never liked it whenever someone told me to just '*get a grip*' or '*change your feelings*', or when I am trying to explain something (which is something very hard for me to do) and then have someone casually comment, '*that's not true*'. In my mind, these are MY experiences, MY emotions, MY truths, and so when someone tries to invalidate them, I get very angry.

However, I have come to realize that my emotions are not who I am. My emotions don't have to control me. I am the one who has the power to control (regulate) my emotions.

Now, I know that you should never change for others. That never works. So for a while, I even *resisted* doing something about my volatile emotions and resulting behavior. I thought, "*Well, if I change, that means THEY are right, and I am wrong.*"

But DBT taught me something that changed my way of thinking: if I entertain misery, I stay miserable. If I don't do anything to be happy, I stay unhappy. In short, if I don't do anything to get out of my funk, I am just making myself suffer longer. And I didn't want to suffer any longer. I was tired of my OCD, anxiety, and anger issues. They were dominating and derailing my life, and I truly wanted to live a better life.

So, Emotion Regulation, in many ways, is about understanding yourself. It is about understanding your emotions, why you're even feeling that way, and how to change unwanted emotions and manage extreme emotions—because you no longer want to suffer from them.

IMPORTANT: Emotion Regulation skills are NOT about getting rid of emotions. Emotions are part of what makes us human. So the goal is not to get rid of or invalidate them. The objective is simply to identify emotions that are negative, harmful, or non-beneficial to us and to regulate these feelings so that we feel better about ourselves and life in general.

I won't lie to you. Unlike altering your body chemistry (physical condition), changing your emotional state is more difficult. But I promise you that it can be done! How? Start with the Emotion Regulation exercises below. And please do not do them just once. It takes multiple efforts over time to learn new behaviors, so please keep at it until they become almost second nature to you.

Worksheet: Check the Facts

Check the Facts is an exercise where you pause, reflect, and fact-check your emotions. This helps you make logical sense of a situation (arrive at Wise Mind, page 379) and not overreact.

First, let's do a reflective exercise. Look back and think of a few situations where you overreacted. It can also be an event that, at the time, you thought was a big deal, but it turned out to be unimportant.

Question: What emotion do you want to fact-check?
Example: my anger

Your answer:

Question: What happened? What triggered this emotion?
Example: My sister skipped my bridal shower. I was furious because she was in charge of the party giveaways.

Your answer:

Question: What assumptions did you make about the event?
Example: My sister deliberately tried to ruin my bridal shower.

Your answer:

Question: What did you do?

Example: I sent very angry, accusatory text messages to my sister and told her she was no longer welcome at my wedding.

Your answer:

CHECK THE FACTS!

You listed your assumptions above, but <u>WHAT ELSE</u> happened?

Example: My brother-in-law had an accident at work, and my sister had to rush to his side. She was so distraught she completely forgot about my bridal shower.

Your answer:

Question: Why do you think you reacted that way? What were you afraid of?

Example: My sister and I have not been on the best of terms for years, and although things were a lot better, I was afraid it was just all a façade, and she was still out to get me.

Your answer:

Question: Looking back, on a scale of 0-5, did your emotion fit the facts? (0 = not at all, 5 = yes):

Example: 0, not at all

Your answer:

Question: If your emotion DID NOT fit the facts, what would you do differently?

Example: I would not jump to conclusions and give her the benefit of the doubt. I would also not have acted on my emotions and sent those angry text messages.

Your answer:

Question: If your emotion DID fit the facts, would you do anything differently?

Example: Yes. I would not have acted impulsively and sent angry text messages to my sister because by letting my anger get control of me, I ruined my bridal shower for myself. Instead of enjoying the party and my friends, I was consumed by anger at my sister throughout the event.

Your answer:

IMPORTANT: **Check the Facts** can be used whenever you're in a negative situation. It is not just for past events. However, I suggest you do the above exercise at least two (2) more times. That is, think of past events when you may have overreacted and, as a result, made the situation worse. This is to get you accustomed to the process of fact-checking your emotions.

Worksheet: Opposite to Emotion

Sometimes, even when we fact-check our feelings and find that our emotions do not match the facts, we still want to do what we want to do instead of what we should do.

To prepare you for such situations, below is an **Opposite to Emotion** table. Column A lists down unhealthy emotions; on Column B, write down what you would normally want to do when you feel these emotions; and then, on Column C, write an *opposing action* to your original natural urge.

The next time an unpleasant situation occurs, refer to this table and do what you wrote in Column C. (I have done the first emotion as an example for you.)

A	B	C
Emotion *What you are feeling.*	**Emotion-Driven Behavior** *What you would normally do because of this emotion. (If your natural urge is to do something other than what's listed below, please list them on a separate sheet.)*	**Opposite Action** *Write down an opposite action to what you're feeling.*
Sadness	*Self-isolate; not want to be with anyone at all*	*Call a few friends and meet up with them.*
Guilt	Shut down, self-criticize, or even blame others (deflect)	
Anger	Shout, sulk, do something aggressive like breaking something	
Fear	Run away from a situation	

A **Emotion** *What you are feeling.*	B **Emotion-Driven Behavior** *What you would normally do because of this emotion. (If your natural urge is to do something other than what's listed below, please list them on a separate sheet.)*	C **Opposite Action** *Write down an opposite action to what you're feeling.*
Emptiness	Binge-eat	
Loneliness	Get back together with a toxic ex, say sorry to a friend even though it is not my fault just so we can be friends again	
Frustration	Throw things around the room	
Helplessness	Cry and feeling depressed	
Resentment	Talk ill about someone/something	
Feel free to add more emotions and scenarios in the extra rows below.		

A	B	C
Emotion	**Emotion-Driven Behavior**	**Opposite Action**
What you are feeling.	*What you would normally do because of this emotion. (If your natural urge is to do something other than what's listed below, please list them on a separate sheet.)*	*Write down an opposite action to what you're feeling.*

Interpersonal Effectiveness

Relationships are important in life. They provide the foundation for our overall happiness and well-being.[6] A meta-analysis of 148 studies revealed that people with strong social interactions have a 50% lower risk of early death.[7] Healthy connections also allow us to recover more quickly after stressful experiences because we know we have the support of others.

DBT's Interpersonal Effectiveness skills focus on creating and sustaining healthy relationships not just with others but with ourselves. You see, often, in our desire to be in good standing with others, we tend to give in too much and lose ourselves. This is not healthy for us in the long run.

So, Interpersonal Effectiveness is actually all about balance. We learn to prioritize ourselves and respect our own wishes (**ME**) while at the same time considering the needs and desires of others (**THEM**).

When we know how to balance ME + THEM, then we can strengthen our current relationships, learn how to find and keep new relationships, and are able to end unhealthy or toxic relationships.

One of the most powerful things I have learned under this DBT skill is that often, I don't get what I want out of a situation because I do not know how to ask for them effectively. I either demanded something, which of course, rubbed the other person the wrong way making them unwilling to give in to my request, or I was not assertive enough and let people walk over me. In both situations, I don't get what I want, which, of course, would anger me.

Hopefully, the following DBT exercises will help you as much as they helped me in my relationships.

Worksheet: FINDING FRIENDS

As much as we'd like to believe otherwise, relationships don't just happen. Often, we have to work to find people we like and exert effort to get them to like us. Accomplish the following worksheet to help you find friends and keep them to reduce any feelings of isolation or loneliness.

1. **Find close opportunities.** It is easier to find friends and keep them if you know you'll have regular contact with them. So list down at least three (3) places that you frequent where you can meet new people.

Examples: at school, at the office, at the local Starbucks

Your turn:

1. _____
2. _____
3. _____

2. **Find similarities.** It is easier to make friends with people who already like some of the same things that we do. And it is easier for the other person to like us in turn because research shows that we all tend to like people who remind us of ourselves.[8,9,10] When you do find them, let that be your conversation starter!

Example: "Hi, I couldn't help but overhear you're into cooking reality shows? Cool! Me too. Do you watch MasterChef?"

Your turn:

_____
_____
_____

3. Practice good conversation skills. If you're an introvert like me, it is hard to not only start a conversation with someone but also to keep it going! Following are some important tips to keep in mind.

- **Ask and respond.** Practice the art of ending your conversations with a question. Keep in mind, though, that since you just met the person, ask general questions. For example, *"This is not the first time I have seen you here.*
- ***Do you live nearby?"*** is too personal, and the other person will most likely not be comfortable sharing something so private yet. So keep the conversation light.

  Example: I noticed you ordered the Caramel Macchiato. This is my first time visiting this café, any other recommendations?

  Your turn:

  _____

  _____

  _____

- **Engage in small talk.** It may sound silly but small talk is exactly what's required when meeting someone new.

  Examples:
  - *Amazing day, isn't it?*
  - *Don't know about you, but it is those sinful cronuts that make me come here all the time. How about you?*
  - *You work at [company]? Do you know Mike over there at Accounting?*

  Your turn:

  _____

  _____

  _____

- **Share 'just enough'.** Just as you don't want to ask personal questions, it is equally important not to overshare too. Simply put, you guys are not at that stage yet, so it is best to share 'just enough' about yourself. If you're not sure, take your cue from the other person.

  Examples:
  YOU: I don't know about you, but it is those sinful cronuts that make me come here all the time. How about you?
  NEW FRIEND: Oh, they look way too sinful for me. But I can't help myself from ordering the French Toast every morning!
  YOU: Ah, a breakfast person, me too! But I am not into anything sweet in the morning. What would you recommend instead?

  Your turn:

  _____
  _____
  _____

- **Don't interrupt.** No one likes to be interrupted. Even though you're just excited to agree with the other person, don't jump into the conversation too quick because it gives the impression that you're not listening to them. Think of a few ways you can train yourself to stop interrupting people. (I have filled in the first few lines to give you an example.)

  1. *Pause for 5 seconds before speaking.*
  2. *Repeat what they said when they're done speaking before you say what you want to say. (Example: Wow, did you just say you like French Toast too?)*
  3. *Bite your inner lip to prevent yourself from interrupting.*
  4. _____
  5. _____
  6. _____
  7. _____

8. _____
9. _____
10. _____

- **Prepare some discussion points.** *What to talk about?* This is often what stomps people from meeting someone and carrying on a conversation. Personally, because of my anxiety disorder, I would really overthink this. It is like I can't relax and just be in or enjoy the conversation because some part of my brain is already trying to plan the next topic. To get over this, I had to go 'back to basics'.

    Let's go back to the first item in this worksheet, i.e., **Find close opportunities..** So this actually narrows down the *where*, right? From here, just come up with a few general topics that fit the situation.

    For example, if you plan to meet new people at your **corner coffee house**, then the discussion points could be about the *local neighborhood, coffee specialties, baristas, the coffee shop menu,* etc. If you want to introduce yourself to a **co-worker**, then discussion points could be about a *work project, a looming deadline, a new colleague or boss, how you (or they) ended up working there,* etc.

I know it is hard to find friends, but be brave! If we wait for people to come to us, we may never have friends. So, have the courage to put yourself out there. Remember, no risk, no reward.

Worksheet: DEARMAN

DEARMAN helps you get your messages across without damaging your relationships. It helps you be more assertive while keeping the other person's feelings in mind. Fill out your response against each acronym in the spaces provided below.

 escribe the situation.

When you are describing an incident or situation, do so clearly. Avoid mentioning your opinions and stick to the facts.
Example: I have been working beyond my hours, without overtime pay, for the third week now.
Your turn:

_____

_____

 xpress how you are feeling about the situation.

Use **'I'** statements when communicating. **'You'** statements can be taken by the other person as accusatory, which increases the chances of conflict.
Example: I believe I deserve compensation moving forward.
Your turn:

_____

_____

Assert yourself.

Say what you want to happen clearly but not aggressively. This will help the other person understand you better.

Example: I would like overtime pay. Can you please arrange this?

Your turn:

_____
_____

Reinforce your request.

Let the other person know that your request is important. So say how much you will appreciate it if you get what you want or need.

Example: I would really appreciate it if you arranged that. I will probably be even more productive because I know my extra hours are not taken for granted.

Your turn:

_____
_____

Mindfulness.

Stay mindful of your words and emotions; stay focused and remain on topic no matter what the other person says.

Example: So, I hope you understand why I am requesting this. (Note: Aside from your words, ensure your body language is also mindful. For example, don't raise your voice and maintain a relaxed composure.)

Your turn:

_____

 ppear confident.

Show confidence through your words and body language. Do not apologize. Also, be consistent with your demeanor. For example, do not say what you want in a confident voice and then lower your voice as you continue your message.

Example: Sit or stand up straight, straighten your shoulders, maintain eye contact, and then say: I hope I am getting across to you because my stand on this won't change.

Your turn:
_____
_____
_____
_____

 egotiate.

Negotiate if the person you're talking to doesn't want to grant your request. This will allow you both to find an acceptable solution to the problem. You can offer a solution or ask the other person what they think should happen moving forward.

Example: I can do extra work this week and no further. But if you really want me to do extra hours next week, then I am willing to receive 75% overtime pay instead of full overtime pay. What do you think?

Your turn:
_____
_____
_____
_____

Worksheet: GIVE

GIVE aims to keep or improve our relationships with others *while* we try to get what we want from the interaction. Often, people say no to a request not because they don't agree with us but because of *how* we ask for it. (No one likes to be bullied into something or made to feel guilty if they don't agree with us!)

GIVE teaches us how to be effective in communicating what we want so that others are *induced* to grant our requests.

G	**I**	**V**	**E**
Gentle	**Interested**	**Validate**	**Easy Manner**
Be gentle. Do not offend the other person when communicating what you want. So that the other person doesn't feel assaulted, be kind and respectful.	**Act interested** in the other person by actively listening to them.	**Acknowledge** sentiments and emotions of the other person. Demonstrate that this discussion is not one-sided.	Adopt a **friendly and easy-going** manner. People will feel more at ease and will be more receptive to your requests when you have an engaging and pleasant attitude.
What do you want to DO?			
List 3 ways you can ask for something in a *gentle* way. *(e.g., use a friendly voice)*	List 3 ways you can show that you are *interested* in what the other person is saying. *(e.g., face the other person with your whole body; don't look at your phone)*	List 3 ways you can offer *validation* to others. *(e.g., repeat what the other person just said)*	List 3 ways to show that you are *easy to get along with*. *(e.g., smile, present an "open" demeanor by not crossing your arms or legs)*

G	I	V	E
1.	1.	1.	1.
2.	2.	2.	2.
3.	3.	3.	3.
4.	4.	4.	4.

What do you want to __SAY__?			
Example: I am angry about this situation but I can put that aside so we can arrive at a mutually-beneficial conclusion.	*Example: Will you give me some feedback? I am interested to get your viewpoint on this.*	*Example: You said you did not slam the door on me on purpose. So, does that mean you did not know I was behind you?*	*Example: I can see that we are both a bit flustered now. I don't want a fight, just clarification. Shall we discuss this later?*

DBT for Anger Management

You might be wondering if Dialectical Behavior Therapy is truly effective when dealing with anger issues. My personal experience is that it is very effective, and science agrees. Twenty-one (21) articles studying the effects of DBT on anger and aggressive behavior were peer-reviewed and found that DBT "shows a positive impact on the reduction of anger and aggressive behaviors".[11]

Acceptance and Change. The fact that you have this book in your hands says that you know you have anger issues and that you want to change because you want to lead a happier life. Well, congratulations! That's already the first step to Acceptance and Change in DBT!

DBT ACCEPT Skills

Anger is a strong emotion, and often we're reactive or impulsive to it. **Mindfulness** teaches us to be more in the moment and how to be fully aware of our surroundings and ourselves. Learning Wise Mind (page 379) in particular, teaches us to walk the middle path and always consult our emotions AND sensibleness (logic) before we do anything regarding our anger. Again, science agrees, as numerous studies have shown that Mindfulness is highly effective in reducing stress and anger and reducing aggressive behavior.[12,13,14]

Often, we lash out when angry because we cannot tolerate our anger. It consumes us, and we can't just bottle it up. **Distress Tolerance** teaches us the skills we need to deflect (not deny!) and tolerate our anger as it is happening, which is a good thing. Why? Because research has shown that high distress tolerance levels have a positive effect on our blood pressure during times of anger[15] and lowers our anger reactivity[16,17].

DBT CHANGE Skills

When we're angry, it doesn't help anyone (most of all ourselves) if we *stay angry*. **Emotion Regulation** skills teach us how to change unwanted emotions and how to manage extreme emotions so that we don't do or say something we will regret.

When we are angry, we are in a heightened sense of physiological arousal (e.g., blood pressure is elevated, body muscles are tensed, breathing exhilarates, etc.). As you can imagine, *staying* in this state is not good for you, so it is in your best interest to be able to regulate your emotions as quickly as you can. (*Plus, if you don't regulate your anger, chances are very high that you will react aggressively to other things and people around you, even if they have absolutely nothing to do with what prompted your initial anger.*)

Studies have shown that emotion regulation skills lead to "less anger experience" during times of anger[18] and make us more intentional and flexible (as opposed to impulsive) when responding to anger[19].

Interpersonal Effectiveness

When I look back at my anger issues, I realize that most of them were triggered by my family. This is not to assign blame; that's not part of DBT. I simply accept this as fact. So, for me, learning **Interpersonal Effectiveness** skills was crucial for successful anger management. After all, "anger is a common cause of strained negotiations".[20]

Even if your anger issues don't stem from people but more from situations, you'll find that most situations are often caused by humans, directly or indirectly. Again, this is not to assign blame. This is just to make you aware that, for the most part, dealing with your anger means dealing with people (yourself included!).

So, the better you are at interacting with others (interpersonal effectiveness), the more probable it is that you will avoid frustrating circumstances which can drive you to anger and aggressive behavior.

I hope that I have shared enough here to make you realize that DBT can be very useful when it comes to handling your anger issues. Don't worry; I'll share more DBT tools (exercises) with you in the succeeding pages. But for now, let's dive into ANGER itself.

A long time ago, a college friend, one of the first friends I truly had, asked me, *"Why are you always so angry?"* I found it very hard to explain, so I said, *"I JUST AM!"*.

To this, my friend replied, *"Well, you always seem angry and miserable, but that doesn't explain much, so don't blame me if I can't help you."*

The following chapter explains ANGER.

Believe me, it wasn't what I thought it was.

What is Anger?

"Holding on to anger is like drinking poison and expecting the other person to die." - Buddha

 *Before you read up on what anger is all about, please take this quick **Miller-Patton Anger Self-Assessment** exercise on Appendix A (page 339).*

Find out with just a few questions if you're handling your anger well... or if anger is handling you.

Anger 101

Anger is an emotion characterized by hatred toward someone, or something you believe has purposefully wronged you.

Anger, in itself, serves a purpose. It can help you communicate negative feelings. For example, if someone keeps crossing your boundaries, anger can prompt you to speak up so that others learn to respect your wishes. However, anger is not always about a person. You can be angry about certain situations. For example, if you're angry about the fact that you need to drive half an hour to the nearest grocery store, this may prompt you to find a solution to the problem, such as moving to a different place that suites your lifestyle better. So, anger can lead to better situations.

Anger itself does not get us in trouble; it is how we handle our anger that usually does that.

When we are angry, it is hard to "think straight," so we tend to give in to impulse and do something we will most likely regret later. This reaction is called the *amygdala hijack*.

Amygdala Hijack

The *amygdala* is an almond-shaped form in the middle of the brain, and it forms part of the limbic system, which is a group of structures in the brain that help control our emotions (how we feel) and behavior (how we act).

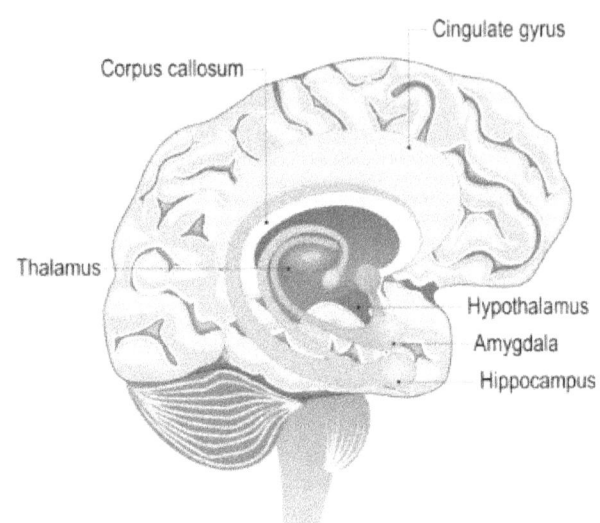

Under normal circumstances, the amygdala processes external frightening or threatening inputs and instructs our brains and bodies on how to respond. This is why the amygdala is strongly linked to our fight-or-flight response. In other words, when we detect a threat or danger, the amygdala produces hormones to get the body ready to either resist the threat or run from it.

The term **amygdala hijack** was first used by psychologist *Daniel Goleman* in his best-selling book "*Emotional Intelligence*" in 1995.[21] He describes it as **a strong emotional reaction that is out of proportion to the situation**.

Basically, the Reasonable Mind is bypassed, and Emotional Mind takes over. (No Wise Mind (page 379) here.) Later, when the information is processed by the part of your brain that lets you think (the prefrontal cortex), you realize that your reaction was completely disproportionate to the situation.

Physically, what happens is that when emotions (such as anger) run high, blood and oxygen flow to the amygdala (emotional hub) rather than the prefrontal cortex (thinking hub), reducing our ability to think and solve problems.

An amygdala hijack is useful in real life-threatening situations. For example, when you are crossing the street and a runaway car is hurtling toward you, reacting without thinking here can save your life.

The problem is that TODAY, we're faced with so many daily stressors that amygdala hijacks kick in easily, causing us to overreact. For example, if you're super busy trying to send out an already late report and your partner tries to talk to you, this may trigger the amygdala to take over, and you end up banging your keyboard and shouting at your partner.

Even though an amygdala hijack seems like a "natural reaction", it doesn't mean you need to give in to it. It may feel like everything is happening in mere seconds, but there's actually a process that your anger goes through.

The Anger Cycle

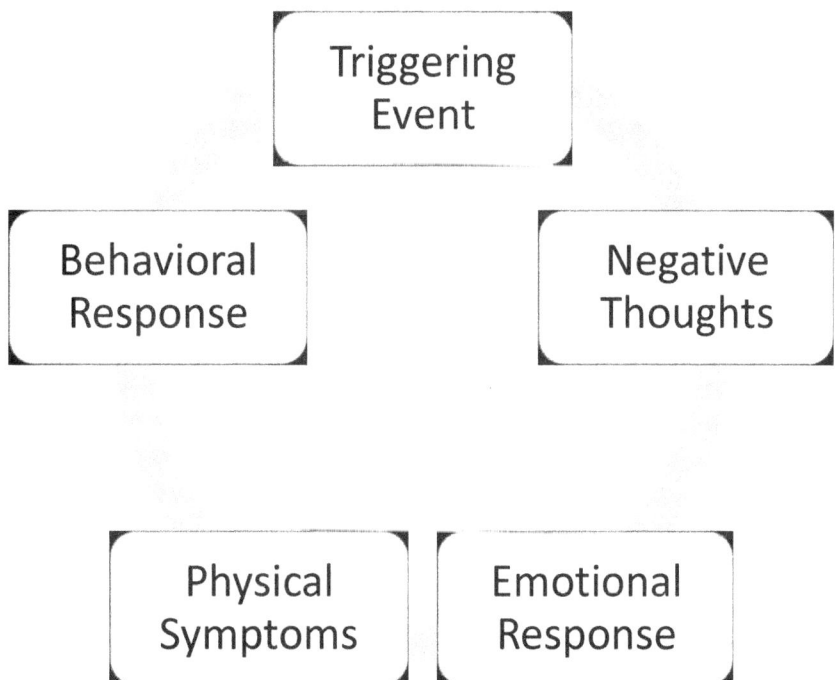

The **Triggering Event** is what caused your anger to begin with. Examples:
- A sibling who barged into your room and invaded your space.
- A co-worker who took credit for your hard work.
- Someone who cut you off while driving.

Negative Thoughts** or illogical thoughts fill your mind as a result of the triggering event. Examples:
- I absolutely HATE my sister/brother!
- [Colleague] is one lazy bastard who wants me to do all the work.
- The idiot who cut me off doesn't have a clue about driving rules and doesn't deserve to be on the road.

A negative **Emotional Response*** then arises as a result of your negative thoughts. Examples:

- **Shame/guilt.**
  I shouldn't hate my sister/brother. What's wrong with me?
- **Anxiety.**
  What is [colleague] going to do next? Give me more work? Ambush me on our next meeting? I am so stressed!
- **Rage.**
  That driver! I better not see that driver ever again because I don't know what I'll do!

As your negative thoughts and emotions consume you, **Physical Symptoms** begin to show. Examples:

** DBT founder Dr. Marsha Linehan believes that *Negative Thoughts* and *Emotional Response* are interchangeable. Sometimes, a triggering event prompts negative emotional responses, which then cause negative thoughts (and vice versa).

- Red face.
- Racing heartbeat.
- Clenched fists.
- Sweating.
- Clenched jaw and teeth.

Finally, your negative thoughts and emotions and their resulting physical symptoms become too much for you to bear, and a corresponding negative **Behavioral Response** ensues. Examples:

- You start arguing with your sibling.
- You explode and start yelling at your colleague.
- You drive fast and past the driver who cut you off. You get out of the car and start yelling and berating the other driver.

Actually, there's one more part of the cycle, the **Aftermath**.

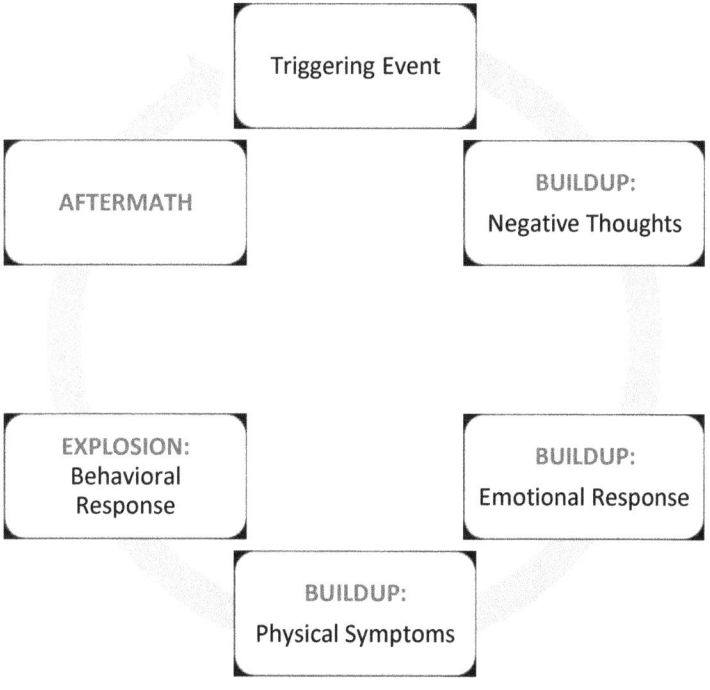

The **Aftermath** is dependent on your Behavioral Response. For example, say that you did react negatively to the situation; this may result in real-life negative consequences for you. Examples:

- Your argument with your sibling escalated to violence.
  Aftermath: Your parents ground you both, and you miss an important school event. A worse scenario is if one of you pushes the other (e.g., down the stairs), resulting in serious injury.
- Your argument with your colleague reaches the higher-ups.
  Aftermath: You get reprimanded or, worse, terminated.
- The driver who cut you off videotapes your outburst and calls the police.
  Aftermath: Jail time.

One thing I'd like to point out because this is what happened to me is that **Aftermath** comes one way or the other.

On many occasions, I kept my anger deep inside. I may not have always reacted aggressively or violently on the outside, but because I was not handling the Buildup phase of my anger effectively, the Aftermath for me was that it all contributed to my anxiety and depression mental health issues.

This is why I strongly advise applying DBT skills to address the Buildup phase of the anger cycle. Examples:

- Negative Thoughts -> Do the Grounding Technique exercise (page 383).
- Emotional Response -> Apply DBT Emotion Regulation skills (page 386).
- Physical Symptoms -> Engage in Mindful Breathing (page 378) or TIPP (page 266).

These are just some of the DBT skills that will help you get through the **Buildup** phase of anger, and as a result, you can avoid the **Explosion** and negative **Aftermath** phases. (See REAL LIFE Tools to Effectively Manage Your Anger (page 443) for more DBT exercises.)

It also helps to understand how you express or unleash anger. Do you lash out? If you do, do you do so physically or verbally? Are you quick to anger or slow to anger? Is the target of your anger others or yourself? Let's go and find out.

The 10 Different Types of Anger

When you are angry, what *kind* of angry are you? You might be thinking, "*Does it matter*"? Yes, it does. If you know what kind of anger you're feeling at any given time, you'll be able to understand—and manage—it better.

1. **Assertive Anger** uses frustration to bring about good or positive change. This is anger with a cause. You show your anger in ways that make things different around you without lashing out, screaming, or being aggressive with someone.

2. **Behavioral Anger** is a manifestation of anger that is often aggressive. You feel overwhelmed by your feelings of anger that you lash out, often, at the person who made you angry, but at other times, you can keep your volatile emotions in and then lash out at others.

3. **Chronic Anger** is a long-lasting, all-around resentment of people, frustration over situations, and anger at oneself.

4. **Judgmental Anger** is a reaction to a slight that you believe others have done to you.

5. **Overwhelmed Anger** is a feeling of uncontrollable anger. It happens when you feel like you can't do anything about a situation or circumstance, which makes you feel hopeless and frustrated.

6. **Passive-Aggressive Anger** is a form of avoidance. This is when a person tries to stay away from any kind of conflict. This may mean having to bury any frustration or anger you might be feeling. However, it often slips out anyway, and you may engage in passive-aggressive comments, sarcasm, and even procrastination.

7. **Retaliatory Anger** is a natural reaction to being confronted or attacked by someone else. It is done to get back at someone for something they did wrong.

8. **Self-Abusive Anger** comes from feelings of shame. If you've been feeling hopeless, unworthy, embarrassed, or ashamed, you might keep those feelings inside and show your anger through negative self-talk, self-harm, drug use, or even eating disorders.

9. **Verbal Anger** is an aggressive and abusive type of anger. Usually, the angry person tries to hurt the target of their anger by shouting, screaming, ridiculing, blaming, or criticizing them.

10. **Volatile Anger**, also known as "sudden anger," is when a person gets angry over both big and small things that bother them. Since it is an explosive type of anger, it is often over as quickly as it starts. (This does not mean that there's no damage done by the outburst, though.)

Do you see yourself in any of the above? Please note that you don't necessarily have to fall into one anger type.

For me, I used to swing a lot between **Behavioral Anger**, **Chronic Anger** and **Passive-Aggressive Anger**. Later, I would find out that these were actually symptoms of my General Anxiety Disorder (GAD), but I didn't realize that my *gender* also had something to do with how I expressed my anger.

Male and Female Anger

It is a myth that men get angrier than women. Males may *display* their anger more often than females, but studies show that women get angry just as often and just as intensely as men.[22,23] It is also been discovered that *men feel less effective when pushed to control their anger*, while *women appear to be better able to control immediate instinctive reactions to rage*. Brain biology may have a hand here.

Brain Biology

The amygdala is the same size in both men and women, but a second part of the brain, the *orbital frontal cortex*, is smaller in men. Since this is the part of the brain that helps control aggressive impulses, it partly explains why men are less successful at keeping their tempers in check.

Societal Norms

Of course, let's not forget how society also plays a role in how men and women express anger. As children, when boys come home angry because someone teased them or fought with them, we don't ask how they feel or teach them how to process emotions. Most parents would say, "*toughen up*" or worse, "*get even!*". Sadly, this makes fighting look like the best way to express anger and solve problems. But we don't say the same things to little girls. In fact, we do the opposite. If little girls get upset or show anger, we tell them, "*that's unladylike*".

Yes, the above is a generalization, guilty of gender stereotyping and double standards, but it is also a fact. Luckily, times seem to be changing, but we cannot dismiss society's role in how men and women process and express anger. And these societal expectations do not stop in our youth.

As adults, an angry woman is seen as dramatic or emotional. One study even revealed that a woman who expresses anger is *"perceived as less competent, lower status, and having a lower salary"* than men and unemotional women.[24] As you can see, society generally encourages men to show anger and frowns on women who do.

But that's not fair, is it? Especially when we consider the following female biological differences.

Premenstrual Syndrome

Premenstrual syndrome (PMS) is a group of physical, emotional, and behavioral changes that start about a week before a female's menstrual cycle. About 75% of women globally experience PMS[25], and research shows that women with PMS experience anger more and have less control over their anger.[26]

Science has yet to explain why PMS is strong in some women and not in others. Still, it is clear that it is caused by the wildly changing levels of estrogen and progesterone hormones in a woman's body during the menstrual cycle. These hormone fluctuations influence *serotonin* levels, and low serotonin levels are linked to feelings of sadness, irritability, sleep issues, and food cravings.

Menopause

As women leave their reproductive years, *perimenopause* (the transition to menopause) kicks in. We've already learned above that *estrogen* and *progesterone* levels fluctuate during the menstrual cycle, resulting in low *serotonin* levels. During the perimenopause stage, these hormones are even more out of whack, resulting in intense emotions such as anger and rage.

As women transition into menopause, the roller-coaster of hormones can result in a lack of sleep, hot flashes, fatigue, low metabolism (resulting in weight gain), and others.

Menopause is not just a biological change. Often, these years signal many changes in a woman's life, such as kids leaving home, facing the realities of aging, waking up and realizing that you and your partner have grown apart, etc. All these changes, happening all at once, may be too much to handle and result in anxiety, depression, or anger.

So far, we've talked about WHAT anger is.

- Anger is an emotion characterized by hostility.
- Anger can make us react "out of proportion" to the situation (amygdala hijack).
- Anger may come on fast but there's a cycle that it goes through: trigger->buildup->explosion->aftermath.
- There are 10 different types of anger.
- There's a difference in how males and females experience and display anger.

However, everyone's "anger source" is different. One person's trigger may mean nothing to another. Different people also show their anger in different ways. So, in the next chapter, let's talk about YOUR ANGER.

Why Are You Angry?

> *"Sometimes when I am angry, I have the right to be angry, but that doesn't give me the right to be cruel". - Bede Jarrett*

By now, you have learned that anger is part of life and that it is one of the most primitive emotions we can experience as humans. However, anger can change how we think about risks.

A 2003 study has shown that anger makes us more impulsive and makes us think that bad things are less likely to happen.[27] In short, *if we don't take a moment to think, anger can make us reckless.* So let's take a moment to think. This chapter is all about you reflecting on your anger.

The Source of Your Anger

As mentioned before, anger is a reaction. To what? Usually, when people are angry, they immediately point to a person or a situation as the reason why they are angry. But neither is the real source of our anger, this is: the realization of our own impotence or powerlessness over a given situation. So, anger is really a coping mechanism.

If something unpleasant happened and we thought we could change the situation, we would have already done it, right? And in doing so, we wouldn't be frustrated or angry about it. However, since **we do not have control** and **cannot change the situation**, we are faced with the fact that **things are not as we want them to be,** and so **we get angry**.

It is also important to note that **anger is a secondary emotion**.[28] Researchers at *The Gottman Institute*[29], led by psychologists John and Julie Gottman, created the *Anger Iceberg* to illustrate that anger is just the tip of the iceberg. Beneath the anger is a host of underlying thoughts, feelings, and emotions that cause it.††

---

†† The underlying reasons in this graphic are not all inclusive. Other thoughts, feelings and emotions (or a combination thereof), may be the source of your anger.

Now that you know that anger is a response that usually stems from an underlying emotion, you can move on to exploring your triggers. These are the people, thoughts, feelings, and/or experiences that prompt or provoke your anger.

Clinical psychologist Nicole Lippman-Barlie, Ph.D. [30] encourages people to view anger as a communication tool. That is, *what is your anger trying to tell you?* Once you find the answer, you can prioritize that over your anger.

In my case, I figured out that my anger was not just a symptom of my anxiety disorder. Anger resulted from the *extreme loneliness* I have been feeling for years.

I spent most of my high school life alone. I did not have any friends even though the school I attended had over 5000 students. Every single day, I would eat lunch alone. And since there was no one to talk to, I'd soon be finished with lunch, so I would go to the library to hide or sleep. After school, I usually went to the arcade or internet cafe because I did not want to go home. If I did go home, I would stay in my room and play video games on my computer or N64. This was my way of escaping my own life.

Since I did not interact much with others, the few times I did usually ended in disaster. I would mumble my words, get all fidgety, and break into a sweat. This would then make me so upset and embarrassed that I would get very angry and find myself in a fit of rage.

In the beginning, I found it hard to accept. But eventually, I came to terms with the fact that I was *choosing* to lash out because it was harder to accept that no one liked me enough to be my friend.

Sadly, I did not know all this during my teen years. However, as an adult, knowing this enabled me to address my feelings of isolation and loneliness over my anger.

At this time, I was already aware of DBT, so I could apply the Interpersonal Effectiveness skills (page 394) I learned (see Worksheet: Finding Friends, page 395). Once I could address my loneliness, the anger I felt inside started to lose its grip on me.

So isolation and loneliness were my triggers or prompting events. These were the *underlying emotions* in my personal *Anger Iceberg*. What about you? Do you know what's causing your anger?

Following are three (3) worksheets to help you arrive at the REAL SOURCE of your anger. You don't have to do both Anger Triggers 1 (page 425) and Anger Triggers 2 (page 426). I have included two worksheets here because some prefer one type of exercise over the other. (Of course, you can also do both exercises if you want.)

Worksheet: Anger Triggers 1

Is your anger prompted by anything specific, or is it provoked by just about anything? Please think about each category below carefully. Is there a specific person or place that's always making you angry? Any specific thoughts or emotions making your blood boil? Write down your responses below.

Category	Your Replies
People *Example: mom, dad, my colleague Dave somehow always rubs me the wrong way, my ex*	
Places *Example: local café where I caught my partner cheating*	
Things *Example: pictures of my ex*	
Thoughts *Example: when I think that I am nowhere near my life goals*	
Emotions *Example: loneliness, sadness*	
Situations *Example: being ignored, when I binge-eat, being told I am wrong*	

Worksheet: Anger Triggers 2

If you find it hard to isolate what's prompting your anger *by category*, then perhaps the following worksheet is for you. Put a checkmark below **S** for sometimes, **A** for always, or **N** for never for each of the anger prompting events below to indicate how much of an anger trigger it is for you.

Potential Trigger	S Sometimes	A Always	N Never
When I am ignored			
When people don't keep promises			
When someone is crossing my boundaries			
When people don't understand me			
When others don't pull their weight			
When I am all alone			
When I am treated unfairly			
When somebody is mean to me			
When I am judged			

Potential Trigger	S Sometimes	A Always	N Never
When somebody doesn't think of my wants or needs			
When others are late			
When others are selfish			
When someone is trying to control me			
When people expect too much from me			
When I am disrespected			
When I am feeling threatened			
When someone embarrasses me			
When I don't know what's going on (facing the unknown)			
When I can't get help			
When I get rejected			

Potential Trigger	S Sometimes	A Always	N Never
When someone is lying			
When someone is insulting me			
When someone is giving me unsolicited advice			

Feel free to add any other potential trigger for you in the spaces below.

Worksheet: Anger Iceberg

Hopefully, after doing the **Anger Trigger** worksheets (pages 425 and 426) in the previous pages, you can fill out the underlying thoughts, emotions, and experiences causing your anger.

If you cannot fill out this worksheet now, that's okay. Go through the rest of this book if you need more clarity about your anger, and just come back to this worksheet when you're ready.

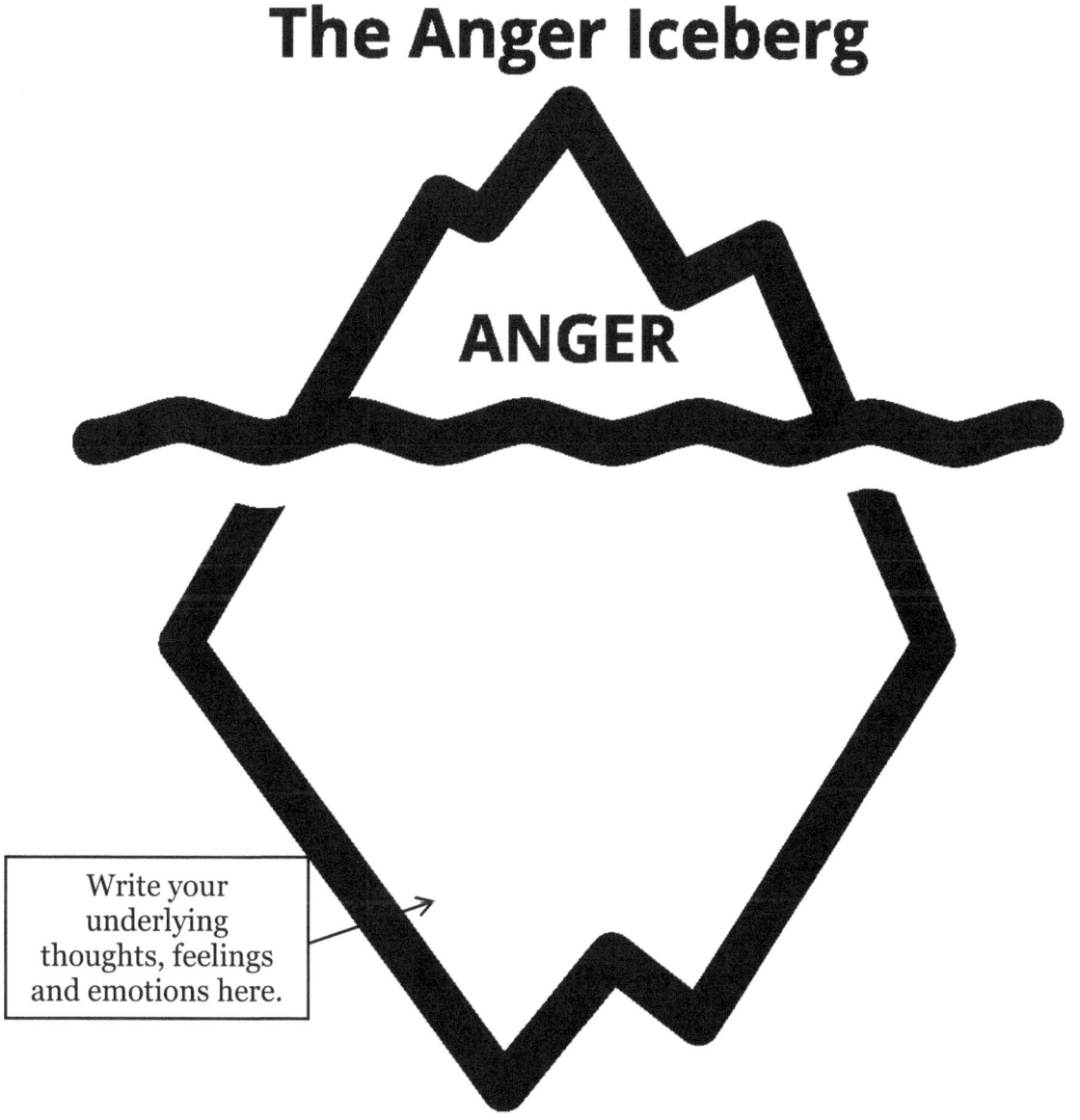

How Your Anger Grows

It is normal to feel as though your anger is intensifying over time. As we've learned in the previous section, anger results from our realization that things are not how we want them to be. If that continues for a considerable time, our anger flourishes due to *continuous unmet needs*.

Here's what my friend Ellen had to say about this:

"I am the eldest of three kids. When I was two years old, my twin brothers were born. From that moment on, the whole family doted on them. As a child, my wishes were always bypassed by whatever my younger brothers wanted. I started to "act out" at school (e.g., pulling a friend's hair, throwing books, scratching someone's arm, screaming, etc.). This prompted my parents to compare me even more to my twin brothers, who could do no wrong. By the time I was a teenager, my anger was uncontrollable. Everything at home triggered me. I just couldn't help but lash out at everything. Since no one paid any attention to me anyway, I ran away from home when I was 16.

For the first time, I felt free and felt like I could just be myself. I think it was the first time I felt any form of happiness. I supported myself by working two jobs during the day and attending night classes. Eventually, I found administrative work for a local construction company. However, after some time, I started to show burnout symptoms, and I could sense my anger issues returning, so I went to see a mental health professional. During this time, I learned that my anger stemmed from continuous unmet needs. What unmet needs? The need to be seen and valued for who I am.

Once I learned that my anger was a result of my feelings of being ignored, which, of course, stemmed from my childhood, I was able to address it by learning better ways of communicating what I needed."

So, if you feel your anger is growing or has been growing over the years, I encourage you to do the following.

1. **List the Top 3 things that anger you.** (**Tip**: Reflect on the previous section, <u>The Source of Your Anger</u> (page 421) and its worksheets.)

    Examples:
    a. When my partner does not actively listen when I am talking.
    b. When my mom guilt trips me to visit every weekend.
    c. When my boss hands extra work on a Friday.

    Your turn:

    _____
    _____
    _____

2. Identify the need that your anger may be expressing.

    Examples:
    a. The need to be heard (NOT ignored).
    b. The need to own my weekends.
    c. The need to be considered; that my time is also valuable.

    Your turn:

    _____
    _____
    _____

3. Develop a simple plan to address your unmet need(s).

   Important: *If you feel you're not ready to come up with a simple step-by-step plan at this stage to address your unmet needs, that's okay. Go through the rest of this book to learn more tools to handle your anger, and just return to this worksheet when you're ready.*

   Example situation: My partner does not actively listen when I am talking.

   (1) Have a sit-down with my partner (e.g., no kids, no phones, no distractions).

   (2) Tell them exactly how I feel (e.g., I feel completely ignored and unimportant when you're not giving me attention when I talk to you. I feel irrelevant.)

   (3) Discuss how to make things better. (e.g., I understand you need to decompress when you just get home, so I'll do my best not to download on you then. But you need to tell me when is the best time to talk and how you intend to actively listen to me.)

   Your turn:

How Do You Express Your Anger?

Now that you have at least a clue as to the source of your anger let's discuss how you express your anger.

Most of the time, anger comes out in one of three ways:

- **External**. Other people can see a clear, outward sign of anger or aggression. This could include yelling, arguing, swearing, throwing or breaking things, having a temper tantrum (e.g., crying uncontrollably, pulling your hair, etc.), or being physically or verbally abusive to yourself or other people.

- **Internal**. This kind of anger is directed at yourself, not at other people or things, even if they caused your anger. This could include negative self-talk, self-denial of simple pleasures or even basic needs, self-harm, or self-isolation.

- **Passive**. This kind of anger is often shown in indirect and subtle ways, like ghosting, stonewalling or gaslighting someone, sulking, being sarcastic (depending on the situation), not helping on purpose or making snide remarks.

Why is it important to know how you express your anger?

As I keep mentioning in this book, anger is a valid emotion, and you shouldn't suppress or deny its existence. However, if you remember the quote at the start of this chapter, a right to be angry doesn't give you a right to be cruel—to others or yourself.

The three ways of showing anger above are all **destructive** ways of showing anger. Expressing your anger in any of these ways usually comes at a cost. (See The Costs of Your Anger, page 435)

So what's the alternative? REAL LIFE Tools to Effectively Manage Your Anger (page 443) will teach you how to effectively manage your anger (Mindfulness and Distress Tolerance) and how to express your anger in empowering, not destructive, ways (Emotion Regulation and Impersonal Effectiveness).

But before we dive into all of that, here's a quick recap of what we discussed in this chapter:

- Anger can make us reckless so it is important to understand the source of our anger.
- Anger is a coping mechanism. We find it hard to accept that things are not going our way and instead of understanding and fixing the situation, we react with anger.
- Anger is a secondary emotion (Anger Iceberg).
- To understand your anger, you must know your "prompting events" (anger triggers).
- Unaddressed anger is not moving on. It is an opportunity for anger to worsen over time.
- Anger is often expressed in one of three ways: external, internal, and passive.

The Costs of Your Anger

"For every minute you remain angry, you give up sixty seconds of peace of mind". - Ralph Waldo Emerson

Anger is a process that happens in both the body and the mind. As a result, anger can hurt your physical and mental health, especially if you express it in destructive ways. But these are not the only 'costs' to you. Uncontrolled, aggressive, explosive anger can also have serious financial, emotional, social and relationship costs.

Physical Costs of Anger

It is NOT healthy to be angry. As you have learned in Anger 101 (page 409), anger prompts the "fight or flight" response of the body. At this stage, adrenal glands release stress hormones such as adrenaline and cortisol into the body. The brain sends blood away from the gut and toward the muscles to get ready for any physical activity. The body's temperature increases, your heart rate, blood pressure, and breathing speed up too, and your skin begins to sweat.

As you can imagine, *chronic anger* can thus lead to *chronic stress*, leading to a host of health problems. Some of the short-term and long-term health issues that have been associated with uncontrolled anger are:

- migraines
- digestion problems
- insomnia
- high blood pressure (*hypertension*)
- high cholesterol

- skin problems
- strokes
- heart attacks

When I was growing up, whenever I got angry, and someone said, *"Careful. Think of your heart!"* I would get angrier because I thought they were making fun of me. Now I know that it is literally true!

Studies show that *anger increases your risk of getting different types of heart diseases, leading to death by up to five times the normal rate.* So, the angrier you are, the more likely you will get heart disease.[31,32,33]

Explosive anger can also lead to serious injury. Here's what my friend Norman had to say.

"My brother and I were the poster kids for 'sibling rivalry'. We did not support each other; we had to one-up each other. Our bodies are covered with cuts, scrapes, and stitches because we would get really physical when we got angry at each other. One day, I was up in the attic trying to find something when my brother followed suit and angrily accused me of trying to steal his skates. I saw red. I shoved him, and he fell down the stairs and broke his arm in three places. We were never "close," but that event made it clear that we didn't want each other in our lives moving forward."

Emotional Costs of Anger

As illustrated in the [Anger Iceberg](#) (page 429) anger is a secondary emotion. It could signify sadness, humiliation, fear, embarrassment, rejection, frustration, confusion, and other unhealthy emotions. If we stay angry, these unhealthy emotions will lead to emotional stress, affecting every aspect of our lives.

Destructive anger can also lead to a loss of self-esteem. Sometimes, we can't help it and let our anger out in explosive ways, which may feel good at the time, but it usually leads to guilt and shame. We end up feeling like this because we realize that our reaction was exaggerated, misdirected, or unjustified on some cognitive level. When this realization kicks in, we are not proud of ourselves, damaging our self-esteem.

There is also what we call "emotional aftershocks" resulting from anger outbursts. For example, say you couldn't control your anger and yell at your staff. You call them incompetent and, for good measure, rip and throw your keyboard across the room. Your staff feels humiliated. At best, you will no longer have their respect (a least not in the near future). At worst, your staff starts to lie, backstab and gossip about you at work. You're not a robot, so this begins to wear you down emotionally.

Also, consider this: if you let anger be the dominant emotion in your life, you reduce the amount of time you have to be happy. Anger, nurturing anger, and even trying to recover from anger all take time. Wouldn't you rather use that time to pursue things that make you happy?

Mental Costs of Anger

DBT teaches us that *choosing to stay in a negative state prolongs our own suffering*. That's certainly true in my experience. Isolation and loneliness were some of the root causes of my anger. Since I did not do anything to address these, I stayed angry—for years.

My chronic anger aggravated my anxiety disorder (GAD), and my passive-aggressive ways (i.e., I ruminate or think A LOT about my anger, but I don't always do something about it because I am always afraid I'll lose control and lash out) led to my depression.

Social Costs of Anger

No one likes to be with angry people. Just as nobody likes to be around a "downer", people also don't like being around someone who's always annoyed, irritated, or exasperated most of the time.

"Angry people" are seen as hard to deal with and exhausting. Many people also don't like to socialize with "angry people" because they don't want to be on the receiving end of that person's anger. Others still simply want to avoid any potential conflict or confrontation.

Regardless of the reason, the result for the person with anger problems is the same— *social ostracization*. Now, you may think, *"So what?"*

Humans are hard-wired with the need to belong.[34,35] On the emotional front, it hurts to be excluded, but you also miss a lot when you're not part of a group. Examples: a friendly neighbor who lends you a ladder so you can clean your top windows, a colleague who tells you about an opening you never even heard about, a cross-cultural friend who shares with you the joys of their food despite you never leaving the city you were born in, and so on.

Studies also show that a healthy social circle contributes to maintaining good physical and mental health.[36,37]

Financial Costs of Anger

Uncontrolled, problematic anger can have serious financial consequences. Studies show that anger problems may result in involuntary job loss[38] and make you handle your finances poorly[39].

For example, suppose you express your rage at your supervisor. In that case, you may be passed over for every chance of promotion, or worse, you may even face termination because you're not a "team player" or not "leadership material".

Anger may also lead to poor money decisions. For example, suppose you're angry because you're not financially where you want to be in life. In that case, you may act recklessly and spend money on lottery tickets, join quick-money schemes, and make poor investment choices, which may result in even more financial problems.

As for me, the financial costs of my anger came due to my inability to finish whatever it was I started. During my academic years, I kept switching majors because the minute things got difficult, I would get very angry and start blaming others, the environment, or life in general. Since things were not working in my favor, I figured I was studying the wrong thing, so I would switch to another major.

In total, I have studied in seven different programs and changed majors six times. The financial impact of that, not even considering the lost years when I could have been steadily working, is something I have never calculated. Why? I cannot alter the past, so I accept my choices. The best thing I can do is learn new behaviors so that I can change and not keep on making the same decisions. (See DBT Fundamentals: Acceptance and Change, page 370.)

Relationship Costs of Anger

Studies show that the people we know and love the most are the very ones we will most likely unleash our anger on, undeserved or not.[40] Perhaps, we do this because we feel "comfortable" with them and that at some level, no matter what we do, we hope we will be understood and forgiven. However, this is not always the case. Anger can leave long-lasting wounds on the people we care about, and it has the potential to destroy even the most "established" relationships.

In our rage, we may blurt out a loved one's secret, unjustly blame or accuse someone, verbally or physically hurt someone, and so on. These actions make it very difficult for the people we love to trust us again. It also makes them feel they cannot talk to us honestly because we might misunderstand and react angrily again. In the end, the result is the same: a breakdown in the relationship.

This is what my friend Monica had to say:

"When it comes to relationships, I am very insecure. No one would believe this because, on the outside, I am probably the most level-headed, non-dramatic, stick-to-the-facts woman you'll ever meet.

Greg and I got married after a year of dating, and he started to see that angry side of me; that side that would always accuse him of lying and cheating for no real reason and angrily threaten him with divorce. One time, about three years after being married, in a fit of rage, I violently threw a drinking glass over his head while he was sitting at the dinner table, the shattering glass echoing between us. Greg quietly got up, cleaned the mess, and went to bed. It made me angrier. I wanted to fight. He wanted to sleep?!

The following day, I was still seething with anger, and as per my usual script, I threatened him with a divorce. This time, he looked up at me and said, "I don't want that, but if you really do, I won't stop you." We broke up because, well, why would I back down? My anger was propelling me to take this path.

Years later, and after much therapy, I would understand the real reason for my uncontrollable anger: deep-seated abandonment issues. I never saw Greg again, but I heard he re-married and now has two beautiful girls. I would be lying if I said I never fantasize about what could have been."

In my anger journey, I can tell you that I have suffered all the different costs of anger mentioned in this chapter.

I have spent years suffering from insomnia, migraines, and a weak immune system (*physical costs*), an endless cycle of anger, shame, and regret (*emotional costs*), the worsening of my OCD and anxiety disorder, which led to depression (*mental costs*), the continuation of my isolation and loneliness (*social costs*), and going through six academic majors (*financial costs*).

As for *relationship costs,* my relationship with my family continued to be fragile at best and volatile at worst. Romantic relationships were not affected because, well, I did not have any.

I truly believe that had I continued down this path, my mental health problems, aggravated by my anger issues, would have continued, and at some point late in life, I would probably look back at an unhappy and unfulfilled life. Luckily, I reached for help, discovered DBT along the way, and changed the course of my life.

In the next chapter, I'll gladly share with you the DBT skills and tools I used to manage anger in real life. But before I do, here's a quick rundown of what we discussed in this chapter:

- Anger is a physical and mental process.

- Anger can wear down your body and cause various health problems.
- Anger that doesn't go away can cause emotional stress, which can affect every part of our lives.
- Anger can wear your mind down and lead to a number of mental health problems.
- Anger can lead to social ostracization.
- Anger can negatively affect your finances.
- When we're angry, we hurt the ones closest to us. As a result, anger can damage our most valued relationships.

REAL LIFE Tools to Effectively Manage Your Anger

"The boiling water that does not cool down only dries out!"
— Ernest Agyemang Yeboah

In Chapter 3 (page 421) you learned that we usually express our anger in destructive ways. In Chapter 4 (page 435) you learned that if you continue to express your anger destructively, you will eventually pay a very hefty price for it. As such, learning healthy and empowering ways to manage and express your anger is crucial. But before you can do that, you must understand the link between anger and vulnerability.

Anger and Vulnerability

As you have learned, anger is our response when we sense a threat, perceive that someone has done us wrong, or experience any form of injustice or unfairness. In many ways, anger keeps us "safe". How? Well, if we focus on anger itself, then we don't need to dig deep and find out WHY we are angry. Often, understanding the WHY is more painful and harder to accept.

As I have previously shared with you, I stayed angry for years because I didn't want to know why I was so alone and isolated in this world. I already had OCD and anxiety disorders, so I don't think I could have dealt with the physical and emotional pain of not being loved. I know that's not true today, but back then, I thought I only had two options: be angry or accept that no one cares about me. I chose anger.

The anger made me feel that I had some semblance of control in my life. Being angry was better than being invisible. But here's the bottom line: anger wasn't better. It did not solve anything, and I was just getting more and more miserable!

With professional help, I learned that letting myself *feel vulnerable* is the first step to healing and stopping my anger from controlling my life. Believe me; I know this is not easy; to "not be angry" means to experience fear.

Remember, this is how it is in a nutshell: when we sense threat or danger, wrongdoing, unfairness, or injustice, the amygdala is triggered. The amygdala is the part of our brain that controls our emotions (*how we feel*) and behavior (*how we act*). So, what are we left with if we don't go into anger? Fear or anxiety, right? And NO ONE likes feeling this vulnerable.

I know this all sounds scary, but I have learned that vulnerability doesn't mean giving up control and letting other people hurt me. It is about being honest and open with myself about the things that hurt me or cause me sadness.

Once I gave myself permission to feel vulnerability, I started to understand my anger, how to effectively deal with it when it happened, and how to get rid of the things that made me angry in the first place. And guess what? Since I fixed what was causing my anger, I was no longer angry.

Top 8 Tips to Be More Vulnerable

Vulnerability or emotional exposure is not a weakness. In fact, it takes a lot of strength and courage to allow yourself to feel vulnerable. Understandably, years of hiding your true self and denying your wants and needs mean that feeling vulnerable takes some getting used to. So, the following are some tips to help you be okay with feeling vulnerable.

1. **Discover yourself and learn to love the person you uncover at the end of that journey.** We spend so much time twisting and turning ourselves into the people others expect to see that we lose who we really are in the process. So my advice is to take the time to get to know yourself.

Here's what my friend Kara had to say:

"Everyone was an over achiever in my family. You can say that I was considered the weakest link. Overtime, I just absorbed this belief. I wouldn't share my thoughts because it probably wouldn't be as great as what others would say. I wouldn't go against anyone because, well, what did I know? I developed the mindset that people are always "better" than me.

Unsurprisingly, as an adult, I suffered from very low self-esteem, which manifested into self-abusive anger. During therapy, I realized that as much I loved my family, I needed to get away from them. I took a job that took me to India. Despite everyone in my life telling me that I shouldn't do it and that I was making a big mistake, I went ahead with it. I was at a place where I just wanted to be on my own, and it was the best decision I had ever made.

Contrary to my own belief, I was not weak at all. I was strong and very capable of finding solutions to problems on my own. I did discover that I had this tendency to hide myself, my real thoughts, and my real feelings for fear of being reprimanded or overstepping someone, so I still have work to do. But I am just so glad that I had the courage to take the step to discover me."

2. **Be honest.** No one is perfect, and part of being vulnerable is knowing your weaknesses, your "less-than-lovable" sides, and acknowledging and admitting mistakes you have made. It is also about learning to communicate what you

need from others, including your expectations and boundaries. (**Tip**: If you need help establishing boundaries, see How to Set Boundaries on page 484.)

3. **Stop seeking the approval of others.** Be 100% okay with who you are, regardless of what others think. Vulnerability is often associated with weakness because it exposes us to other people's opinions and judgments. But if we stop valuing other people's opinions about us above our own, then we will be free to be who we want to be without fear.

In my teens, I was always trying to be friends with everyone. Please note that a healthy sense of *belongingness* is good for our well-being.[41] However, overdoing this is not good because this is when you will lose yourself. This is what happened to me.

I was always seeking the approval of others; what they thought of me was more important than what I thought of myself. This meant I was always trying to change myself into the person I thought other people wanted me to be. In the end, the "friendship" I was looking for never happened, and I'd go back to feeling anxious, depressed, and angry.

Today, whenever I look back, I realize that I shouldn't have spent so much time and effort caring about what others thought of me. For one, I hardly kept in touch with any of them. Most importantly, I should have paid more attention to myself, learning to know and love myself.

4. **Learn how to say "sorry".** I have learned that my anger issues were very much connected to my ego. In the past, I would much rather be enraged than say sorry because that meant (1) I did something wrong and (2) I needed to take responsibility for my actions.

Saying sorry is something my whole family struggles with. You see, in the Chinese culture, saving face and not looking bad is very important so it's rare for anyone in my family to apologize or admit fault. This was just not "normal" to me.

I also thought that apologizing showed people that I had low self-esteem. I had it backward.

Over the years, I have come to the conclusion that the most secure, confident people have no qualms apologizing at all. They're 100% okay with admitting mistakes and saying sorry precisely because they have great self-esteem.

A friend also shared something very powerful with me. She said, *"Apologizing doesn't always mean admitting wrongdoing. Even if you didn't do anything wrong, can't you merely be sorry that your actions caused someone else's feelings to be hurt?"*

Further, saying sorry, even if you did not do anything wrong, opens the lines of communication, enabling you to build trust and reconnect with the person who got hurt.

5. **Take chances.** They say that a human being's greatest fear in life is the unknown. If we are unsure of the outcome, there's a big chance of loss or failure. But we forget there's also an equal possibility for gain and success. So learn to take chances. Sure, the results may not be what you thought they would be—they could be better.

After I graduated from university, I had the opportunity to move to Korea and teach English in a public school. This was a VERY big move for me; many changes would happen. Ultimately, I decided to take the chance, and it was the best decision of my life! I grew a lot as a person and ended up staying in Korea for three years.

So if ever you're presented with an opportunity for change (e.g., striking up a conversation with someone you like, asking for a raise, raising your hand to lead a team, etc.), take the chance. You never know when such an opportunity will present again.

6. **Write down your fears.** Find a safe and quiet space, and then write down all your fears. They don't need to be in any order; just let all those fears tumble out of you. Keep the list and revisit it in a day or two. When you read them again, take a really good look at them. This will give you a better idea of how significant your fears are as a result.

Examples:
I'm afraid my relationship won't last.
I'm afraid of speaking in front of a group.
I'm afraid to reconcile with my parents.

After some time, revisit these fears and really deliberate on them. (**Tip**: Use Wise Mind, page 379.)

For example: *I'm afraid my relationship won't last.* Instead of fearing what MAY happen, why not focus on what IS happening. How long are you in the relationship? How has this relationship helped you and your partner develop, individually and as a couple? What other great ways can you grow this relationship?

7. **Get comfortable with sharing personal information.** We are NOT in the habit of sharing too much about ourselves because we fear many things: rejection, disappointment, abandonment, and so many other insecurities. But if you want to be more comfortable with being vulnerable, you have to learn to share more about your real self. Start with simple guilty pleasures like admitting to like a particular reality TV show, having a fondness for 80's pop songs, checking celebrity gossip sites from time to time, and so on.

8. **Don't be afraid to ask for help.** It is easy to isolate yourself from others when you're hurting or feeling unsure. However, a crucial component of vulnerability is admitting to loved ones that you need them, even if it is just to listen.

How Does Vulnerability Help Me With My Anger?

> *"You can't get to courage without walking through vulnerability."* – Brené Brown

Anger is a shield. We use it to protect ourselves from feeling and experiencing deep physical, mental, and emotional pain. At this stage, your anger is probably an "automatic response," so it is hard to just "get on and deal with it." However, suppose you're comfortable with feeling vulnerable. In that case, you'll be much more open and ready to adopt the DBT skills and exercises in the next pages.

Worksheet: Vulnerability List

Getting comfortable with vulnerability is not a switch you can just turn "on." You need to get used to it. Following are a few things you can do to practice feeling vulnerable. Write down the date you did each one and your thoughts about them.

Notes:
- You don't need to do the items in any order. Just do the ones you're comfortable doing for now.
- Feel free to do any activity more than once.
- Not all of them may apply to you, so feel free to skip a few and add your ideas to the list.

Activity	Date	Thoughts
Example: *Greet a complete stranger.*	*Aug. 1*	*I was uncomfortable, but the experience was NOT as bad as I thought it would be.*
Example: *Greet a complete stranger.*	*Aug. 2*	*I greeted them, but the person did not greet me back. First, I was annoyed because I put myself out there, but I am OKAY with it. I realized I don't control other people's actions, only my own.*
Greet a complete stranger.		
Ask for feedback.		
Say sorry to someone.		

Activity	Date	Thoughts
Ask someone for help.		
Make an unpopular suggestion.		
Share an unpopular opinion.		
Go somewhere you know you'll need to wait. (e.g., a popular coffee shop, grocery store during peak hours, etc.) *Note: The vulnerability part here is exposing yourself to feelings of frustration (due to impatience). IF you're feeling overwhelmed and feel yourself getting angry, leave the situation.*		
Join friends on a night out knowing there's a big chance of changes in plans during the night.		
Take a cooking class. *Note: Actually, you can take any class you want. The vulnerability part here is knowing you're not in control of the situation. You're deliberately surrounding control to the class teacher. You are here to follow.*		

Activity	Date	Thoughts
For singles: Go on a blind date.		
For married couples: Schedule a time to talk to your partner about anything that's bothering you or them. *Note: The vulnerability part here is opening yourself to your partner. Avoid interrupting if they have something to say that hurts or offends you. Just hear them out and wait for your turn to say anything. IF you're feeling overwhelmed and feel yourself getting angry, take a break. DO NOT respond in anger.*		
Do something you know you're not good at.		
Share one personal thing with someone you trust.		
Call or reach out to someone you have lost touch with.		
Call out someone constantly breaking your boundaries.		
Tell someone you care.		

Activity	Date	Thoughts
Say NO to someone.		
Feel free to add more activities to the extra rows below.		

Mindfulness Skills for Anger Management

When we are angry, it feels like everything is happening so fast. Amygdala hijack (page 410) kicks in, and before we know it, we say or do something we usually regret. Sometimes, though, anger doesn't come over us quickly; it can be a feeling that simmers just beneath the surface. Still, anger has the power to dominate, whether it rises suddenly in a flaming burst or burns quietly over time. And when that happens, we either lash out or internalize the feeling, neither of which is good.

Mindfulness helps calm the amygdala, the part of the brain that is linked to fear and emotion. In fact, a 2013 study revealed that after eight weeks of practicing mindfulness, the amygdala seemed to shrink. As the amygdala shrank, the pre-frontal cortex, which is linked to higher-order brain functions like being aware, focusing, and making decisions, got thicker.[42]

In short, mindfulness weakens the part of the brain that focuses on emotions and strengthens the part that helps us think logically and make decisions. By practicing mindfulness, or being in the moment, we teach ourselves to be less controlled by strong emotions like anger.

Worksheet: Mindful Body Scanning (Anger Observation)

This Mindfulness exercise will help calm your nerves, focus your thoughts, and center your being when feeling angry.

1. Sit or lie down, whatever is most comfortable for you. Close your eyes.

2. Breathe in deeply for a count of four (4), and then exhale for a count of four (4). Do this two (2) more times. (Three rounds in total).

3. Starting with the top of your head, become aware of your scalp. Is it feeling tight because of your anger? If so, take a deep breath in and as you exhale, deliberately relax your head. If it helps, shake your head gently from side to side. Imagine your scalp loosening because of this.

4. Next, move on to your forehead. Is it *scrunched* because of your anger? If so, take a deep breath in and as you exhale, deliberately relax your forehead. Release all those angry lines.

5. Next, move on to your eyebrows. Is one arched more than the other because of your anger? If so, take a deep breath in and as you exhale, deliberately relax your eyebrows. Release all that tension.

6. Next, move on to your cheekbones. Are they tight and elevated because of your anger? If so, breathe in and as you breathe out, relax your cheeks.

7. Continue down until you've covered your whole body.

After you have done this exercise a couple of times, you'll gain knowledge about how your body physically reacts to anger. For example, not everybody scrunches their forehead and brings their eyebrows together when angry.

For me, my top physical anger expressions are: (1) clenched jaw, (2) tight shoulders, and (3) clenched fists. I never knew this about myself until I started doing the above exercise whenever I felt angry. When I learned this about myself, I could calm down faster by zeroing on these three body parts. Here's what I do:

1. Clenched jaw? I take a deep breath in, and as I exhale, I force myself to smile a bit. I take a deep breath in again, and as I exhale, I smile a bit wider, and so on.
2. Tight shoulders? I take a deep breath in, and as I exhale, I force myself to relax my shoulders. I take a deep breath in again, and as I exhale, I slowly round my shoulders.
3. Clenched fists? I take a deep breath in, and as I exhale, I open my hands wide. I take a deep breath in again, gently closing my fists as I do so, and as I exhale, I open my hands wide.

There's no rule about how many 'rounds' of breathing you need to do. It all depends on how angry you are at the moment and how fast you can calm down. As always, practice makes progress. Before you know it, this will all become a habit for you.

Worksheet: Mindfully Angry (Anger Description)

Sometimes, all it takes to deal with anger is simply to recognize it. Yes, this is hard to do when you're really angry, but doing so lessens the effect of your anger. If we fight, hide, or deny our anger because we don't like how it makes us feel, our anxiety and negative feelings about the situation tend to worsen. As what DBT teaches us, this just prolongs our suffering (from anger).

1. Sit or lie down, whatever is most comfortable for you. Close your eyes.‡‡

2. Imagine a stack of paper next to you. In simple words, describe your anger. Write down every word that comes to your head. It can be an emotion, a person, a place, an activity, a color, anything!

   For example, on a piece of paper, imagine writing the word "**red**" or the phrase "**seeing red**." Mentally take that piece of paper, crumple into a ball and throw it in your imaginary waste basket.

It is important that you do this exercise non-judgmentally. Just describe the anger, don't evaluate it. Don't stay on it either (ruminate). Write and release. Write and release. Write and release.

---

‡‡ If you prefer, make this a physical exercise rather than a mental one. That is, grab a stack of paper, a pen and a place a wastebasket near you.

When you write down your anger descriptors, you're accepting your current state. When you release them, you're helping yourself calm down.

Distress Tolerance Skills for Anger Management

Anger is such a powerful, overwhelming emotion. So much so that we cannot help ourselves from lashing out, internally or externally. But basically, we do this because we cannot tolerate our distress.

Remember the Anger Cycle (page 411)?

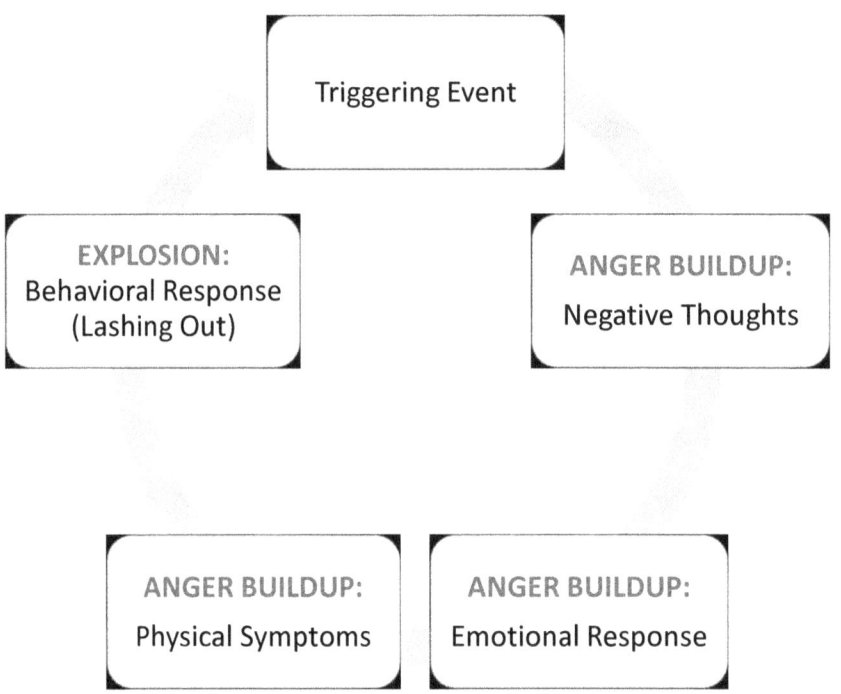

But what if you can tolerate that emotional distress (Anger Buildup)? If you're able to do that, then you can prevent the next process (Explosion), right?

The following DBT Distress Tolerance exercises will help you build the skills you need so that your (anger) cup never flows over.

Worksheet: Radical Acceptance

Radical Acceptance is based on the idea that *we suffer because we are attached to our anger, not because anger is bad in and of itself*. By getting angry and telling yourself that this situation "should not be happening," you miss the point that the situation is already happening, with or without you, with or without your consent.

This does NOT mean that you give up and give in. Instead, Radical Acceptance means that you know that denying your anger-related thoughts and feelings won't change the situation. If you fight, ignore or deny anger, you get stuck in thoughts like, *"Life is so unfair!"*, *"Why me?!"*, *"I don't deserve this!"*, *"this is NOT right!"*

Remember too that Radical Acceptance is NOT the same as approval or consent. Instead, it means accepting with your whole mind, body, and spirit that you cannot change the present situation, even if you don't like it. By radically accepting the things you cannot change, you avoid getting stuck in anger.

I'll be the first to admit that learning to accept something we don't like is very difficult. Whenever I got frustrated, it was very hard for me to radically accept the situation when every fiber of my being was trying to go to my default mode: *anger*.

However, humans are not born with anger. Yes, we have the potential to feel every emotion on the planet, including anger, but anger styles and anger responses are all learned.[43] So, this means that we can unlearn it.

It takes time to unlearn the old and learn the new, but it is not impossible. The following worksheet will help you learn how to apply Radical Acceptance when you're angry.

1. OBSERVE. Notice HOW you are fighting reality or questioning it.

Example: Oh no, this shouldn't be happening! (This is denying the situation).

Your turn: *(List down the ways you may be ignoring, fighting, or denying your anger.)*

_____
_____
_____

2. REMEMBER. Remind yourself that the current situation (reality) is the way it is and cannot be changed.

Example: I don't like it, but it is what it is.

Your turn: *(Write down your own anger acceptance statement.)*

_____
_____
_____

3. RATIONALIZE. Remind yourself that there are reasons behind this current situation. Recognize that past events have led to this exact moment. It did not just happen; there are reasons why things happened this way.

Example:
Situation: I am furious at [colleague] for stealing my marketing idea.
Possible Reason 1: I let [colleague] pass his workload to me before, so this probably let them think they can always get away with things like this.
Possible Reason 2: When [boss] asked for ideas, I did not speak up.

Your turn: *(Write down your reasons.)*

_____
_____
_____

4. ACCEPT. Practice acceptance of the situation involving your whole being.

Examples:

Accepting with my mind: I am okay. I accept this. It is all good.

Accepting with my body: do <u>Body Scanning</u>

Your turn:

_____
_____
_____

5. PRACTICE OPPOSITE ACTION. List down everything that you would do, assuming that you have indeed radically accepted the situation.

Example:

Situation: I was furious at [colleague] for stealing my marketing idea.

(1) I did Body Scanning, so I am physically relaxed now. I will NOT have an angry demeanor when I meet [colleague].

(2) When I meet [colleague], I will not replay the meeting in my mind.

Your turn:

_____
_____
_____
_____
_____
_____

6. COPE AHEAD. Close your eyes and imagine radically accepting something you do not want to. Visualize acceptance anyway. That is, play in your mind what you're going to do.

Example:

Situation: I find it very hard to accept reading the new marketing materials because they will have [colleague]'s name as the author.

Visualizing acceptance:

(1) When I receive the new marketing materials, I will read them without resentment. I will treat them just like any marketing material in the company.

Your turn:

_____
_____
_____
_____
_____

7. ATTEND. Pay attention to your physical reactions while you consider what you need to accept.

Example: While visualizing acceptance, I can feel myself starting to clench my fists. I should do some deep breathing and open my hands wide each time I exhale.

Your turn:

_____
_____
_____
_____
_____

8. ALLOW. Give yourself permission to feel disappointed, upset, or grieve.

Example:

Situation: I am furious at [colleague] for stealing my marketing idea.

Allow: I am feeling really sad about the missed opportunity.

Your turn:

_____
_____
_____

9. ACKNOWLEDGE. Recognize that even in the face of hardship, life is still worth living!

Example:
Situation: I am furious at [colleague] for stealing my marketing idea.
Acknowledge: I'll get through this. Another opportunity will present itself, and next time, I'll have an even better idea to share.

Your turn:

_____
_____
_____

10. PROS & CONS. Whenever you're unable to radically accept a situation, chances are you'll feel an overwhelming need (urge) to act on your anger. Use the **Pros & Cons** table below to help you fight your urge.

Pros & Cons is about considering the positive and negative aspects of acting and not acting on your anger. The goal is for you to see that tolerating your anger is better than acting on your anger impulses.

Example:

Situation: [Colleague] stole my marketing idea and presented it as theirs.

Urge: Lash out.

Your turn:

Your Situation:

_____

Your Urge:

_____

	Acting on Your Urge	**Resisting Your Urge**
PROS	*Example:* *I'll feel some relief.*	*Example:* *I won't regret anything tomorrow.*
CONS	*Example:* *I might physically harm someone.* *My boss may frown at my "short-temper."*	*Example:* *I might internalize my anger.*

Worksheet: STOP

Often, when we are angry, we don't have time to think. Mindfulness (page 232) and Radical Acceptance (page 223) skills are the PAUSE buttons you can apply to prevent lashing out. Sometimes, though, the desire to act on your anger impulses (urges) is so strong that you can barely contain yourself. In this scenario, adopt the **STOP** skill below. It will help prevent you from acting on impulse and make a stressful or hard situation even worse.

 top.

Stop! Freeze. Don't move a muscle.
Physically freezing for a moment prevents you from acting impulsively (which is acting in Emotion Mind).

Example: A co-worker has taken credit for work you've done, and you have this insane urge to punch them in the face. Instead of doing so, FREEZE in your tracks.

 ake a step back.

Take a physical and mental step back from the situation. Take a deep breath and continue to do so for as long as necessary until you are in control. Remember this: we hardly ever need to make a split-second decision about anything, so give yourself time to think before you act.

Example: You're very angry at your partner for volunteering YOUR time this weekend to a cause you don't even believe in. Before you say or do something you'll regret, FREEZE and then TAKE A PHYSICAL STEP BACK. Of course, don't just leave. That will lead to even more misunderstandings. Say to your partner, "Wait, I am not okay with what you did. I need a moment," and then leave the room.

bserve.

Take note of what is going on within you and around you. Do this one-mindfully and non-judgmentally. That is, literally observe things as if you're making a list.

Example of observing yourself: I am sitting. My face feels hot. My breathing is ragged.*
Example of observing your surroundings: There's a ball on the floor. There's a half-filled water glass on the table. My partner is looking at me.

* Since you notice that your breathing is ragged. Make a deliberate choice to practice Mindful Breathing (page 378).

What are you observing?

_____
_____
_____

 roceed mindfully.

You've taken a break from your emotions, and now it is time to proceed mindfully. Enter Wise Mind (page 379) and ask yourself, "*What do I want to happen?*", "*How do I make this situation better?*", "*How do I honor my feelings AND be reasonable about this situation?*"

Example: Okay, I don't want to go, but my partner says it is only for an hour. I can deal with that. But I need to tell them that (1) moving forward, they should respect MY time, so they need to ask me first before if I am okay with whatever they're planning, and that (2) since I am compromising, I'll hold to that one hour, and if it goes further, my partner will understand and NOT get angry if I leave.

What do you want to do to proceed mindfully?

_____
_____
_____

Worksheet: ACCEPTS

Distraction is one of the best ways you can ride out your anger. The following DBT exercise is called **ACCEPTS**. It is a great way to build your frustration tolerance levels because it can give you the space you need to process your anger. It helps you divert your attention, which helps calm your emotions down.

 ctivities.

Make a list of stimulating and attention-demanding activities that you enjoy doing. The goal is to draw yourself completely into doing something fun so that you don't spend any mental, physical, or emotional resources on your anger.

Examples: solve a puzzle, engage in coloring by number by getting a coloring book or downloading an app like Color by Number for Adults, follow a new exercise routine on YouTube

Your turn:

_____
_____
_____

 ontributing.

Turn your attention to others' needs. Contributing will make you feel good and take your mind off your own problems.

Examples: de-clutter and donate old clothes, volunteer to clear a neighbor's front yard, check your kitchen cabinets and find at least 10 food items to donate, etc.

Your turn:

_____
_____
_____

Comparisons.

Recall an infuriating situation in the past that's worse than your current frustration.

Example: I got so frustrated with my brother not answering my text messages that I sent a very angry message listing down all the things he owed me and called him ungrateful. Our relationship has never been the same since.

Your turn:

_____
_____
_____

Emotions.

Do something completely opposite to how you feel. So think about what you would normally do when you're angry and then deliberately do the contrary.

Examples:

I want to SCREAM! (Opposite: Be quiet and meditate.)

I want to clench my jaw and fists. (Opposite: Smile and open your hands wide.)

Your turn:

_____
_____
_____

ush away.

Actively push your anger away. Select your desired action from the list below. Feel free to include extra choices as well.

- ☐ Go somewhere where you can be alone and then, in your loudest voice, say, **STOP! GO AWAY!**
- ☐ Write down your "anger words" (e.g., *pissed, furious, red, boiling*, etc.) on a piece of paper, and then let them go by burning the paper. (Alternatively, see [Mindfully Angry](#) on page 457.)
- ☐ Take a stroll. Pick up a leaf. Imagine that the leaf represents your anger, and then let it go and watch it drift away from you. If this is too gentle for you, pick up a stone. Imagine it representing your anger, and then throw it as hard and as far away from you as you can.

☐ Others:

_____
_____
_____

T houghts.

Transport yourself to a happy time in your life (happy thoughts).

Examples: watch a feel-good movie; look at a picture of a loved one, relive a surprise that family or friends did for you

Your turn:

_____
_____

S ensations.

Distract your angry thoughts and feelings by subjecting yourself to different physical sensations. Select what you want to do below, and feel free to include extra choices as well.

- ☐ Suck on a lemon wedge.
- ☐ Eat a few pieces of really hot (spicy) spicy chips.
- ☐ Hold ice cubes.
- ☐ Chew intensely sour gum.
- ☐ In winter, walk out in the cold.
- ☐ Others:

_____
_____
_____

Emotion Regulation Skills for Anger Management

Anger can be long-lasting. Some people get angry quickly, they lash out and explode, and then they are done. For others, like me, anger stays for days on end.

One of the reasons anger is so hard to regulate is because it IS a powerful emotion. But then again, it is a power we give. By not regulating anger and moving forward, we give it the fuel it needs to stay and dominate our lives.

Emotion Regulation is all about influencing the anger we have, when we have it, how we experience it, and how we express it. It is that we are controlling anger instead of the other way around.

The DBT exercises below will help you up-regulate positive emotions, which in turn down-regulate our susceptibility to anger. The goal is simple: regulate your anger so that you feel less angry.

Worksheet: BPE

A happy person is not easily angered. **BPE** stands for **B**uild **P**ositive **E**xperiences, and it is an exercise designed to increase positive emotions in your life, thereby reducing your capacity for anger and other negative emotions.

Build Positive Experiences I

Write down 10 experiences that make you instantly happy. These are positive events that make you feel better while doing them or immediately thereafter.

1. Example: walking my dog
2. Example: tending to my herb garden
3. Example: meditating
4.
5.
6.
7.
8.
9.
10.

Build Positive Experiences II

Choose one experience from the list above, and then resolve to do it every day. What you decide to do and how long you wish to do it is not important. The goal is to do it EVERY SINGLE DAY. (Daily happy habits!)

Example: meditating

I will <u>meditate</u> every day for <u>30 minutes in the morning</u>.

Your turn:

I choose: _____

I will _____ **every day for** _____.

Build Positive Experiences III

Write down 10 experiences that have the potential to give you long-lasting happiness. These are positive events that you may need to plan for, but when achieved, their positive impact on your life is long-term.

1. *Example: take a cooking class*

2. *Example: get a gym membership*

3. *Example: go on a weekend getaway alone*

4.

5.

6.

7.

8.

9.

10.

Worksheet: PLEASE

Your physical health has a direct impact on your emotional health and vice versa.[44] So, to create positive emotional change, it is crucial to take care of your body too.

This DBT exercise emphasizes the importance of taking care of our physical health because an unhealthy body makes it difficult for us to manage our emotions.

PL **P**hysical **Il**lness

Don't wait to see a doctor and take any prescribed drugs if you're feeling physically sick. It is also advisable to reach out to someone (e.g., a friend, a family member, a neighbor, etc.) so that you are not by yourself through this time. If you don't want to consult a physician or are physically unable to do so, then, by all means, pursue a holistic approach to wellness. The idea is to GET HELP so that your illness doesn't worsen.

When was the last time you were physically ill?
_____

Did you see a doctor?   Y / N
Why or why not?
_____
_____

E Balanced Eating

Make sure you're consuming a nutritious, balanced diet. Avoid anything that comes from a bag or a jar (processed food). As much as possible, eat food in its natural form. For example, if you want to put strawberry jam on your toast, which is high in sugar, put real strawberries instead.

Below is a quick, **7-day Healthy Swaps** log. It is important to note that the objective here is NOT to lose weight. The table below is simply a tool you can use to make you aware of any unhealthy food choices you may be making today and to swap them for healthier ones.

If you're already doing this, great! I encourage you to move on to more detailed food journaling using apps like MyFitnessPal.

Note: Please always consult your doctor or a nutritionist before making any drastic food changes in your diet.

7-Day Healthy Swaps		
Day	**Current Food Choice**	**Swap**
Monday	*Example: white bread*	*Example: wholegrain bread*
Tuesday		
Wednesday		
Thursday		
Friday		
Saturday		
Sunday		

Avoid Unhealthy Substances

Consuming unhealthy substances such as caffeine, alcohol, and prohibited drugs can exacerbate your anger, so avoid taking them. Instead, consume water or lemon water, green tea, healthy smoothies, etc.

S Sleep

Adults need seven (7) or more hours of quality sleep each night.[45] If you don't, you'll have low energy levels, which makes you more likely to give into anger and display aggressive behaviors.[46]

To check if you're getting enough sleep, try this **7-Day Sleep Log**. Just jot down the time you sleep and the time you wake up and calculate your total sleep hours.

7-Day Sleep Log			
Date	**Sleep Time**	**Wake Time**	**Total Sleep Hours**
Monday	*Example:* *11:30 PM*	*Example:* *6:00 AM*	*Example:* *6.5 hours*
Tuesday			
Wednesday			
Thursday			
Friday			
Saturday			
Sunday			

Exercise

Engage in at least 30 minutes of active daily movement. If you haven't worked out in a while, start with something shorter (e.g., 10 minutes) and less intense (e.g., walking). Note that you don't have to join a gym or subscribe to a class. You can do yoga, follow a YouTube Zumba class, power walk in a nearby forest, etc.

7-Day Exercise Log		
	Exercise Activity	**Time Spent**
Monday	Example: indoor cycling	Example: 1 hour
Tuesday		
Wednesday		
Thursday		
Friday		
Saturday		
Sunday		

Are you exercising enough? Y / N

If not, list down ways to increase your active hours.

Example: wake up an hour earlier, set out my exercise clothes and shoes, and put them in the bedroom, so it is the first thing I see when I wake up

I wanted to increase my daily steps, so I bought a pedometer to motivate me. If you're interested in joining a gym, then subscribe to one that's near your workplace or home.

The goal is to make exercising an "easy choice" and a seamless part of your daily routine.
1.
2.
3.
4.
5.

Worksheet: COPE AHEAD

Coping ahead is identifying situations that are likely to make you angry. In Why Are You Angry (page 421) you listed down your anger triggers. Revisit your list, select one, and then PLAN AHEAD how to handle it. You can also write down below a specific event or situation that happened to you recently or a long time ago.

Triggering Event or Situation:

Example: Mom telling me that I am too fat.

Your turn:
_____
_____
_____

What DBT skills do you want to use to handle this situation?

Example: Wise Mind (page 379), Opposite to Emotion (page 391), DEARMAN (page 399)

Your turn:
_____
_____
_____

Imagine the situation happening RIGHT NOW.
(Be as detailed as you can.)

Example: Mom's entering the door wearing her favorite red blouse. She greets me while looking at me up and down at the same time and says, "Oh, you look like you have gained a few."

Your turn:
_____
_____
_____

Role-play; imagine in your mind how the situation is going to unfold.

Example: I excuse myself, walk to my room and quickly do Wise Mind. I decide what Opposite Action I am going to do. (I'll be cheerful because what I really want to be is defensive.) And then I am going to apply DEARMAN.

Your turn:
_____
_____
_____

Take a break. Imaginary role-playing can be mentally exhausting, and since you're thinking about a situation that angers you, it is highly possible that the role-playing itself will make you angry. As such, it is important to take a break after doing this exercise.

Example: I'll do Mindful Breathing (page 378) and then do one of my short-term BPEs (page 301).

Your turn:
_____
_____
_____

Interpersonal Effectiveness Skills for Anger Management

One of the most devastating costs of anger is the deterioration of relationships. Our volatile emotions and actions can result in lasting scars on the people we value and love the most.

In my case, I was caught in a vicious no-win situation. I felt extremely alone and isolated, which was one of the things that made me very angry. But my anger kept me from having real, deep relationships with other people. So, as the years went by, I just got lonelier and angrier.

Interacting with others has also always been so awkward for me, so I was very glad to learn the Interpersonal Effectiveness exercise Finding Friends (page 395). It was exactly what I needed to get the ball rolling in terms of meeting people and trying to forge friendships.

The fact that my personal boundaries were always being crossed at home was another big reason for my chronic anger.

In Chinese culture, there are no "boundaries." Privacy is an alien concept, and I grew up with my mom constantly barging into my room. In my parents' minds, it is *their* house, so they don't need permission to enter any of its rooms. I have also experienced my mom throwing away some of my stuff because *she* did not think they were important to me and to be respected.

In Chinese culture, we don't really "talk" about feelings. In fact, if you "talk back" to your parents, you're considered a defiant, ungrateful child, so there wasn't really much I could do in terms of setting boundaries at home. Of course, that did not mean I did not get angry when my boundaries were crossed, and since I couldn't show anger, I internalized it.

When I left home, I did not internalize my anger anymore. Whenever my boundaries were crossed, I did the exact opposite; I lashed out.

Again, I was caught in a loop. I did not communicate my boundaries, so people kept crossing them. Each time my boundaries were crossed, I would get furious.

When I finally realized the importance of setting boundaries, I got stumped again! This time, I was surprised to realize that I had trouble defining my boundaries and claiming my right to them.

So, let's start with identifying personal boundaries. After that, I'll share the DBT tools you need to start communicating them effectively so that you can get the outcomes you want from your interactions with other people.

How to Set Boundaries

> *"Anger is our reaction to the violation of our boundaries."—Kathleen Dowling Singh*

When our boundaries are always being crossed, we get frustrated, overwhelmed, and angry. So it is important to set healthy boundaries because they communicate what you will and will not tolerate. Note, though, that a "healthy boundary" doesn't mean saying "No" all the time. It means knowing when to say "Yes" and when to say "No."

If you're finding it difficult to figure out where you want to draw the line between yourself and other people, the following exercise is for you.

Worksheet: Anger Boundary Journaling

STEP 1. Pick an area in your life where you're often angry.

- FAMILY
- WORK
- PARTNER
- FRIENDS
- DIGITAL WORLD
- MYSELF
- OTHER

STEP 2. Is a specific person or event making you feel this way?

Example: My older sister

Your turn: _____

STEP 3. What do you think is the underlying reason for your anger in this situation? What are you really feeling behind your anger?

(Remember, anger is a secondary emotion.)

Example: Embarrassment

Your turn: _____

STEP 4: Which boundary is being violated? (You can choose more than one.)

- PHYSICAL
- EMOTIONAL
- VERBAL
- TIME
- SEXUAL
- RELATIONSHIP
- OTHER

STEP 5: Describe, in the simplest of words, your current situation.
Example:

> **Area:** Family || **Person:** Sister || **Underling emotion:** Embarrassment || **Crossed Boundary:** Emotional, Relationship || **Situation:** My older sister always comments on my weight regardless of where we are, at home, while out dining, in front of friends.

Your turn:
_____
_____
_____
_____

STEP 6: Plan how you can re-instate your boundary.

Example: This is a sample plan using <u>DEARMAN</u> (page 399).

<u>D</u>*escribe.*
For so many years, I have been receiving comments on my weight.

<u>E</u>*xpress.*
I feel very embarrassed each time that happens. When I was younger, I just cried about it in secret. But it is been a constant source of anger and frustration for me.

<u>A</u>*ssert.*
I want that to stop.

<u>R</u>*einforce.*
This is important to me, so I would really appreciate it if you stop commenting on my weight, especially in front of everyone.

<u>M</u>*indfulness.*
So, I hope you understand my request.

<u>A</u>*ppear confident.*

The plan: I won't apologize to my sister. I'll maintain eye contact. I'll ask her to sit, but if she stands up, I will too.

***Negotiate*.**

If my sister is not taking me seriously, I'll say, "I understand my role in this too, you know. I have let it go on for years. So I'll understand if this doesn't change overnight. But we are adults now, so you should know how I really feel about this."

Your turn:

_____
_____
_____
_____
_____
_____
_____
_____
_____
_____
_____
_____
_____
_____
_____
_____
_____
_____
_____
_____
_____

Worksheet: FAST

The following is an *assertiveness exercise.* It will teach you how to achieve your objectives, maintain relationships, and enhance self-respect. In relationships, you might sometimes go against your values and beliefs in order to be liked or get what you want. The FAST exercise will help you become more effective at self-respect.

F air.

Be reasonable when you talk about what you want and what you need. Don't get too emotional, dramatic, or talk in anger. Just stick to the facts.

Example: I don't think talking about your child's schoolmate passing away is an appropriate topic on my kid's birthday. Let's please change the subject.
NOT: Oh My God! Are you trying to sabotage my kid's birthday party?!

Your turn:

_____
_____
_____
_____

A pologies are not necessary.

Don't apologize for asking. Keep in mind that you have a right to make the request. The other person will also take you more seriously if you make your request with greater assertiveness.

Example: A kid's birthday party should be a fun, happy time, no?
NOT: I am so sorry! I did not mean to be insensitive.

Your turn:

_____
_____

S tick to your values.

Don't give in merely because the other person is uncomfortable or unwilling to comply with your request. This is especially true if complying with your request would violate your moral principles or boundaries.

Example: If the guest talks about the same thing again, say, "[Name], we talked about this already. Please show some respect for my child's birthday party."

Your turn:

_____
_____
_____
_____

T ruthfulness.

Don't lie or exaggerate to get what you want.

Example: I'll be more than happy to spend some time with you later to discuss. But for now, please stop.

Your turn:

_____
_____
_____
_____

Anger and Unfairness

A sense of unfairness or injustice is one of the things that make most people angry. This is because humans have an innate sense of fairness. The basic principle is really "give and receive," and in our minds, this means 50% give and 50% receive. When it is not equal, that's unfair, and we get hopping mad.

Science says that unfairness, injustice, or impartiality evolved in humans to foster cooperation.[47] When we experience unfairness, the *anterior insula* in our brain activates. This area is associated with empathy and disgust, indicating that we are hard-wired to find unfairness repulsive. In response to this injustice, the amygdala (the brain's emotional hub) is also stimulated, leading to feelings of anger and rage.

How to Deal with Unfairness

\# 1. **Stop ruminating.** Dwelling on unfairness prolongs your own suffering from it. It does not change the situation, and by focusing on the unfairness, you're magnifying it, leading to even more feelings of rage. (**Tip**: Practical Radical Acceptance, page 223.)

\# 2. **Cool off—literally.** Subjecting yourself physically to cold temperatures shocks your internal panic button. For example, you can splash cold water on your face, take a cold shower, hold ice cubes, and so on. (See TIPP, page 266.)

\# 3. **Pause and think.** Anger may be our biological reaction to unfairness, but it doesn't mean we need to act on our anger impulses. Prevent the amygdala hijack from happening by using Mindfulness techniques (page 232). Often, when we take the time to think, we realize that the unfairness we perceive may not be as big or serious after all. (It may not even be there at all once you objectively and non-judgementally gather facts about the situation. (**Tip**: See Check the Facts., page 388.)

4. **Accept what's under your control and what's not.** We respond to unfairness with anger, but which aspects should we really focus on?

For example, we cannot change someone else's actions or behavior; we only have control over our own reactions. We cannot go back and relive our childhoods and correct any unfairness that happened; we can only change how we conduct ourselves as adults (today and onwards). We cannot change unfairness or tragedies that occurred in the past; we can only actively support causes that aim to prevent these in the future.

So, whenever you experience unfairness, don't dwell on "what happened?" and "this is wrong!" move to acceptance of the event (because it already happened) and then go to "how can I help?" or "how can I prevent this in the future?"

How to Prevent Yourself from Exploding

All the tools, tips, and exercises in this book to manage your anger take time and practice, so be kind and patient with yourself as you learn new behaviors. However, I do understand that in the real world, anger can come on fast and furious. Here's what my friend Melinda had to say:

"I have been ignored and taken for granted for years in my family, especially by my youngest brother. Things changed positively for me when I started working and living away from home. I started working on my deep resentment and anger issues and am happy to say that I now live a happy life with my husband and three kids. However, some days, the anger still strikes like a lightning bolt.

About a month ago, I received an SMS out of the blue from my brother, whom I hadn't spoken to in three years. No "hi" or "hello." Just "Melinda, your secretary emailed me about a paper I need to sign. I live far from the city and don't have time for this. Just figure it out." My brother lived half an hour from the city. I very calmly messaged him back that I would send my staff to him, so he's not inconvenienced in the least. He did not reply.

All of a sudden, all of my frustrations came out again: all the years of suppressing my anger to keep peace in the family, all the "giving" and "understanding" extended, all the hesitations for wanting to ask for even the smallest of things, all the changes in MY plans to accommodate theirs, all the stuff I just swallowed... I could feel my anger rising as I stared at my brother's name on my phone. I wanted to explode. But I did not.

I went into the bathroom and splashed my face with icy cold water. It was winter, so the water was really cold! I put on my winter boots and jacket and took a walk. When I came back home, I made myself a comforting cup of latte macchiato. I picked up my phone again and deleted my brother's name from the Contacts list."

When you're faced with extreme anger that catches you off-guard, don't explode. This is not because you don't have a right to your anger. This is because if you explode, you're giving up more of your power to the other person or the situation. So, here's a rapid-fire list of things to do. You don't need to do them all or in sequence. The objective is to do something quick to experience immediate relief.

1. Engage in deep, mindful breathing.
2. Cool your body down.
3. Walk away.
4. Ground yourself using your five senses (page 383).
5. Find a place where you can SCREAM as loud as you can.
6. Sit down and grab the armrests (or the bottom of the chair) really hard.

7. Grab a stress ball.

8. Close your eyes and go to a "happy place" (mentally escape).

9. Close and open your hands repeatedly.

10. Recite a mantra. (Examples: relax; I am in a good place now; release, release, release, and so on.)

Healthy Ways to Communicate Your Anger

You are angry. You have taken a pause, evaluated the situation and the best recourse is to communicate your anger. This doesn't mean getting physically and verbally abusive or grabbing something and throwing it at someone. These are all destructive ways of expressing anger. The following are healthy ways:

1. **"P" before "S."** Process before speaking. For example, if you're mad because your partner left the dirty dishes (yes, again!) on the kitchen counter when the dishwasher is just right there, don't shout, *"Why are you so lazy?!"* Process what the situation really makes you feel. In this example, you may feel tired (by the repeated "offense") and rejection (because you already talked to your partner about it before). Address the underlying issue.

2. **Rehearse** the conversation in your mind. (**Tip**: You can use the DEARMAN (page 399) and FAST (page 488) templates.) Using the above example, you can say, *"Babe, I saw the dishes out on the kitchen counter. I just want to explain why it frustrates me. You see, if you don't do it, it comes across to me as if you want ME to do it. You're handing the responsibility of it to me. What can we do to change this?"*

3. **Do not communicate angrily.** Using angry words and having an angry demeanor will not get you the results you need. (**Tip**: See GIVE, page 322.)

4. **Do not bring up past transgressions.** We cannot change the past. Bringing up past "offenses" may only bring aggression to the discussion. Focus on moving forward.
5. **Do not mind-read.** When expressing your anger, don't jump the gun and state why you think the situation happened. (*Example: You interrupted my presentation deliberately to suck up to the boss!*) Give the other party a chance to express their views about the situation.

Anger can be very tiring and draining. It is truly worth your while to learn how to handle it effectively so that it doesn't run your life. Here's a quick rundown of what we discussed in this chapter:

- Allowing yourself to feel vulnerable is the first step to addressing your anger.
- Mindfulness is the Pause button you need to slow down the anger cycle.
- Distress Tolerance helps tolerate the situation as it is happening so that you don't explode and lash out.
- Emotion Regulation is the process of adjusting your emotions away from anger so that you're not easily controlled by it.
- Interpersonal Effectiveness is about healthy relationships with yourself and others.
- Identifying and setting your boundaries is one of the most effective ways you can prevent situations that cause anger.
- Anger can come on fast, and you may find yourself quickly on the verge of exploding. Stop yourself from it by adopting the techniques mentioned in this chapter.
- You can achieve the best results from anger when you express it in healthy ways.

In the next chapter, I'll share tips on how you can live a life less angry. Why? Learning how to handle unhealthy anger is great. But learning how to prevent it is even better!

Living a Life Less Angry

One of Dr. Marsha Linehan's goals with DBT is for people to reach a stage where they feel that life is worth living. Anger leads to so much pain and results in so much loss that it is crucial to live a life less angry!

This book has tackled so many ways to handle and get over unhealthy anger that I hope that you'll soon find more space in your life for happiness. To help you, the following are what I call my "anti-anger tips." These are life changes that I encourage you to adopt to help you get rid of unhealthy anger in your life.

HANGRY is Real

Hunger + Angry = Hangry

You know that saying? Don't argue with someone who's hungry? Well, it turns out it is true. Hunger really does make us prone to anger. A recent study showed that "hunger was associated with 37% of changes in irritability, 34% in anger and 38% in pleasure, which suggested the emotions were caused by fluctuations in hunger."[48]

The quick solution here is not to be in a situation where you experience hunger. However, we are what we eat, so what we eat also affects our moods and emotions. So, the best way is to consume a healthy, balanced meal. Here are a few tips on how you can fuel up wisely so that you don't end up fuming.

1. **Drink PLENTY of water.** Eight (8) glasses of water are the general rule, but please do adjust this depending on your height, weight, overall health, and lifestyle.

2. **Eat high-fiber foods.** These food items keep you satisfied for longer periods of time because they take time to break down in the body. High fiber foods include dark, leafy vegetables, wholegrain foods, nuts, seeds, etc.

3. **Pack healthy snacks.** When hungry, our tendency is to grab something fast and easy, which, unfortunately, almost always means something unhealthy. To resist the temptation, make it a habit to always bring healthy snacks with you, such as fruit slices, unsalted nuts, dark chocolate, etc. Meal prepping is the key here. For example, on weekends, plan your meals and snacks for the week and prepare them already.

4. **Execute "Plan B."** Forgot to pack a healthy snack? Avoid giving in to unhealthy food choices by knowing in advance where you can get healthy foods. For example, is there a *Subway* sandwich store nearby? If so, know the healthiest option there. "Plan B" is thus, head onto Subway and order x.

5. **Don't skip meals.** Skipping meals leads to hangry. In addition, it slows down your metabolism and may even cause you to overeat on your next meal.

Note: The above list is not comprehensive. Nutrition is a very broad and deep topic beyond this book's scope. Please talk to your doctor or a nutritionist to receive proper and customized nutritional advice.

Get Enough Sleep!

The importance of a good night's sleep is possibly today's most underrated health habit, and science reveals that sleep debt can increase feelings of anger.[49] Unfortunately, we do not sleep enough. Adults, according to the Centers for Disease Control and Prevention (CDC), should sleep for at least seven hours every night. However, over 60% of adults around the world say they don't sleep as well as they want.[50]

Following are a few tips on how to get enough good quality sleep.

1. **Turn off your screens** at least an hour before bed. The hormone that makes us feel tired, *melatonin*, is not produced as a result of the blue light from our displays. Using an app like *Twilight* for your phone or *f.lux* for your laptop is a good place to start.
2. **Unwind before going to bed** by reading a book, listening to soothing music, or engaging in meditation or light yoga.
3. **Make your bedroom conducive to sleeping.** Today's bedrooms are multi-purpose (e.g., workplace, children's playroom, etc.) Bring it back to its original purpose by de-cluttering, installing dim lights, hanging blackout curtains, and removing all devices.
4. **Cool down your bedroom.** Room temperatures between 60 and 67°F is best for Rapid Eye Movement (REM) sleep, the stage where dreaming, learning, memory, emotional processing, and healthy brain development occurs. If your room is too hot or too cold, you'll keep waking up, which prevents you from reaching REM and deep, restorative sleep.
5. **Practice gratitude.** You can write your positive thoughts on a journal you keep beside your bed, or you can simply lie down, close your eyes, and just mentally list down the people, events, and things for which you are grateful that day. Personally, doing this relaxes my body and mind, and I fall asleep mid-way.

Be Accountable for Your Own Emotions

"Why does he make me so angry all the time?!"
"Why does mom always invade my privacy?!"
"Argh! Why did my boss give such impossible deadlines?!"
"This is crazy! Why is that checkout lady so slow? Can't she see this line is so damn long?"

When we are angry, the tendency is to assign blame. Someone or something caused feelings of rage... as if we don't have a say in our own emotions. In truth, external factors *prompt* our anger, but when we are in an actual angry state, that's on us.

Anger is a *personal* emotional state. It is based on your personal preferences, prejudices, and life experiences. This is why what infuriates you might not bother anyone else at all.

So the next time you feel anger, try not to look outward. Take responsibility for your own emotions and try to figure out WHY you have allowed yourself to be angered by the situation. Whatever happened, you are entirely accountable for what happens next.

Assigning blame:
 "Why does Adrian make me so angry all the time?!"
Taking responsibility for your emotions:
"I am easily angered by Adrian because he reminds me of an abusive ex."

Assigning blame:
"Why does mom always invade my privacy?!"
Taking responsibility for your emotions:

"I need to have a serious talk with mom about my boundaries."

Assigning blame:
"Argh! Why did my boss give such impossible deadlines?!"
Taking responsibility for your emotions:
"I knew the deadlines when the project started. I am super frustrated because I did not speak up during meetings about why the deadlines were impossible to meet."

Assigning blame:
"This is crazy! Why is that checkout lady so slow? Can't she see this line is so damn long?"
Taking responsibility for your emotions:
"I could have gone shopping during non-peak hours, but I chose this moment even though I KNOW it is always busy here at this time. So, I guess I am really just angry at myself. LOL."

Setbacks

Things don't always go as planned. Setbacks happen. And when they do, it is easy to get flustered and angry.

When setbacks happen, one way to combat any negative reactions is to practice *gratitude*. For example, instead of getting mad at yourself because you gained two pounds, be happy and grateful that you lost 10 pounds the month before. Instead of focusing on the fact that your friends are "always late" for lunch dates, focus on the fact that they are your true friends who would do anything for you.

Another technique is called *reframing*, which is changing the way you look at things. For example, instead of being furious that you missed a turn and added 20 minutes to your drive, reframe the situation by thinking, *"I have actually always been intrigued by this route. I guess today I'll finally get to see it."* Here's another example: your neighbor shrieks at the presence of your cat outside, and you hear a nasty swear word against you come out. Instead of getting mad, think, *"That's got nothing to do with me or Elsa (the cat). He's just having a bad day."*

Let It Go

Imagine a cup on your desk. If you fill it up with anger, it will overflow, spill out all over your desk and ruin all the papers you have spread in front of you. You need to "throw out" or release your anger so that you can your cup is ready to receive new, healthy, and positive emotions. Here are some tips on how you can let go of anger.

1. **Start from a place of peace.** Breathe, relax, and calm yourself. (See Distress Tolerance, page 252.)

2. **Check your perspective.** When we are angry, everything is magnified. Check the facts (page 388) and see if they fit the level of your anger.

3. **Go ahead and comfort yourself.** Cuddle with your pet, buy a plant, re-watch your favorite Netflix series, etc.

4. **Write down what you feel.** Don't censor yourself and let it all out. Put into writing the words and emotions that want to explode from you, and then burn the piece of paper.

5. **Get a birthday balloon**, blow it out and then pop it.

6. **Light a candle.** Stare at the flame. Make it the target of your rage, and then blow the candle out.

7. [Express your anger in healthy ways](#) (page 493).

8. **Forgive**. Many people think forgiveness is giving others a pass. However, I have come to realize that forgiveness is actually very healing for the *forgiver*.

Most, if not all, of my anger issues stem from my childhood. But I cannot go back and change that. Holding a grudge against my parents is also not the solution because it just makes me a prisoner of my childhood and prolongs my suffering. So, I have chosen to forgive. I did not have a sit down with my family and said, "*I forgive you guys*." Instead, one day, I found myself sitting on a park bench, and I just acknowledged that my immigrant parents were doing the best they could with what they had and knew, and I said, "*I forgive*".

Live a Positive Life

> *"Darkness cannot drive out darkness: only light can do that." – Martin Luther King Jr.*

When you fill your life with light, darkness has a very hard time penetrating it. Truth be told, when I started this journey, my only goal was to stop being angry. Anger was just costing me too much. As I started to change, I found many aspects of life improving too. So my final tip to live a life less angry is to live a life more happy.

1. **Ask yourself what makes you happy**. So many people want to be happy and yet have a very hard time identifying exactly what makes them happy. I should know; I was one of them. So ask yourself what makes you happy, and don't just focus on the "big stuff." In fact, go for the simple stuff first, and then do your best to fill your days with a lot of these "little things."

Here are a few of the things that make me happy and how I have expanded them to amplify my happiness.

- A strong, hot cup of coffee in the morning.
  So I invested in a good coffee machine. I also figured out what coffee beans I liked best and started buying only that.
- A nice, tasty smear of butter on really good bread.
  I switched to grass-fed butter and started buying artisan bread from a local bakery.
- People greeting me on my long forest walks.
- I don't wait to be greeted anymore. I initiate it.

2. Set and claim your **boundaries**. (**Tip**: See How to Set Boundaries on page 484.)

3. Engage in **self-care**. Exercise daily and eat well for your health. Ask for help when you need it. Take breaks more often. Read a book just because. Get enough sleep. Say no if you want to. Say yes if you want to. Don't bother with what other people think of you. Smile.

4. **LIKE yourself.** This may come as a surprise, but many people don't like themselves or what they've become. Somehow, it became common and okay to self-bash and self-criticize. One way to counter this is to talk to yourself as you would a friend: be gentle, be kind, and be supportive.

Why don't you do this right now? Write down three (3) things you like and appreciate about yourself.

Examples:
I like how I make people smile.
I like how I love taking long walks and appreciate nature.
I like how I'm open to learning new behaviors to control my anger.

1. _____
2. _____
3. _____

5. **Leave the past.** Don't live in the past because that means you miss today, and you'll cloud tomorrow. "Leave the past" is not just about letting go. It's also about consciously, deliberately living in the moment. Most people are

either thinking about the past or worrying about the future, and that just
makes you miss today, doesn't it? So, just enjoy and live today to its fullest.

6. Acknowledge your **accomplishments**.

Why don't you do this right now? Write down three (3) accomplishments you did the past week that you're proud of. It doesn't matter what they are or if they're "big" or "small" accomplishments.

Examples:
I took 10,000 steps a day for five (5) consecutive days.
I took a chance and volunteered to lead our latest marketing campaign at work.
I started waking up 15 minutes earlier than usual.

1. _____
2. _____
3. _____

7. Wake up expecting **happiness** and go to sleep practicing **gratitude**.

8. Build and keep **healthy relationships**, and end toxic ones. For example, call up an old friend you haven't communicated with in a while, message three (3) friends, ask them how they are and let them know you're thinking about them, block a bully on social media, delete and block an ex who has been harassing you, and so on.

Please go ahead and add your own ideas to living a positive life.
_____
_____
_____

Conclusion

An angry life is a hard one to live. I am filled with gratitude that you have chosen this book to guide you to live a life less angry. Again, please remember that addressing anger is not a linear process. There will be roadblocks and setbacks, but nothing that you cannot overcome.

Here's a quick recap of all that we covered in this book:

- Dialectic Behavior Therapy (DBT) and its main fundamentals (Acceptance and Change) and its core skills (Mindfulness, Distress Tolerance, Emotion Regulation, and Interpersonal Effectiveness).
- What anger is: what happens in the brain when anger is triggered, the anger cycle, and the basic differences in anger in men and women.
- Understanding the source of your anger (Why Are You Angry?) and how you may be destructively expressing it.
- The physical, emotional, mental, social, financial, and relationship costs of anger.
- The DBT tools and skills you can apply to effectively manage anger in your life.
- How you can live a life focused on happiness and not anger.

Learning new behaviors is never easy, but it is not impossible. You got this book because you know that anger is not good for you. So please keep on trying to manage your anger because that is what's good for you.

What we think, we become. – Buddha

Appendix A – Miller-Patton Anger Self-Assessment

The **Miller-Patton Anger Self-Assessment** exercise was created by licensed marriage and family therapists Mark S. Miller, MA, and Patricia Patton, Ph.D. of Emerge from Anger.[51]

Warning: This self-assessment explores aspects of anger and contains depictions of self-harm, alcohol abuse, eating disorders, and others. Please read with care.

If you agree with the statement, circle TRUE; if you disagree, circle FALSE. If any statement is not applicable to you (i.e., statements related to partners), you can skip them.

STATEMENT	True or False?	
1. I use foul language, including slurs, sarcasm, and name-calling.	True	False
2. People say I become furious too easily.	True	False
3. It takes me a very long time to cool down.	True	False
4. I still get upset when I reflect on the wrongdoings of people against me or the unfairness of life.	True	False
5. I frequently criticize and judge other people, even when they don't seek my opinion or assistance.	True	False
6. To stop people from nagging me, I engage in passive-aggressive tactics like ignoring them or making promises to do things, only to "forget" about them.	True	False
7. I make aggressive gestures and attitudes, such as clenching my fists, glaring at others, making banging noises, and others.	True	False
8. I spend a lot of time thinking about what scathing responses I should have made at the time or how I can exact revenge when someone does or says something that enrages me.	True	False
9. Following an angry outburst, I resort to self-destructive activities to calm down, such as gambling, excessive eating, vomiting, or self-harm.	True	False

STATEMENT	True or False?	
10. Sometimes, after an occurrence that makes me really upset, I get physical sickness (headaches, nausea, vomiting, diarrhea, etc.).	True	False
11. Forgiving someone who has wronged me is really difficult, nearly impossible. Even if they have expressed regret and made an effort to make amends, I just can't give them a pass and forgive.	True	False
12. I constantly have to win a debate and establish my "rightness."	True	False
13. I frequently rationalize my actions and attribute my irrational conduct to other individuals or external factors (like job stress, financial problems, etc.)	True	False
14. When I am frustrated, I respond so negatively that I ruminate, or I have trouble falling asleep at night because I keep thinking about the things that have upset me.	True	False
15. I frequently despise myself for losing my anger after arguing with someone.	True	False
16. There are moments when I am so enraged that I "see red" and think of killing someone or myself.	True	False
17. I occasionally lose track of what I say or do when I am angry.	True	False
18. I am aware that some people "walk on eggshells" around me to avoid upsetting me	True	False

STATEMENT	True or False?	
because they are terrified of me when I get angry.		
19. When I have been furious, I have slammed doors, hurled things, smashed things, or punched walls.	True	False
20. Even when there was no proof that my partner was being unfaithful, I was unnecessarily possessive and jealous of them, accusing them of cheating.	True	False
21. On occasion, I have had my partner perform sexual acts they don't want to, or I have threatened to cheat on them if they don't comply with my demands in order to satisfy my sexual needs.	True	False
22. I have occasionally chosen to ignore my spouse in an effort to hurt them while being extra kind to other family members or friends.	True	False
23. In order to exert control and manipulate my partner's emotions and behavior, I have made them dependent on me or socially isolated. This has prevented them from leaving me or ending our relationship.	True	False
24. I have threatened people in order to get my way or win a debate.	True	False
25. I feel like I have been betrayed a lot in the past, and I find it very hard to trust people.	True	False

Scoring the Miller-Patton Anger Self-Assessment Quiz

Important: The Miller-Patton Anger Self-Assessment test is an informal screening test to help you learn more about your emotions and outward displays of anger. It is NOT meant to be a formal evaluation.

- If you circled **True** to 10 or more of the statements above, you most likely suffer from moderate-to-severe anger issues.
- If you circled **True** to five of the statements above, you are most likely at risk of having an anger problem.
- Even if you circled **True** to only one of the questions, it would still be beneficial for you to learn the anger management techniques in this book to improve your coping skills.
- If you circled **True** to **Statement #16** and believe you may engage in self-harm, please dial 911 (or your local support hotline) for immediate assistance.

Review Request

If you enjoyed this book or found it useful…

I'd like to ask you for a quick favor:

Please share your thoughts and leave a quick REVIEW. Your feedback matters and helps me make improvements to provide the best books possible.

Reviews are so helpful to both readers and authors, so any help would be greatly appreciated! You can leave a review here:

http://tinyurl.com/dbtskills-bundle-review

Or by scanning the QR code below:

Also, please join my ARC team to get early access to my releases.

https://barretthuang.com/arc-team/

THANK YOU!

Further Reading

Be sure to check out my other bestselling DBT books in the Mental Health Therapy series. Here are some titles you can find:

- DBT Workbook for Kids
- DBT Workbook for Teens
- DBT Workbook for PTSD
- DBT Workbook for BPD
- DBT Workbook for Emotional Eating
- OCD Workbook For Adults

You can get them here:

https://tinyurl.com/mental-health-therapy

About the Author

Barrett Huang is an author and businessman. Barrett spent years discovering the best ways to manage his OCD, overcoming his anxiety, and learning to embrace life. Through his writing, he hopes to share his knowledge with readers, empowering people of all backgrounds with the tools and strategies they need to improve their mental wellbeing and be happy and healthy.

When not writing or running his business, Barrett loves to spend his time studying. He has majored in psychology and completed the DBT skills certificate course by Dr. Marsha Linehan. Barrett's idol is Bruce Lee, who said, "The key to immortality is first living a life worth remembering."

Learn more about Barrett's books here:
https://barretthuang.com/

References

1 Linehan, M. (2015). *DBT skills training manual*. The Guilford Press.

2 Carey, B. (2011, June 23). *Expert on mental illness reveals her own fight*. The New York Times. Retrieved August 1, 2022, from https://www.nytimes.com/2011/06/23/health/23lives.html

3 Influence Digest. (2018, February 9). *Research has shown that you can condition yourself to do anything*. Influence Digest. Retrieved August 1, 2022, from https://influencedigest.com/psychology/research-shown-condition-yourself-anything/

4 Linehan, M. M., & Dimeff, L. (2001). Dialectical Behavior Therapy in a Nutshell. The California Psychologist. https://www.ebrightcollaborative.com/uploads/2/3/3/9/23399186/dbtinanutshell.pdf

5 Levine, M. (2012, July 12). *Logic and emotion: Delving into the logical and emotional sides of the human brain*. Psychology Today. Retrieved August 1, 2022, from https://www.psychologytoday.com/intl/blog/the-divided-mind/201207/logic-and-emotion

6 Holt-Lunstad, J., Smith, T. B., & Layton, J. B. (2010). Social relationships and mortality risk: A meta-analytic review. *PLoS Medicine, 7*(7). https://doi.org/10.1371/journal.pmed.1000316

7 Mejia, Z. (2018, March 20). *Harvard's longest study of adult life reveals how you can be happier and more successful*. CNBC. Retrieved August 1, 2022, from https://www.cnbc.com/2018/03/20/this-harvard-study-reveals-how-you-can-be-happier-and-more-successful.html

8 Byrne, D. (1961). Interpersonal attraction and attitude similarity. *The Journal of Abnormal and Social Psychology, 62*(3), 713–715. https://doi.org/10.1037/h0044721

9 Montoya, R. M., Horton, R. S., & Kirchner, J. (2008). Is actual similarity necessary for attraction? A meta-analysis of actual and perceived similarity. *Journal of Social and Personal Relationships, 25*(6), 889–922. https://doi.org/10.1177/0265407508096700

10 Laursen, B. (2017). Making and keeping friends: The importance of being similar. *Child Development Perspectives, 11*(4), 282–289. https://doi.org/10.1111/cdep.12246

11 Frazier, S. N., & Vela, J. (2014). Dialectical behavior therapy for the treatment of anger and aggressive behavior: A Review. *Aggression and Violent Behavior, 19*(2), 156–163. https://doi.org/10.1016/j.avb.2014.02.001

12 Wright, S., Day, A., & Howells, K. (2009). Mindfulness and the treatment of Anger Problems. *Aggression and Violent Behavior, 14*(5), 396–401. https://doi.org/10.1016/j.avb.2009.06.008

13 Momeni, J., Omidi, A., Raygan, F., & Akbari, H. (2016). The effects of mindfulness-based stress reduction on cardiac patients' blood pressure, perceived stress, and anger: A single-blind randomized controlled trial. *Journal of the American Society of Hypertension, 10*(10), 763–771. https://doi.org/10.1016/j.jash.2016.07.007

14 DeSteno, D., Lim, D., Duong, F., & Condon, P. (2017). Meditation inhibits aggressive responses to provocations. *Mindfulness, 9*(4), 1117–1122. https://doi.org/10.1007/s12671-017-0847-2

15 Onyedibe, M. C., Ibeagha, P. N., & Onyishi, I. E. (2019). Distress tolerance moderates the relationship between anger experience and elevated blood pressure. *South African Journal of Psychology, 50*(1), 39–53. https://doi.org/10.1177/0081246319832540

16 Hawkins, K. A., Macatee, R. J., Guthrie, W., & Cougle, J. R. (2012). Concurrent and prospective relations between distress tolerance, life stressors, and anger. *Cognitive Therapy and Research, 37*(3), 434–445. https://doi.org/10.1007/s10608-012-9487-y

17 Ellis, A. J., Vanderlind, W. M., & Beevers, C. G. (2012). Enhanced anger reactivity and reduced distress tolerance in major depressive disorder. *Cognitive Therapy and Research, 37*(3), 498–509. https://doi.org/10.1007/s10608-012-9494-z

18 Mauss, I. B., Cook, C. L., & Gross, J. J. (2007). Automatic emotion regulation during anger provocation. *Journal of Experimental Social Psychology, 43*(5), 698–711. https://doi.org/10.1016/j.jesp.2006.07.003

19 Renna, M. E., Quintero, J. M., Fresco, D. M., & Mennin, D. S. (2017). Emotion regulation therapy: A mechanism-targeted treatment for disorders of

distress. *Frontiers in Psychology, 8.* https://doi.org/10.3389/fpsyg.2017.00098

20 Fabiansson, E. C., & Denson, T. F. (2012). The effects of intrapersonal anger and its regulation in economic bargaining. *PLoS ONE, 7*(12). https://doi.org/10.1371/journal.pone.0051595

21 Goleman, D. (2006). *Emotional intelligence: Why it can matter more than Iq.* Bantam Books.

22 ScienceDaily. (2000, January 31). *Comparison of anger expression in men and women reveals surprising differences.* ScienceDaily. Retrieved September 3, 2022, from https://www.sciencedaily.com/releases/2000/01/000131075609.htm

23 Esquire (Ed.). (2020, August 21). *American rage: The 'esquire'/nbc news survey.* Esquire. Retrieved September 1, 2022, from https://www.esquire.com/news-politics/a40693/american-rage-nbc-survey/

24 Brescoll, V. L., & Uhlmann, E. L. (2008). Can an angry woman get ahead? *Psychological Science, 19*(3), 268–275. https://doi.org/10.1111/j.1467-9280.2008.02079.x

25 Casper, R. F. (2021). *Patient education: Premenstrual syndrome (PMS) and premenstrual dysphoric disorder (PMDD) (Beyond the Basics).* UpToDate. Retrieved September 1, 2022, from https://www.uptodate.com/contents/premenstrual-syndrome-pms-and-premenstrual-dysphoric-disorder-pmdd-beyond-the-basics

26 Yeşildere Sağlam, H., & Basar, F. (2019). The relationship between premenstrual syndrome and anger. *Pakistan Journal of Medical Sciences, 35*(2). https://doi.org/10.12669/pjms.35.2.232

27 Lerner, J. S., Gonzalez, R. M., Small, D. A., & Fischhoff, B. (2003). Effects of fear and anger on perceived risks of terrorism. *Psychological Science, 14*(2), 144–150. https://doi.org/10.1111/1467-9280.01433

28 Reilly, P. M., & Shopshire, M. S. (2019). ANGER MANAGEMENT for Substance Use Disorder and Mental Health Clients. Rockville, MD; U.S. Department of Health and Human Services.

29 Lisitsa, E., Fraser, C., & Benson, K. (n.d.). *A research-based approach to relationships*. The Gottman Institute. Retrieved September 1, 2022, from https://www.gottman.com/

30 *Nicole Lippman-Barile, Ph.D on mindbodygreen*. mindbodygreen. (n.d.). Retrieved September 1, 2022, from https://www.mindbodygreen.com/wc/nicole-lippman-barile-ph-d

31 Kawachi, I., Sparrow, D., Spiro, A., Vokonas, P., & Weiss, S. T. (1996). A prospective study of anger and coronary heart disease. *Circulation, 94*(9), 2090–2095. https://doi.org/10.1161/01.cir.94.9.2090

32 Davidson, K. W., & Mostofsky, E. (2010). Anger expression and risk of coronary heart disease: Evidence from the Nova Scotia Health Survey. *American Heart Journal, 159*(2), 199–206. https://doi.org/10.1016/j.ahj.2009.11.007

33 Montenegro, C. E., & Montenegro, S. T. (2018). Anger and cardiovascular disease: An old and complicated relationship. *Arquivos Brasileiros De Cardiologia*. https://doi.org/10.5935/abc.20180176

34 Baumeister, R. F., & Leary, M. R. (1995). The need to belong: Desire for interpersonal attachments as a fundamental human motivation. *Psychological Bulletin, 117*(3), 497–529. https://doi.org/10.1037/0033-2909.117.3.497

35 Over, H. (2016). The origins of belonging: Social Motivation in infants and young children. *Philosophical Transactions of the Royal Society B: Biological Sciences, 371*(1686), 20150072. https://doi.org/10.1098/rstb.2015.0072

36 Williams, V. (2022, March 4). *Mayo Clinic Minute: The benefits of being socially connected - mayo clinic news network*. Mayo Clinic. Retrieved September 1, 2022, from https://newsnetwork.mayoclinic.org/discussion/mayo-clinic-minute-the-benefits-of-being-socially-connected/

37 Lin, S., Faust, L., Robles-Granda, P., Kajdanowicz, T., & Chawla, N. V. (2019). Social network structure is predictive of Health and Wellness. *PLOS ONE, 14*(6). https://doi.org/10.1371/journal.pone.0217264

38 Adler, A. B., LeardMann, C. A., Yun, S., Jacobson, I. G., & Forbes, D. (2022). Problematic anger and economic difficulties: Findings from the Millennium

Cohort Study. *Journal of Affective Disorders, 297*, 679–685. https://doi.org/10.1016/j.jad.2021.10.078

39 Ngo, S. (2016, February 22). *How anger can hurt your finances*. Wall St. Watchdog. Retrieved September 8, 2022, from https://www.wallstwatchdog.com/money-career/how-anger-can-hurt-your-finances/

40 South Richardson, D. (2014). Everyday aggression takes many forms. *Current Directions in Psychological Science, 23*(3), 220–224. https://doi.org/10.1177/0963721414530143

41 Arslan, G. (2021). School belongingness, well-being, and mental health among adolescents: Exploring the role of loneliness. *Australian Journal of Psychology, 73*(1), 70–80. https://doi.org/10.1080/00049530.2021.1904499

42 Taren, A. A., Creswell, J. D., & Gianaros, P. J. (2013). Dispositional mindfulness co-varies with smaller amygdala and caudate volumes in community adults. *PLoS ONE, 8*(5). https://doi.org/10.1371/journal.pone.0064574

43 *Anger styles are learned*. Mental Help Anger Styles Are Learned Comments. (n.d.). Retrieved September 1, 2022, from https://www.mentalhelp.net/anger/types/

44 Pally, R., & Olds, D. (2018). Emotional processing: The mind-body connection. *The Mind-Brain Relationship*, 73–104. https://doi.org/10.4324/9780429482465-4

45 Watson, N. F., Badr, M. S., Belenky, G., Bliwise, D. L., Buxton, O. M., Buysse, D., Dinges, D. F., Gangwisch, J., Grandner, M. A., Kushida, C., Malhotra, R. K., Martin, J. L., Patel, S. R., Quan, S., & Tasali, E. (2015). Recommended amount of sleep for a healthy adult: A joint consensus statement of the American Academy of Sleep Medicine and Sleep Research Society. *SLEEP*. https://doi.org/10.5665/sleep.4716

46 Saghir, Z., Syeda, J. N., Muhammad, A. S., & Balla Abdalla, T. (2018). The amygdala, sleep debt, sleep deprivation, and the emotion of anger: A possible connection? *Cureus*. https://doi.org/10.7759/cureus.2912

47 Brosnan, S. F., & de Waal, F. B. (2014). Evolution of responses to (un)fairness. *Science, 346*(6207). https://doi.org/10.1126/science.1251776

48 Swami, V., Hochstöger, S., Kargl, E., & Stieger, S. (2022). Hangry in the field: An experience sampling study on the impact of hunger on anger, irritability, and affect. *PLOS ONE, 17*(7). https://doi.org/10.1371/journal.pone.0269629

49 Krizan, Z., & Hisler, G. (2019). Sleepy anger: Restricted sleep amplifies angry feelings. *Journal of Experimental Psychology: General, 148*(7), 1239–1250. https://doi.org/10.1037/xge0000522

50 Philips Global Sleep Survey. (2019). The global pursuit of better sleep health. Source: https://www.usa.philips.com/c-dam/b2c/master/experience/smartsleep/world-sleep-day/2019/2019-philips-world-sleep-day-survey-results.pdf

51 *Marriage and family therapist: Emerge from anger: Santa Clarita.* Emergefromanger1. (n.d.). Retrieved September 1, 2022, from https://www.emergefromanger.com/

Indexes

Acceptance and Change, 367, 370, 373, 406, 439, 505
Aftermath, 413, 414, 415
Amygdala, 409, 410, 411, 417, 419, 444, 454, 490, 518
amygdala hijack, 409, 410, 411, 419, 454, 490
Anger Cycle, 411, 458
Anger Iceberg, 422, 424, 434, 436
Anger Management, 406, 454, 458, 472, 483
Behavioral Response, 413, 414
Borderline Personality Disorder, 367
Boundaries, 446, 484, 503
BPD, 367
Build Positive Experiences, 473, 474
CBT, 367
Check the Facts, 388, 390, 490
Cognitive Behavior Therapy, 367
DBT, 363, 364, 365, 366, 367, 368, 369, 370, 371, 372, 373, 375, 376, 379, 382, 386, 394, 406, 407, 408, 412, 414, 415, 424, 437, 439, 441, 449, 457, 458, 468, 472, 475, 481, 484, 495, 505, 514
Dialectical Behavior Therapy, 363, 366, 370, 406, 514
Distress Tolerance, 375, 382, 385, 406, 434, 458, 494, 500, 505
Dr. Marsha Linehan, 364, 366, 367, 412, 495
Emotion Regulation, 375, 386, 387, 407, 414, 434, 472, 494, 505
Emotional Mind, 410
Emotional Response, 412, 414
GAD, 362, 363, 417, 437
General Anxiety Disorder, 362, 417
Grounding, 382, 383, 414
Hangry, 495

Interpersonal Effectiveness, 375, 394, 407, 424, 483, 494, 505
Miller-Patton Anger Self-Assessment, 506, 510
Mindful Breathing, 414, 466, 482
Mindfulness, 375, 376, 377, 379, 406, 434, 454, 455, 465, 486, 490, 494, 505, 515
Negative Thoughts, 412, 414
Obsessive-Compulsive Disorder, 362
OCD, 362, 363, 370, 382, 386, 441, 443
Radical Acceptance, 368, 369, 370, 459, 465, 490
Reasonable Mind, 410
Setbacks, 499
Sleep, 478, 496, 518, 519
Social ostracization, 438, 442
TIPP, 382, 414, 490
Triggering Event, 412, 481
Unfairness, 490
Vulnerability, 443, 444, 446, 449
Wise Mind, 379, 380, 381, 388, 406, 410, 466, 481, 482
Worksheet: ACCEPTS, 468
Worksheet: Anger Boundary Journaling, 485
Worksheet: Anger Iceberg, 429
Worksheet: Anger Triggers 1, 425
Worksheet: Anger Triggers 2, 426
Worksheet: BPE, 473
Worksheet: Check the Facts, 388
Worksheet: COPE AHEAD, 481
Worksheet: DEARMAN, 399
Worksheet: FAST, 488
Worksheet: FINDING FRIENDS, 395
Worksheet: GIVE, 402
Worksheet: Grounding Technique Using Your 5 Senses, 383

Worksheet: Mindful Body Scanning (Anger Observation), 455
Worksheet: Mindful Breathing, 378
Worksheet: Mindfully Angry (Anger Description), 457
Worksheet: Opposite to Emotion, 391
Worksheet: PLEASE, 475
Worksheet: Radical Acceptance, 459
Worksheet: STOP, 465
Worksheet: TIPP, 385
Worksheet: Vulnerability List, 450
Worksheet: Wise Mind, 380

www.ingramcontent.com/pod-product-compliance
Lightning Source LLC
Chambersburg PA
CBHW080213040426
42333CB00044B/2635